Vs.

Published by Avalonia

BM Avalonia
London
WC1N 3XX
England, UK

www.avaloniabooks.co.uk

Vs.
Copyright © Kim Huggens 2010
Individual authors and artists retain the copyright to their original work.

First Edition, February 2011

ISBN 978-1-905297-36-8
Design by Satori

Cover Image "Polarity" by Emily Carding (c) 2010

British Library Cataloguing in Publication Data. A catalogue record for this book is available from the British Library

All rights reserved. No part of this publication may be reproduced or utilized in any form or by any means, electronic or mechanical, including photocopying, microfilm, recording, or by any information storage and retrieval system, or used in another book, without written permission from the authors.

Vs.

DUALITY AND CONFLICT
IN MAGICK, MYTHOLOGY AND PAGANISM

WITH ESSAYS BY

Chrissy Derbyshire, Diane M. Champigny, Ellie Horne,
Emily Carding, Gareth Gerrard, Guy Gaunt, Jon Hanna,
Jonathan Carfax, Karen F. Pierce,
Katherine Sutherland, Katie Gerrard, Kim Huggens,
Magin Rose, Melissa Harrington, Michael Howard,
Payam Nabarz, Rachel Donaldson, Sophia Fisher,
Sophie Nussle, Trystn M. Branwynn and Vikki Bramshaw

Edited by
Kim Huggens

Published by Avalonia
www.avaloniabooks.co.uk

Vs.

TAT TVAM ASI
THOU ART THAT ~ THAT THOU ART

Vs.

TABLE OF CONTENTS

The Contributors..7
Introduction by Kim Huggens...15
Cover Art: 'Polarity' by Emily Carding................................21

The Tale of the Twins by Trystn M. Branwynn....................25
Gods of Light and Darkness by Michael Howard...............35
Toads and Diamonds by Chrissy Derbyshire 46
Constellations by Payam Nabarz..52
Vodou Maryaj by Sophia Fisher..61
Recognition of the Divine by Ellie Horne 65
The Divine Human by Rachel Donaldson...........................71
A Lantern to the Cave by Guy Gaunt..................................80
Sun and Moon by Emily Carding...91
Sir Gawain And the Green Knight by Katherine Sutherland....100
The Momentum of Polarity by Gareth Gerrard 108
Marassa Dossou-Dosa by Kim Huggens............................115
Brothers at Arms by Magin Rose 130
Riders upon Swift Horses by Karen F. Pierce 150
The Scorpion & the Bridal Bed by Vikki Bramshaw 169
Inanna and Ereshkigal by Sophie Nusslé...........................180
Are Freyja and Frigga the Same Goddess? by Katie Gerrard.........191
Hidden Children of The Great M/Other by Melissa Harrington....201
Polarity Magick by Diane M. Champigny 212
Exoteric Neopaganism by Jon Hanna 216
Coniunctio by Frater Jonathan Carfax 228
Of the Nature of the Soul by Plato 236
Extract from Thunder, Perfect Mind 240

Index..242

Vs.

THE CONTRIBUTORS

Vikki Bramshaw

Vikki Bramshaw is a priestess and author of esoteric initiatory witchcraft. Having trained for 10 years under respected elders, she now runs her own working group in Hampshire. Just some of her passions are theurgy, initiatory rites and Hellenic and Sumerian mythology. Her first book, *Craft of the Wise: A Practical Guide* was released with O-Books (John Hunt Publishing) in 2009, and her essay *'Swaying with the Serpent: A Study of the Serpent Girdled Hekate'*, features in *Hekate: Her Sacred Fires* edited by Sorita D'Este (Avalonia Books, 2010). In addition to her magical training Vikki successfully completed several courses as part of her ongoing research, including The Origins of Human Behaviour with Oxford University. She is also a trained Holistic Healer with the Scottish Healing Association, and is currently studying counselling & transactional analysis with Peter Symonds College of Winchester. Also see: www.vikkibramshaw.co.uk

Trystn M. Branwynn

Trystn M Branwynn was born in St. Louis, MO, in September 1967. His parents moved across the country keeping up with (first) his father's military duties and later second career. He began to display a fascination for the Occult in his mid teens and had several experiences that served to propel him further along this road. At the age of 17 he entered the U.S. Marine Corps, and while in the service was drawn strongly to the work of Aleister Crowley. It was during this phase, in 1987, that he met the Magistra of a small Traditional group that met in Carlsbad, CA (he was stationed on nearby Camp Pendleton) and began the learning and working process that has since defined his life. He currently resides in the state of Washington with a Siamese cat – 'The True Imperial Scion' - Josephine, a Betta – 'Tart', and two rabbits, Peony and Zen. He has served with two Cuveens, and married and divorced three times, and now prefers to spend his time working - both at Magic and at his day job, fishing for salmon, and enjoying life.

Emily Carding

Emily Carding lives in Cornwall with her amazing husband, ethereal daughter and the glorious Albus Dumbledog. Here she creates various offerings, such as *The Transparent Tarot, The Transparent Oracle*, and *The Tarot of the Sidhe* for Schiffer Books. She has also contributed book covers, articles and artwork for several previous works from Avalonia Books. To date these titles include *Towards The Wiccan Circle* (Cover), *Both Sides of Heaven*, (Cover and article - *'The Salvation of the Sidhe'*,

From a Drop of Water (Article – *'Nimue: The Archetypal Priestess'*), and *Hekate: Her Sacred Fires* (Cover, Article - *'Painting Hekate'* and internal illustrations). Emily speaks at specialist Tarot events around the world and also works as a storyteller, the perfect combination of her experience in Theatre and knowledge of folklore, myth and magick! She is currently working on lots. You'll just have to wait and see... Her website can be found at www.childofavalon.com

Frater Jonathan Carfax

Jonathan Carfax has gotten to thinking about the Jewish mystical concepts on reincarnation into inanimate objects, because he is sure a nice mahogany hat stand may be a future incarnation. When he isn't wearing the Phrygian cap associated with the Qabalistic Society of Guardians, he likes to sport a moushwa headscarf as an initiate of the Puerto Rican vodou-espiritismo tradition of Sanse. And while many Freemasons don't wear stylish top hats anymore, as a Past Master of an esoterically minded Lodge in Sydney, he would if he could. Probably just as well, as being the co-editor of Absinthe.com.au, documenting the history of la Fee Vert in Australia, requires practical research that does not permit the sort of vertical stability conducive to the wearing of hats (lampshades possibly excepted). Jonathan resides amongst the idyllic vineyards of the Adelaide Hills in South Australia with his partner, son and three cats. None of his cats wear hats, much the pity.

Diane M. Champigny (Thea)

Diane M. Champigny (Thea) is a 3rd Degree High Priestess and Lineage Elder of the Alexandrian Tradition of Witchcraft. She is an active member of the Society of Elder Faiths and has served as a Ritualist and Workshop Facilitator for the Wiccan Educational Society, a Global Pagan Community. Thea is also a Trance Medium, Occult Bibliophile and contributing author to the books *Priestesses Pythonesses Sibyls*, *From A Drop of Water* and *Hekate: Her Sacred Fires* published by Avalonia. Inquiries may be directed to PriestessThea@hotmail.com or visit www.myspace.com/PriestessThea

Chrissy Derbyshire

Chrissy Derbyshire is an author and teacher living in Cardiff. She is a keen lifelong student of folklore and mythology. Her first book, *Mysteries*, was published in 2008 by Awen Publications. It is a selection of poetry and short stories, structured to mirror a descent into and emergence from the Underworld. She was the winner of the Mercian Gathering Bardic Contest 2006, and most recently contributed an essay to the Avalonia Books anthology, *From a Drop of Water*.

Rachel Donaldson

Rachel is a mountain climbing, yogic philosophising, wild food foraging Wiccan who lives in Kent, UK with her partner and their cat (who thinks he is a bear). She has taught yoga for six years and has a passion for yoga philosophy. She previously contributed to the anthology *From a Drop of Water* (Avalonia, 2009).

Sophia Fisher

Sophia Fisher has previously published an article with Avalonia books. She is a *'caballo des mysterios'* in 21 Divisions Vodou and is also initiated as Hounsi Lave Tet in the Haitian Tcha-Tcha lineage, a proud member of Sosyete Gade nou Leve and the proprietor of Baron's Magic and the LaSirena Botanica. Mum to baby Robin and two West Highland White Terriers, when Sophia isn't working or serving the lwa she loves dancing, creative writing and watching hammy horror flicks! Also see www.baronsmagic.com and www.sirenabotanica.com, or alternatively e-mail her sophia@sirenabotanica.com

Guy Gaunt

Guy is a Spiritist Sorcerer who spends most of his time talking to the Spirits - sometimes they talk back, sometimes they don't. He is a member of the Ordo Templi Orientis Antiqua, La Couleuvre Noire and works with Sosyete Gade Nou Leve in the Haitian and 21 Divisions Vodou traditions. He is also a Civil Servant.

Gareth Gerrard

Gareth is an obligate tea drinker, an avid supporter of Welsh Rugby, a molecular biologist and a long time student of esoterica. With a particular interest in the Cymric mythos (and Norse, and Classical) he has lectured and run workshops on a variety of related subjects at many local, national and international conferences, moots and gatherings. He also contributed to an earlier anthology from Avalonia (*Horns of Power*), exploring the myths associated with the Cymric otherworld deity, Gwynn ap Nudd. Originally from Cardiff in South Wales, he now lives in London with his wife, daughter and fat idiot cat.

Katie Gerrard

Katie Gerrard is a writer, researcher and workshop facilitator with a passion for the magic of Seidr and the Runes. She has been studying the different forms of Norse magic and working with the Norse Gods since discovering them in the 1990s, when she was at university in West Wales. Katie lectures and facilitates workshops at national and international events on esoteric subjects, as well as facilitating developmental and employment coaching workshops at a London adult education college. She is the author of *Odin's Gateways* (about working with the runes) and the forthcoming *Seidr - The Gate is Open* (about Seidr and Northern Tradition magical techniques), both published by Avalonia. An essay on the High Seat Rite written by Katie Gerrard appeared in *Priestesses Pythonesses Sibyls* edited by Sorita d'Este. She also regularly hosts Seidr and other Seer and Norse rites within the London area. You can find out more at www.thebirchtree.com

Jon Hanna

Despite his lack of academic qualifications, Jon Hanna has never felt the need to invent any. Jon has never claimed that his grandmothers engaged in witchcraft or any fortune-telling more involved than putting buttons and pennies in apple-pie. Jon has written a book, but it is rumoured to cite sources. Sightings of footnotes have even been reported. He is not secretly bisexual or kinky, being quite happily up front on both counts. Disappointingly, he manages to interact socially and magically with people without trying to seduce them. All of which makes Jon a disgrace to witchcraft and the wider occult tradition, and this biography dull. Things were much better when witches had to make their own entertainment.   Also see: www.hackcraft.net

Melissa Harrington

Melissa Harrington has been Pagan for most of her life, and an initiated Wiccan for nearly quarter of a century. Her interest in Paganism and magic has led her to undertake a degree in psychology and a PhD in theology and religious studies, as well as to work intensively with several magical orders. Melissa is a full-time Mum who lectures part-time in psychology and sociology. She also teaches Wicca and the Western Mystery tradition, frequently speaks on the magical and Pagan lecture circuit, and writes for academic and Pagan publishers. Her favourite time is spent with family and friends in her native Lake District, reading Edwardian literature in the garden, and going for long meditative walks in the bluebell woods.

Ellie Horne

Ellie is an esoteric student and magic practitioner. She studied Buddhism in India and Nepal for 25 years followed by teachings and practice in Western Magical traditions. Her research interests include Thelema, Renaissance Magic, and the Rosicrucian movement. She is a member of ESSWE (European Society for the Study of Western Esotericism) and AMORC (The Ancient and Mystical Order Rosæ Crucis). Ellie is currently studying for a MA in Western Esotericism at The University of Exeter.

Vs.

Michael Howard
Michael Howard is a writer on esoteric subjects and since 1976 he has been the editor of *The Cauldron* witchcraft magazine (www.thecauldron.org.uk). He has also written over thirty books and his latest ones include *Welsh Witches and Wizards* (Three Hands Press, USA 2009), *Wicca: A History from Gerald Gardner to the Present* (Llewellyn, USA 2010) and *West Country Witches* (Three Hands Press 2010).

Kim Huggens
Kim Huggens is a researcher and author, focusing on the maleficerotic magic of the Late Antique period, world mythology, Tarot, and Vodou. She is a Tarot reader of 17 years experience, and co-creator of *Sol Invictus: The God Tarot* with Nic Phillips (Schiffer Books, 2007.) She is the author of the homestudy Tarot book from Llewellyn publications, *Tarot 101: Mastering the Art of Reading the Cards* (June 2010) and also writes articles and papers for various anthologies and journals. Previous work has appeared in *Horns of Power*, *The Mithras Reader vol. 2*, *Priestesses Pythonesses Sibyls*, and *Both Sides of Heaven*. She also edited and contributed to *From a Drop of Water* (Avalonia, 2009.) Kim is a Vodou practitioner and Hounsi Lave Tet with Sosyete Gade Nou Leve, and Body Master of the Tamion Camp of the Ordo Templi Orientis. In her spare time she makes jewellery, sequin flags and spirit dolls, runs Tarot workshops and classes, writes short fiction, and roleplays.

Payam Nabarz
Payam Nabarz is author of *The Mysteries of Mithras: The Pagan Belief That Shaped the Christian World* (Inner Traditions, 2005), *The Persian Mar Nameh: The Zoroastrian Book of the Snake Omens & Calendar* (Twin Serpents, 2006), and *Divine Comedy of Neophyte Corax and Goddess Morrigan* (Web of Wyrd, 2008). He is also editor of *The Mithras Reader: An academic and religious journal of Greek, Roman, and Persian Studies*, Volume 1(2006), Volume 2 (2008) and *Stellar Magic: a Practical Guide to Rites of the Moon, Planets, Stars and Constellations* (Avalonia, 2009). He is a regular contributor to a number of esoteric magazines and anthologies. For further info visit: www.stellarmagic.co.uk

Sophie Nusslé
Sophie Nussle has been a lawyer, a humanitarian, a policy adviser on relief and on AIDS, a complementary therapist and a stay-at-home partner. She is a professional dreamer and has carried her curiosity, her stories, her shamanic and pagan outlook, her enjoyment of life and her

strong commitment to justice to many countries around the globe. She grew up in Geneva, Switzerland, a liminal place at the crossroads of the world. In 2000, she won the *BBC World Service Short Story Competition for the Millennium*, with her story about a Rwandan genocide survivor caught between two worlds in Belgium, *Buried Bananas*. In 2006 she also came out with the companion book to the *Fantastic Menagerie Tarot*, in which she wrote stories and vignettes to accompany every image. She has spent her life trying to bring together her daily life, her writing, her humanitarian commitment and her spiritual practices. Maybe one day she will succeed, with the help of the patrons of duality and polarity!

Karen Pierce

Karen Pierce has been a practising pagan for over fifteen years. Whilst a student she took an active role in running two pagan societies (at Cardiff and Lampeter). In 2004 she completed a PhD on Helen of Troy, and now works as a librarian. Having been born a Gemini she has always had a fondness for the divine twins, and has threatened (much to her partner's horror) that if she ever had twin boys she would call them Kastor and Polydeukes. She is passionate about stone circles and last year embarked on a journey to visit 40 of them in Britain, writing up her experiences as she went along; this journey continues.

Magin Rose

Magin Rose is a writer, illustrator, priestess, runic practitioner and Wiccan. She has a particular fondness for the Greek and Norse traditions. She loves making things, knocking things down and day dreaming. She lives in London with Mr Magin and their three cats who all do their best to keep her feet on the ground. Her work has previously featured in *Hekate: Her Sacred Fires* and *Horns of Power*. For more on Magin's work visit www.maginrose.com

Katherine Sutherland

Katherine Sutherland is an occult scholar and practitioner with wide ranging interests. Also a poet and author of fiction, Katherine is currently working on a children's novel focused on a character not dissimilar to Dr John Dee. Her poetic reworking of the Persephone myth entitled *Underworld* was published in 2009. Katherine is a Priestess in the Fellowship of Isis, and a devotee of the flowing spiritual path that her gods have chosen for her.

Vs.

Vs.

Figure 1 - Alchemic treatise of Ramon Llull,
16th century manuscript

Vs.

INTRODUCTION

by Kim Huggens

In most religions there exists a concept of duality, a recognition that what is *'one thing'* is not *'another thing'*. From this dualism arises an awareness of the necessity of polarity, opposition, paradox, and conflict to achieve a state of union. Consequently, mythology abounds with stories of divine twins both opposing and co-operating with one another; magical bonds are drawn between blood-brothers; and a relationship between both God and human and between person and person is symbolically described with reference to dualistic symbolism and language. In many religions this duality may manifest in the everyday world as a black vs. white moral attitude, in which certain acts are deemed *'evil'* and punished whilst other acts are deemed *'good'* and rewarded. The papers collected in this volume all seek to explore the concept of duality, opposition and polarity within the context of the modern neo-Pagan movement and the sources for its inspiration; it is telling that all of the papers seem to conclude or at least suggest that the view of duality or polarity as antagonistic is an over-simplified one, and one that does not aid the spiritual seeker in his/her journey towards union. Instead, each polarity or pair of opposites works in co-operation to preserve a natural order or to create something new – thus the two opposing forces within the alchemical wedding depicted in the seventh trump of the Tarot pack, the Lovers, shows both the recognition of the Other and division and a yearning for union and the result thereof *(solve et coagula...)*

In Wicca the Oak King and the Holly King battle twice yearly for rule over the land and the hand of the Goddess. In Scandinavian mythology Odin and Loki are blood brothers yet continually harass and challenge each other. In Greece and Rome the Sun and Moon were male and female respectively, imagined in the figures of Helios and Selene or Apollo and Artemis. In the Vodou tradition the divine twins are held in high esteem, forming a necessary part of the universe. In the Tarot a Magician draws energy from Above to Below, and a White Queen and Red King are united in a Sacred Marriage. Medieval alchemy seeks to create the Philosopher's Stone from the

Vs.

union of opposing substances and symbolically represents this process in the imagery and language of polarity and union.

Tension and conflict leads to unity: not just good vs. evil but also masculine vs. feminine, dark vs. light, high vs. low, nature vs. nurture, fire vs. water, Cain vs. Abel, Inanna vs. Ereshkigal, Set vs. Osiris... And the relationships created by the recognition of the Beloved Other: Osiris and Isis, the Hieros Gamos, the Alchemical Wedding of Christian Rosenkreutz, and marriage between two people. For relationship cannot be created without duality: we are divided for love's sake, for the chance of union...

This anthology seeks to draw together a diverse collection of papers examining the theistic concepts of duality, unity, conflict, polarity and paradox from a Pagan, magickal, and mythological perspective, in the hope that we can better understand the nature and necessity of tension between *'one'* and *'other one'* and between human and God, accepting the distance between two ideas and states of being as the foundation of the path towards enlightenment and union. Broadly speaking, the essays contained within can be organized into three categories:

Mythological examinations of divine twins / siblings / lovers / opponents. These papers also look at what these tales reveal about either the culture they originate in, or about our own spiritual journey or sense of self. It becomes clear when reading the papers in this category (which form the largest part of the anthology) that myth is rich in such pairings, and that it speaks to us on a level that often we cannot fully identify. The myths explored here act as psychodramas through which we are able to find a blueprint of our own evolution towards unity.

Practices and methods. The papers in this category seek to explore the techniques used in the modern neo-Pagan movement or the religions that influenced it to transcend duality in its many forms. These essays all make the point that in attempting to transcend duality we automatically fail to achieve unity, since by acknowledging the need to transcend we also acknowledge the existence of the Not-I as well as the I.

Social commentaries. These essays deal with the dualities that can be found in the modern Pagan movement, as well as examining concepts such as external vs. internal, insider vs. outsider, and Self vs. Other.

From the first category we initially find two papers written from a Traditional Witchcraft perspective, both highlighting mythological significances of pairings such as Eve vs. Lilith and Cain vs. Abel. *'The Tale of the Twins'*, by Trystn M. Branwynn, and *'Gods of Light and Darkness: Dualism in Modern Traditional Witchcraft'* by Michael Howard, both serve to highlight the role that such antagonistic pairings play both within their original context and that of the modern magickal understandings of them. Another theme that recurs in this category of papers is that of the Inanna/Ereshkigal or Ishtar/Ereshkigal (and, through association, Inanna/Dumuzi or Ishtar/Tammuz), a pairing discussed extensively by two authors, Vikki Bramshaw and Sophie Nusslé in *'The Scorpion and the Bridal Bed, a Paradoxical Tale of Two Star-Crossed Lovers: Innini & Dumuzi'* and *'Inanna and Ereshkigal: A Necessary Encounter'* respectively. The first focuses on the archaeological and mythological exploration and significance of the opposition between these two Mesopotamian Goddesses, whilst the second relates the tale to the author's own experience of entering the Underworld and returning, using the tale of Inanna as the blueprint for the reflection upon her journey.

Since dualistic concepts tend to come in pairs, it should come as no surprise that a further two subjects are dealt with by another two authors each. The Greek myths are visited by authors Magin Rose and Karen F. Pierce. The first explores the dualities inherent in the mythical brothers Ares and Hephaestus – one a smith and one a soldier, one forging weapons and one wielding them, one lame and one virile – in *'Brothers at Arms: the Smith and the Soldier.'* The second examines the twins Castor and Pollux, as well as their relations with other mythological twins in Greek literature, in *'Riders Upon Swift Horses: The Divine Twins of Greek Myth.'* Finally, the Celtic world gets a thorough mention by authors Katherine Sutherland and Gareth Gerrard in *'Sir Gawain and the Green Knight: the Self and Other as sacred doubles in Arthurian mythology'* and *'The Momentum of Polarity: the Battle of Calan Mai'*. Both papers use as their primary source a famous literary piece, and relate them to both the natural cycles of the world around us as well as our internal evolution.

Norse mythology is visited by Katie Gerrard in her paper, *'Are Freyja and Frigga the Same Goddess?'* in an insightful examination of an issue which has been plaguing modern Pagans for decades! My own paper, *'Marassa Dossou-Dosa: The Divine Twins and Duality in Vodou'* pays a visit across the pond to the African-Diaspora religion of Vodou, and explores the mischievous child-twins served near the beginning of most Vodou ceremonies as both mythological figures but also representatives of the Vodou cosmology. Finally in this category we have a paper from folklorist and storyteller Chrissy Derbyshire, *'Toads and Diamonds: Portrayals of Good, Evil, Virtue and Wickedness in Fairytales'*, which explores a dualistic universe of clearly defined black-and-white morality as shown through the lens of the fairytale genre.

The second category is rather diverse, taking us from the duality of Hand and Eye or Mind and Body present in the automatic writing and dream practices of Austin Osman Spare (Guy Gaunt, *'A Lantern to the Cave: Magickal methods for conscious and unconscious communion'*) through Indian beliefs regarding spirit vs. matter and the techniques engaged in to transcend the duality of both (Rachel Donaldson, *'The Divine Human: Nature/Shakti and Spirit/Shiva'*). Diane M. Champigny offers a paper exploring techniques for sex magick and magick based on energetic exchange between opposites in *'Practical Polarity Magick',* and Payam Nabarz provides a Beltane ritual inspired by the myth of Perseus and Andromeda – a ritual that plays on the opposition between male and female, the ritual energetic tension created between them, and the eventual unity achieved (*'Constellations: Perseus and Andromeda Beltane Rite'*). Sophia Fisher also gives us a paper concerning the Vodou tradition of maryaj – marriage – between human servitor and divine spirit, from both a personal perspective and examining what this practice demonstrates about concepts of division between man and God, or unity between human and divine, in this tradition from the African Diaspora.

The third and final category is brief but invaluable, including a paper by Jon Hanna exploring the concepts of Us vs. Them, Exoteric vs. Esoteric, Major vs. Minor, Self vs. Other, within the context of the modern Pagan movement (*'Exoteric Neopaganism: Towards a Minor Religion'*). Here we also find Melissa Harrington's paper, *'Hidden Children of the Great M/Other'*, looking at the process of Othering at its use within the modern Pagan movement, specifically Wicca.

There are a few papers that do not find their way naturally into a category, because instead they serve beautifully as introductory or background pieces, or even seminal pieces that demonstrate in a broader sense the purpose of this anthology and the underlying themes of the other essays contained within. Firstly, Ellie Horne's *'Recognition of the Divine'* explores the understanding mankind holds of duality and how to transcend it, highlighting the paradoxical nature of such an endeavour and the impossibility of unity whilst the endeavour is underway. Secondly, Emily Carding's *'Sun and Moon: An Artist's Perspective on Polarity and its Role in the Tarot'* highlights, through Carding's own Tarot pack *The Tarot of the Sidhe*, the symbolism that is prevalent in all of the discussed pairings, oppositions and dualities, and the significance thereof. Finally, Jonathan Carfax concludes the anthology with a short piece of prose fiction: *'Coniunctio',* a witty and brilliant exploration of everything discussed in *Vs.* through the characters of Aleister Crowley, Florence Farr, and a young woman attempting to unite her Self and Other on the path towards unity.

In putting together this anthology I realize that both myself and the contributing authors have attempted to comment upon, describe, elaborate upon and analyze an issue that oftentimes transcends language, symbolism and rational thought. To demonstrate that we are not alone through the ages in our attempt, I include at the end of the anthology two extracts from ancient texts – Plato's Charioteer analogy from the *Phaedrus*, and a snippet from *Thunder, Perfect Mind*. Both these pieces, I think, serve to remind us that sometimes the very thing that embroils us in the world of duality – logic, the organized mind, words – can help us transcend it; for there are two paths to unity: the first, silence and the still, quiet mind removed from the need for duality; the second, chaos and over-analysis – just as the mind experiences a moment of utter *'break'* upon considering the sound of one hand clapping or the complex problems of philosophy, so it shoots us off into blissful transcendence.

We are divided for love's sake, for the chance of union. I hope that you enjoy these offerings from authors who all have in common that same yearning towards union.

Yours between two worlds, in two minds, and always Vs.,

Kim Huggens
Possibly in Wales, somewhere between the Autumnal Equinox and Winter Solstice, 2010.

Vs.

Figure 2 - Polarity by Emily Carding

COVER ART: 'POLARITY'

by Emily Carding

When I was asked to paint the cover for *Vs.* I was delighted, as polarity has always been an artistic obsession of mine and a key feature of most of my work. I took the opportunity with this piece, *'Polarity'*, to explore the essence of the concept without the usual framework of a myth, being or story to work within, thus trying to make my portrayal as 'pure' as possible. Here is a summary of some of the symbolism of the piece...

The power of polarity lies in the meeting of opposites, the point at which the two come together, (or separate), and the energy that is produced by that event. The most obvious forces of polarity that surround us on a daily basis are the cosmic forces of the Sun and Moon, and their earthly reflection, the genders of male and female. In *'Polarity'* the Sun and its powerful fiery rays is pictured to the centre of the left-hand side of the picture, and the Moon on the right. Within each of these we can see spirals of energy that are flowing outwards from the centre in opposing directions as an expression of their complimentary yet opposing natures. Reflecting this divide, the central hermaphroditic being is split down the middle, which is also the centre of the image, into male and female. The male side, which would normally be associated with the Solar energy, can be seen on the right of the image with the Moon, and vice-versa, thus generating another layer of polarities.

The central being itself is inspired primarily by Qabalistic symbolism, as the Qabalah is a system which beautifully encompasses polarity on every level from universal to the personal and mundane. The Qabalah gives us one of the most important glyphs in esoteric wisdom as we know it today, the Tree of Life. The Tree of Life is like a map of the universe on both a macrocosmic and microcosmic scale, consisting of two opposing pillars, Severity and Mercy and one central unifying pillar, Balance, upon which are placed ten spheres, or Sephiroth, which encompass the various qualities and levels of existence and can also represent stages on our journey to enlightenment and unification with the Divine.

The two sides of the being represent the pillars of Severity and Mercy, and the cosmic bodies within the figure are points on the central pillar of the Tree of Life, the pillar of Balance. As already noted, the figure is an hermaphrodite, with a clear division between his/her male and female side. The male side is white, representing the pillar of Mercy, which contains the Sephiroth Chokmah, Chesed and Netzach. The female side is black, representing the pillar of Severity and the Sephiroth

Vs.

Binah, Geburah and Hod. The bright star in the brow of the figure represents Kether, or The Crown, the highest and most pure of the Sephiroth. Kether is the point towards which all who seek unity with the divine must strive. I chose a star as the symbol for Kether due to its brilliance and connection to the unreachable yet ever-present divine. In the heart of the figure shines the Sun, a symbol of the Sephira Tiphereth. Tiphereth stands at the very centre of the Tree of Life and so also at the centre of our being. I have also incorporated the ancient Chinese symbol of the yin-yang here, as it is a graceful and simple symbol that beautifully captures the energy of polarities flowing and meeting in beauty and balance. Another nod to this symbol can be seen in the face of the figure, where the eyes are of the opposing colour of each side, demonstrating that there is always a little of our opposing polarity within us, like a seed or connecting point.

Moving further downwards to the area of the genitals, we encounter the Moon, which symbolizes our foundation, Yesod. It is located in this area because of its associations with creation and procreation, as well as instincts and intuition. This is also alluded to in the way that the energy lines from the Sun and Moon to the left and right of the image meet in the centre of the figures legs. Is the figure born from this powerful meeting, or is the cosmos born from the energies within the figure itself?

The figure's feet are firmly planted on the Earth, which corresponds with Malkuth, the Sephira which lies at the bottom of the Tree of Life, also known as the Kingdom. It represents the material realm and the power of manifestation, in which is contained the four elements, Earth, Air, Fire and Water. These four elements may be seen in the colours I have used - some more subtly than others!

Returning to the top of the picture, we can see that the figure is reaching upwards, towards the spectrum of colours that flow crown-like from Kether and the top of the head. The spectrum represents the whole of the universe, which is both within and without each of us. It also can be seen as the veil which stands between us and the higher levels of wisdom and understanding on the Tree of Life, which is beautiful and terrible to behold, and which all who seek enlightenment must climb beyond.

Overall in this image, I have attempted to use colour to capture the essence of polarity to the best of my ability, including where possible complementary colours which oppose each other on the colour wheel and react to give an optical effect of 'flashing' when seen in such close proximity. Even such a simple device can give us one key into understanding the power that is generated when two poles or opposites come together!

Polarity is a universal force that is reflected in the world around us and all cultures within it, so I have tried to be as universal as possible in my choice of symbolism. I hope you have found this small journey through my thoughts behind this image interesting and inspiring!

Vs.

Vs.

Figure 3 - Baphomet, by Eliphas Levi.

Vs.

THE TALE OF THE TWINS

by Trystn M. Branwynn

This tale is as old as human storytelling. It can be found in every culture and every magical and religious system on earth. These ideas don't have to be theistic in nature, nor do they deal exclusively with male figures, even though some of the most well known characters include Cain and Abel; Tubal and Jubal; Jesus and John the Baptist; Yeshua (Joshua) Bar Abbas and Yeshua Ben Miriam (amusingly, Jesus and Jesus); Bran and Beli, Merlin and Vortigern, and Gog and Magog.

We can also look at brother – sister or husband - wife combinations such as Artemis and Apollo; Diana and Lucifer (Dianus); the heretical Jesus and the Magdalene; and Tubal and Naamah. Equally interesting are the female – female relationships such as Inanna and Ereshkigal; Eve and Lilith, and Brigid and Cailleach.

I don't have space within the scope of this article to examine the rich detail of all of these figures and relationships. To do so would require volumes rather than pages, so I must content myself with presenting a few examples and trust the reader search further for more in-depth analysis. As we examine some of these figures, I will present views that sometimes contradict and challenge literal or established ecclesiastic interpretations and present a more *'functional'* or occult perspective. I do this because we can best understand the Twins in terms of their relationship in mythic process; while the literal and dualistic perspectives remain static and speak only to a paranoid worldview of an eternal battle of *'good and evil.'* In functional terms, heresy often presents the very best facets of any magical-religious system.

These complexes of figures carry one common thread: they encompass two figures that appear alternately as lovers and rivals, and share certain commonalties. On the Qabalistic Tree of Life, we can see this diagrammed as Chokmah (Wisdom) and Binah (Understanding) dividing themselves out from the union of Kether in the process of the Fall. They originate and conclude as one being[1] much as a pair of identical twins takes their life from the division of a single ovum.

---

[1] Gray, William G., *Qabalistic Concepts*, pp. 78-84.

Vs.

Many people find all too great a temptation to view these spirits as dualistic and discrete opposites. Cain represents the *'First Murderer'* while Abel is the *'First Victim'*.[2] One is *'evil'* and one is *'good.'* Lilith appears *'dark, monstrous, and terrifying'* while Eve seems all sweetness and light.[3] I find that this very simplistic and surface view takes no note of the commonalties in the figures just as it ignores the fact that these apparent opposites depend upon each other to exist. To put the matter very plainly: both light and darkness must be present for our senses to register either. Further, in purely physical terms, as all radiant energy consists of varying frequencies of light waveforms, *'darkness'* doesn't really exist at all. It is really full of light. So, we can hide in the sun all we like, but until our senses register darkness and shadow, which are necessary illusions, we will never see the light. In occult terms, we must embrace the *'dark'*, and challenge it, in order to find the light within.

Another instructive view might be gleaned from Aristophanes' tale of the origin of love as told by Plato.[4] This story, popularized in song by the musical *Hedwig and the Angry Inch,* tells of a time when humanity comprised three genders. One, called the *'Children of the Sun'*, consisted of two males combined in a single body. A second group, the *'Children of the Earth'*, had two females sharing one form, while the third, the *'Children of the Moon'*, had a body shared by one each, male and female.[5] The story goes on to say that the gods became offended by these beings and so Zeus divided them with the thunderbolt. This left pairs of humans, each yearning for his or her twin. Each one of us desires to reconnect with our second self, which is also a very strong image held by the *'Storm and Stress'* movement in German Romanticism.[6] This imagery speaks very powerfully to the shamanistic philosophy of Traditional Witchcraft, which sees the Witch-Shaman as *'third gendered'* – a union of male and female in a single form. As we shall see, mythology supports this concept strongly.[7]

---

[2] *Genesis 4:1-10.*

[3] Jackson, Nigel and Howard, Mike, *The Pillars of Tubal Cain*, pp.134-148.

[4] Plato, *Symposium, Aristophanes' Speech*, 189c-195a.

[5] Aristophanes' speech is portrayed as an "origin of sexualities" in *Hedwig*. Within the context of Symposium, it appears to mock Creation Myths that can be seen as supportive of any sort of exclusive sexual politics.

[6] Hoffmeister, Gerhart and Tubach, Friedrich, *Germany: 2000 Years*, Volume II, Continuum Publishing Company, New York, NY.

Goethe, J. Wolfgang von, trans. MacNeice, Louis, *Goethe's Faust,* Oxford University Press, New York, NY, 1961.

Wagner, Richard, *Der Ring des Nibelungens,* et al, Bayreuth, Bayern, BRD.

[7] While this information can be gleaned from conversing with a TIW Magister or Magistra, and is widely agreed upon, it remains a matter of Clan and Current Gnosis, and detailed understandings in text form are most likely to be found in private, internal grimoires, however a reference to the concept can be found in the *Robert Cochrane Letters* p. 26.

Vs.

A cosmological symbol for these Twins, or Rivals, can be readily seen in the Zodiac sign of Gemini, called *'The Twins'*. We see this mirrored in the image of its associated Tarot trump *The Lovers*. Various decks depict this concept in their own way, but in his *Book of Thoth*, Aleister Crowley suggests a compelling image for this trump that he titles *The Brothers*. His description reads:

> *"In the middle of the field stands Cain; in his right hand is the Hammer of Thor with which he hath slain his brother, and it is all wet with his blood. And his left hand he holdeth open as a sign of innocence. On his right hand is his mother Eve, around whom the serpent is entwined with his hood spread behind her head; and on his left hand is a figure somewhat like the Hindoo but much more seductive. Yet I know it to be Lilith. And above him is the Great Sigil of the Arrow, downward, but it is struck through the heart of the child. This child is also Abel. And the meaning of this part of the card is obscure, but that is the correct drawing of the Tarot card; and that is the correct magical fable from which the Hebrew scribes, who were not complete Initiates, stole their legend of the Fall and the subsequent events."*[8]

This vision never made the leap from conceptualization to visual realization, but still exemplifies, in the strongest terms, the relationship of Cain and Abel. To the Traditional Witch, Cain is not murdering Abel, nor is he sacrificing his brother. Instead he calls down the thunder from the heavens to quicken him – to pour the power of spirit into Abel's form, releasing the combination from the tyranny of Fate. The result of this action is the creation of Cain, the Master of the Four Winds and the Man in the Moon – according to such sources as the Horseman's Word. Cain appears to us formed of the active principal of awareness and the passive principle of the fleshly vehicle (Abel) combined into one becomes the first sorcerer through the act of sacrificing the person he loves best.

We can also look at Cain and Abel from a cultural perspective to glean some additional keys. The *Book of Genesis* presents Cain to us as the ploughman and the inventor of agriculture (actually horticulture.) He lives in one place to attend his crops, and works to shield them from the effects of unpredictable weather. He digs wells and irrigation ditches to keep them watered during dry periods during summer. He thus establishes himself as master of a stable territory and bitterly resents outside intrusions that could damage his livelihood. Abel, by contrast, is a herdsman. He follows his grazing and browsing herds, completely at the mercy of wind, weather, seasons, and prevailing conditions. He finds farmland, such

---

[8] Crowley, Aleister, *The Book of Thoth*, p. 81.

Vs.

as Cain's, both an obstacle and a danger as his herd animals will attempt to break into farm fields looking for browse and graze and thus incurring the wrath of the farmer whose livelihood they eat. Thus we can see the conflict between the brothers on the level of the conflict between herding folk and territorial farmers. On a magical level we can see the relationship between the Child of Fate (Son of Mary or Son of Man) who obeys the cause-and-effect laws of nature and between its ruling spirits - the Elohim and the Child of Awareness who defy these laws, altering the environment to serve his own needs.[9]

In the later *Gospel of Matthew*'s crucifixion sequence we find two Jesuses in jeopardy. One is the Son of Man, or Son of Fate (Joshua, Son of Bitterness, whom we know as Jesus) whom Luke describes earlier as *'Pleasing to his mother in all things'*,[10] just as Abel found favour with the Elohim. The other, a zealot in jail for murder, Joshua Bar Abbas or *'Jesus, Son of the Father'*, has rebelled and worked to cast down the foreign rule of Rome.[11] He thus sought to transform his world. He made his life's goal to recreate that world in his own image. Joshua Ben Miriam goes to the cross and Joshua Bar Abbas goes free... We need only look to the ritual parallels from a Roman Mystery Faith called the Rex Nemorensis to unlock the keys to this little riddle. The High Priest at Lake Nemi was required to be an escaped slave, a prisoner, and he ascended to his exalted position by assassinating his predecessor.[12]

We can find another interesting point in Wicca's adoption of the twin Year Kings.[13] I find this syncretism puzzling, since Wicca posits the existence of only a single male deity figure, *'The Horned God'*. The obvious explanation for their understanding of this rivalry would be that this God assassinates himself, Woden fashion.[14] This gives us the effect of completely internalizing the rivalry within a single being and points to a Freudian – Crowleyan concept of strife, sacrifice, and union within the psyche between the Id and the Superego or, in occult terms, the Beast and the Archangel. The result of this process would look much like the figure of Baphomet, long regarded as an accurate symbolic image of the God of Witches.

An alternate set of twins within this same system would require an understanding of a Waxing Year Queen (Noctifera) and a Waning Year King (Hades.) Noctifera would then behead Hades at Midwinter, rebirthing herself in the process, and rebirth him at Brigidmas/Imbolc. Her own sacrificial qualities would occur in her

---

[9] *Genesis 4:1–10.*
[10] *Luke 2:51.*
[11] *Matthew 27:16.*
[12] http://en.wikipedia.org/wiki/Rex_Nemorensis.
[13] Farrar, J., and Farrar S., *A Witches Bible: The Complete Witches Handbook,* pp. 93-101.
[14] *Havamal* verses 137–144.

Vs.

defloration at Roodmass/Beltane and complete sacred marriage at Midsummer. I must stress that this understanding is *possible* - but not orthodox - within a Wiccan milieu. To find mythic support for this idea, we must look back into the root mythologies whence Gardner and Sanders drew their inspiration.[15] In Leland's exposition in *Aradia* we find this Goddess presented as the Daughter of Lucifer and Diana. She does carry the keys needed to assume both roles – Lucifer and Noctifer. We find a Lightbringer Goddess of both Sun *and* Moon very akin to Lilith or Naamah. As I mentioned earlier, some of the best facets of any magical-religious system can be found in seemingly heretical views.

We can also find support for this internal conflict within many mythologies. One example is found in the First Branch of the Welsh *Mabinogi*. In the first of three stories that make up the First Branch,[16] Pwyll finds himself carrying out an Underworld Raid in disguise. He wears the face of Arawn, King of Annwfn, and must spend a year and a day in Arawn's Castle, while the King of the Dead rules Dyfed in his stead. Pwyll must overcome several traps – temptations - inherent in the conditions of his sojourn, and so doing both learns and demonstrates the wise restraint that will allow him to win his duel at the ford and make himself Pen Annwfn.

Arawn clearly typifies the instinctual qualities of both the Beast and the War God or Waning Year King in his conflicts with Hafgan. The King of the Dead finds himself eternally unable to refrain from continuing to pummel his rival after the latter falls. This of course, gives him the result of his enemy simply standing up and walking away. Pwyll, whose name can be translated as *'Wisdom'* must restrain himself to a single killing stroke and this clearly marks a trait of the Archangel or Superego. Pwyll must exercise an imposed restraint that the titanic Arawn cannot. We see a clear example of the restraint of Wisdom as opposed to unbridled, instinctual aggression.[17]

One of the most fascinating sets of apparent rivals can be seen in the relationship between Eve and Lilith.[18] In many versions of their story Lilith is the first wife who refuses to submit to Adam demanding *'Why should I lie beneath you...?'* She then leaves, seduces Samael and learns from him the secret name of God, returning to the Garden - first to steal Adam's seed and then, in some versions of the tale, in the guise of the serpent (who can also be the Seraphim – *'Fiery Serpent'* – Samael) offering Eve the fruit of the Tree of the Knowledge of Good and Evil. Whether one sees this fruit as an apple or a pomegranate (*pomme* also means *'apple'*,) it is a fruit

---

[15] Leland, Charles G., *Aradia: Gospel of the Witches*.
[16] Parker, Will, *Four Branches of the Mabinogi: Celtic Mythology and Medieval Reality*, pp. 178-182.
[17] Ibid.
[18] Jackson, Nigel and Howard, Mike, *The Pillars of Tubal Cain*, pp. 134–148.

of the rose family and sacred to Venus. As all such fruits are symbolically associated with female genitalia, one could read the entire sequence: *"When the woman saw that the fruit of the tree was good for food and pleasing to the eye, and also desirable for gaining wisdom, she took some and ate it. She also gave some to her husband..."*[19] as: *"Eve performed cunnilingus upon Lilith, and then showed Adam how."* One gains the knowledge by tasting the forbidden fruit and worshipping at the gates of the temple, and we have a lesbian union of twins that recalls the Greek myth from Plato's *Symposium* mentioned earlier. We also have a likely trio to take the roles shown in many older Lovers cards of the Tarot cards: we see Adam torn between the sweetness and allure of Eve and the dark, transforming power of Lilith.[20]

In Traditional Witchcraft we find our Twins defined a bit more clearly by the cosmological understanding we call *'The Compass'*,[21] but at the same time given its shifting and moving nature, this apparent clarity can appear between several sets of figures and can become somewhat blurred: the seeming lines between the figures shift and evolve in the consciousness. The immediate imagery represents the Waxing and Waning Year Kings, whom Cochrane calls Lucet the Divine Child – we will associate this figure with Apollo for convenience's sake – and Tettens the King of the North Wind, whom we will associate with both Hermes[22] and Hades. The first item to note is that neither of these figures presents us with a whitewashed or clear-cut set of keys. They are closely related and their associations clearly indicate their kinship. Tettens is the King of the Castle of Weeping, which lies behind the North Wind. He also carries the mantle of the Waning Year - King of Winter and the Wasteland. We see him first in the role of the Psychopomp – the Guide to the Underworld – and here his mercurial qualities display themselves clearly. We can call him Woden or Lugus – who are, of course, the Wind and Lightning Gods[23] as well as the Underworld Guides.

Amusingly, we can also find a Tettens or Woden image at the core of the symbols that make up the popular figure of Father Christmas. We can see them even more pronounced in the American Santa Claus and nowhere more clearly than in the poem *A Visit from St. Nicholas*.[24]

The moon on the breast of the new-fallen snow

---

[19] *Genesis 3:6*.
[20] See for instance the Tarot de Marseilles and Tarot Belgique.
[21] Cochrane, Robert, *The Robert Cochrane Letters: An Insight Into Modern Traditional Witchcraft*, pp 163–167.
[22] Cochrane, Robert, *The Robert Cochrane Letters: An Insight Into Modern Traditional Witchcraft*, p. 164.
[23] Parker, Will, *Four Branches of the Mabinogi: Celtic Mythology and Medieval Reality*, pp. 447–480.
[24] Moore, Clement C., *A Visit From St. Nicholas*.

Vs.

Gave the lustre of mid-day to objects below,
When, what to my wondering eyes should appear,
But a miniature sleigh, and eight tiny reindeer,
With a little old driver, so lively and quick,
I knew in a moment it must be St. Nick.
More rapid than eagles his coursers they came,
And he whistled, and shouted, and called them by name;
"Now, Dasher! now, Dancer! now, Prancer and Vixen!
On, Comet! on Cupid! on, Donner and Blitzen!

The most interesting facet of these images lies in the fact that the poet, Clement Moore, had no connection at all to the Northern Traditions in his background and was merely writing to amuse his sick daughter. As we say: *'Awen will out'*. The Old Ones speak through whom they will.

He also presents himself as King of the Dead and Master of the Wild Hunt. In this imagery we clearly see stern Hades or Arawn. We've already commented on his association with strife, change, and conflict and many find it very tempting to label him a War God. He certainly does connect with Ares in this regard, but even more so with the old Nordic Tiw, who is also Father of the Tribes. As King of the Dead, we also find him associated strongly with the power of Time, via the crossroads process of death itself, and thus he carries a strong saturnine quality. Robert Cochrane describes this combination of qualities symbolically in his letters to Norman Gills thus:

> "In the North lies the Castle of Weeping, the ruler thereof is named Tettens, our Hermes or Woden. He is the second twin, the waning sun. The Lord over mysticism, magic, power and death, the Baleful Destroyer, the God of War, of Justice, King of Kings, since all pay their homage to Him. Ruler of the Winds, the Windyat. Cain imprisoned in the Moon, ever desiring Earth. He is visualized as a tall, dark man, shadowy, cold and deadly. Unpredictable, yet capable of great nobility since he represents Truth. He is the God of magicians and witches, who knows all sorcery. Lord of the North, dark, unpredictable, the true God of all witches and magicians if they are working at any decent level at all. A cold wind surrounds him, age and time so ancient that it is beyond belief flows from him. Dark is His shadow, and he bears a branch of the sorrowing Alder and walks with the aid of a blackthorn stick. Sorrow is printed upon his face, yet also joy. He guards, as the rider upon the eight legged horse, the approaches to the Castle of Night. He is also the Champion of the glass bridge after the Silver Forest. Cold is the air as he passes by. Some

say tall and dark, I say small and dark, speaking in a faint voice, which is as clear as ice."[25]

Lucet, or Lucifer, on the other hand, carries the Apollonian keys of the Sol Invictus. Like Woden and Father Christmas, he presents himself as a charioteer, but rules from the Castle of the Rising Sun. He is the spirit of Wisdom and human awareness and thus presents us with a combination of solar and mercurial keys. Like Woden, he descends (falls) and ascends the World Tree or Axis Mundi and survives his act of self-sacrifice. Like Osiris and Pwyll, he descends into the Underworld and makes himself its master. He likewise closely associates himself with Time, and we can find him presented as the stepson of the Old Man, Saturn. In fact, the image of the Fatherless Boy or Magical Bastard presents us with one of his strongest earmarks. He can thus be seen in the Masonic epithet of *'The Widow's Son'* and in the Christian concept of *'The Virgin's Son'*. Cochrane's use of the name of a device that takes the form of a Mercury symbol, and is used to make flaxen cords, serves to heighten the image of the Mercury – Sol combination. As the son of the Widow or the Virgin, we find in him the Son of Fate, whose destiny is to overthrow the dread power of his mother. We also find him presented as a member of not one, but two sets of Twins. The Waxing and Waning Year Kings present themselves readily. But he also appears as twin to Saturn, or Nodens Mecurianus, and Cochrane comments:

"...these two appear as twins, but they may be the same person."[26]

In purely physical terms, we can ask if Light creates Time, Time creates Light; or do they create each other? Are they indeed the same force? Certainly the various Creation myths and many religious systems comment on this relationship, but none appear to attempt to answer the question. The science of Quantum Physics has been weighing in on the question, but it remains, at least for now, a matter for argument in all of the three realms of Magic, Religion, and Science.

All of the mythic process that we've examined in this article points to one conclusion: the reunification of the Twins. The zodiac and Tarot show this if we look directly across the girdle of constellations from Gemini and *The Lovers* to Sagittarius and *Temperance*. The symbol of the Centaur Archer holds both the arrow we heard about from Crowley – the same arrow Cupid prepares to launch in *The Lovers* – and the key of the union of Angel and Beast. I find no accident in the portrayal of the hybrid of Horse (sovereignty

---

[25] Robert Cochrane, *The Robert Cochrane Letters*, pp. 164–165.
[26] Ibid.

bearer) and the Man (King) or of Beast and Human. Temperance likewise shows either the Forge of Spirit or one vessel emptied into the other. Psychologist Sallie Nichols sees this image as an act of balancing, or reconciling[27] but I must disagree and insist that it goes further to express a process of *combining*.

This brings us back to the figure of Baphomet, or Seth, featured in many Tarot *Devil* cards. In this figure, we see a combination of Angel and Beast, Male and Female, Hermes and Apollo, unified into a single figure. Very often, an artist will also include a caduceus at the groin to represent the Kundalini or Fiery Serpent, rising up the Tree – the spine – to cause the explosion of fire (wisdom) from the head. Again, I find no accident in the placement of these symbolic associations in subsequent positions of the zodiac. We progress from Gemini, to the reunion of the Twins in Sagittarius, to the expression of the Devil/Set/Ianus at Capricorn.[28] Of course we find the Master of the Wasteland (or winter) in the ram or goat-horned Set and the Master of the Threshold in the two-faced (unified twins) Ianus. Far from being a figure of horror, the Goat of Mendes becomes an expression of sublime beauty as the Twins reunify to form once again the Omega of the Crown. Here then, as the Twins become one, is Cain: Twins in one body and Master of the Four Winds.

Bibliography
Gray, William G., *Qabalistic Concepts*. York Beach, ME: Red Wheel / Weiser, 1997.
The Holy Bible, New International Version, Authentic Media, 2008.
Jackson, Nigel and Howard, Mike, *The Pillars of Tubal Cain*. Milverton, Somerset: Capall Bann Publishing, 2000.
Plato, *Symposium, Aristophanes' Speech*. trans. Dover, Kenneth. Cambridge: Cambridge University Press, 1980.
Crowley, Aleister, and Harris, Lady Frieda, *The Thoth Tarot Deck*. U.S. Games Systems Inc., 1972.
Crowley, Aleister, *The Book of Thoth*. York Beach, ME: Samuel Weiser Inc., 1989.
Tavaglione, Giorgio, *The Stairs of Gold Tarot*. U.S. Games Systems Inc., 1990.
Farrar, J., and Farrar S., *A Witches Bible: The Complete Witches Handbook*. Blaine, WA: Phoenix Publishing, 1996.
Parker, Will, *Four Branches of the Mabinogi: Celtic Mythology and Medieval Reality*. Oregon House, CA: Bardic Press, 2007.
Leland, Charles G., *Aradia: Gospel of the Witches*. Custer, WA, Phoenix Publishing, 1990.
Cochrane, Robert, John Jones, Evan, and Howard, Mike ed., *The Robert Cochrane Letters: An Insight Into Modern Traditional Witchcraft*. Milverton, Somerset :Capall Bann Publishing, 2002.

---

[27] Nichols, Sallie, *Jung and the Tarot*, pp. 249–259.
[28] Jackson, Nigel and Howard, Mike, *The Pillars of Tubal Cain*, pp. 70-82.

Vs.

Cochrane, Robert. *The Robert Cochrane Letters*, (Writings of Roy Bowers) Clan of Tubal Cain, Shani Oates, Maid,
http://www.clanoftubalcain.org.uk/links.html
Moore, Clement C., *A Visit From St. Nicholas*. Troy, NY: Troy Sentinel, 1823.
Nichols, Sallie, *Jung and the Tarot*. York Beach, ME: Samuel Weiser Inc., 1980.
Olive Bray trans. *The Elder or Poetic Edda,* commonly known as Sæmund's Edda, part I: The Mythological Poems, (London: Printed for the Viking Club, 1908), pp. 61-111.
  http://www.pitt.edu/~dash/havamal.html#runes

Discography
Hedwig and the Angry Inch Soundtrack, "The Origin of Love." Music and lyrics Stephen Trask, recorded by John Cameron Mitchell, 2001. Hybrid Recordings, New York, NY

Vs.

GODS OF LIGHT AND DARKNESS

Dualism in Modern Traditional Witchcraft

by Michael Howard

In a religious or spiritual sense *'dualism'* refers to any belief system or philosophy that divides the universe between two opposing and conflicting principles, even if at some stage they are reconciled or united. Patriarchal religions usually represent these two principles in black and white terms as the forces of light battling with the powers of darkness for rulership of the cosmos and the human soul. A classic example can be found in the 6th century CE Persian text *Zenda-Vesta* where a dualistic cosmology describes a universe divided between two brothers engaged in eternal conflict. These divine twins are Ahura-Mazda, symbolising good, life, fire and the sun, and Ahriman, representing evil, death, darkness and the underworld. Similar divine twins, usually male, can be found in many other pre-Christian religions.

Many forms of modern traditional witchcraft (i.e. non-Wiccan and pre-Wiccan) also have a dualistic system. However, it is far more complicated and subtle than these ancient examples, and not so black and white. Some traditional witches follow a Luciferian tradition or have a Cainite mythos. The archangel Lucifer (from the Latin *luci* or *'light'* and *ferre, 'bearer'*) or Lumiel/Lumial (Hebrew and Arabic for *'Light of God/Allah'*) is said to have rebelled against Yahweh or God. As a result he was cast down to Earth as a fallen angel to become the *'Lord of This World'*. For this reason some witches have accepted the Lightbearer as their saviour and the redeemer of humanity. They believe that as he regains his previous exalted position in Creation and is redeemed, so will 'fallen' humanity do so. However this is a symbiotic relationship because Lucifer, and the rebel angels who followed him into exile, can only be redeemed if humankind spiritually evolves. It is therefore in the Fallen Ones' own interest to help us achieve that aim, hence their title of *'teaching angels'*.

In a radical interpretation of the biblical Garden of Eden myth, Lucifer is seen as the serpent who *'seduced'* the Mother of All Living, Eve. In reality by defying Yahweh and tempting her to eat the forbidden fruit of the Tree of the Knowledge of Good and Evil the serpent enabled primitive humans to *'open their eyes'*, become wise and to achieve the potential to be transformed *'as gods, knowing good and evil'* (*Genesis 3:5*). A similar acceleration of the spiritual and material evolution of the human race took place when the rebel angels known as the Watchers incarnated in human form. They acted as cultural exemplars to teach emerging humankind occult lore and the arts and crafts of civilisation. By mating with *'the daughters of men'* they also created a hybrid half-angelic, half-human race.[29]

Lucifer's *'crime'* of defying Yahweh that led to his exile from heaven or the divine realm is described in the *Qur'an* as a refusal to bow down before the first man, Adam. Allah had wanted him to become the caliph or religious ruler on Earth and, quite understandably, Lucifer, described in Islam as Iblis, objected. He pointed out that he had been created from cosmic fire while Adam was only created from the dust of the earth. In response Allah cursed the archangel and banished him from his presence until the Day of Doom (Judgement Day in Christian mythology) because he would not bow down to his clay-born creation.

In the Judeo-Christian tradition it is said that the Archangel Mikhael or Michael (*'Beloved of God'*) fought with Lumiel or Lucifer and his rebel angels. The outcome of the War in Heaven was that the *'Great Dragon'* was *'cast out into the earth, and his angels were cast out with him.'*[30] Unfortunately for Yahweh many of the company of angels supported Lucifer and, although they had not participated in the war, they began to leave Heaven in protest. In fact so many angels sided with the rebels and were leaving to join them that Yahweh ordered the gates of Heaven to be closed.

For those witches who follow the Luciferian tradition the relationship between Lucifer and Michael is seen in dualistic terms. They are in fact brothers who, from being fellow archangels or *'sons of God'*,[31] became enemies on different sides of a dispute with Yahweh. Esoteric teachings say that before Lucifer's fall from grace he was the angelic regent of the sun and the Solar Logos, the ruler of the solar system. Michael was only the planetary regent or ruler of the third planet Terra or Earth. After the Fall Michael became the solar regent and was appointed commander-in-chief of the divine army, leader of the angelic hosts left behind and the vice-royal of Heaven. In his fallen state Lucifer took Michael's place as the earthly regent and adopted the role of caliph previously given to Adam.

In Islamic lore it is said that each day the Archangel Michael prays and sheds tears for fallen humanity that it may achieve salvation. He also prays at the same time for his brother Lucifer to be redeemed and take his rightful place in Heaven. This reflects the

---

[29] *Genesis 6:1-4.*
[30] *Revelations 12:7-9.*
[31] See *Job 1:6* and *2:1-2.*

belief in some Traditional Craft circles that Lucifer and Michael are in fact the twin serpents of light and dark. Although Michael is depicted in Christian iconography as crushing a dragon or serpent underfoot or pinioning it with his spear or lance, in reality they are one and the dual aspects of the same spiritual force. This is illustrated in the saying: *'The Light is in the Darkness and the Darkness is in the Light.'*

Figure 4 - St. Michael the Archangel, crushing the fallen angel Lucifer

Vs.

Another dualistic aspect of the Luciferian tradition is the belief that Lucifer and Jesus are brothers. This is apparently also held by the Church of Jesus Christ of Latter-Day Saints or the Mormons. In their case it is allegedly based on the biblical reference to the pre-Fall Lucifer and Jesus as both *'sons of God'* (see the *Book of Job*). In the Luciferian tradition Lucifer is believed to have incarnated as various sacrificial saviour gods throughout history. This was an attempt to progress the evolutionary and spiritual development of the human race. These avatars include Attis, Mithras, Mani, Quetzalcoatl and, of course, Jesus.

In the *Old Testament*, the *Dead Sea Scrolls* and the *Qur'an* the brotherly rivalry between Lucifer and Michael is reflected on the earthly plane in the myth of the warring brothers Cain and Abel. It says that when Eve gave birth to her first-born son Cain she said *'I have gotten a man from the Lord [Adonai]'*.[32] A Christian tradition says Eve was attended at the birth of Cain by the Archangel Michael acting as the midwife. The biblical account adds that *'And she again bore his brother Abel'*, suggesting to some biblical scholars that they may have been twins.

The first woman's cryptic comment about getting a child from *'the Lord'* refers to an ancient tradition that Cain was of supernatural origin. In Jewish Kabbalistic lore Cain was said to be the product of an illicit mating between Eve and Samael, the Hebrew name for the serpent in the Edenic myth and the ruler of the Hebrew version of the underworld, who is also identified with Lucifer. For this reason in the original Greek translation of the *Old Testament* Cain is referred to as *'the evil one'*.[33]

In the Bible Cain is described as *'a tiller of the ground'* and Abel is a *'keeper of sheep'*.[34] Specifically Cain is a farmer while his brother is a shepherd or nomadic herdsman. Because of these occupations the fraternal rivalry between the two siblings, and its eventual violent conclusion, has been interpreted in human evolutionary terms by some historians. The myth of Cain and Abel is seen as symbolic of the struggle for supremacy in late Neolithic times in the Middle East between nomadic herdsmen and early farmers and city builders.

The conflict between the brothers is triggered by Cain making an offering or sacrifice to Yahweh. As it says in the *Old Testament*: *'And in process of time it came to pass, that Cain brought of the fruit of the ground an offering unto the Lord'*. In response Abel offered up a blood sacrifice of a first-born animal from his flock. Yahweh was pleased with Abel's offering and respected him for it. In contrast he had no respect for what Cain had offered and rejected it. In Yahweh's

---

[32] *Genesis 4:1*.
[33] Ginzburg, Louis. *The Legends of the Jews*, pp. 105-9.
[34] *Genesis 4:2*.

Vs.

commandments to Moses he had made clear his preference for sacrificial offerings of *'cattle, sheep and goats'*.[35]

Following his rejection by Yahweh, Cain went to the field where his brother was tending his flocks and he *'rose up against Abel his brother and slew him'*.[36] No apparent reason is given for Cain's sudden fratricidal action. It can only be presumed that he was jealous of Abel's special relationship with Yahweh and his new role as the *'chosen one'*. Although Cain secretly buried his dead brother's body Yahweh knew what had happened and was led to the corpse by a raven.

He promptly cursed Cain saying that henceforth he would be exiled to become a wanderer on the Earth and would struggle to get a living from the ground. Ironically he is doomed to become a nomad like his murdered brother. Cain protested that he would be singled out and hunted down by those who wanted to avenge Abel's death and if they found him he would be killed. Yahweh then set a *'mark'* on Cain *'lest any finding him should kill him'*. Oddly he also said that if anyone should kill or do harm to the first murderer, divine vengeance would be taken on them sevenfold.[37]

The nature of this mysterious *'Mark of Cain'* has always been a matter for speculation. Some writers have suggested it was Cain's bright red hair. This was a colouring also associated with other biblical villains such as Jezebel, Delilah, King Herod, Mary Magdalene and Judas. Others say the Mark was extreme hirsuteness, a ritual tattoo, a limp caused by a lame leg, or even some unusual physical deformity such as horns or a blackened face. My first occult teacher, Madeline Montalban, founder of the Luciferian-based Order of the Morning Star, told me that the Mark was a special symbol that could be seen in the aura of those of the *'witch blood'* or *'elven blood'* spiritually descended from Cain.

In Hebrew Cain and Abel are known as Qayin and Hevel and in Arabic they are described in the *Qur'an* as Kabil and Habil. The latter names suggest they might have been twins, albeit with different fathers! In the *Torah* the name Qayin is said to mean a *'metal smith'* or metallurgist and is derived from the Hebrew root word *kaneh* meaning *'to create, form or shape'*. An alternative linguistic origin is from the word *'acquisition'* or *'to acquire'*. This perhaps relates to Cain's role as the farmer who acquires land. In contrast Abel's name means *'breath of wind'*, suggesting that he wanders free where he wills.

The ancient philosopher Philo of Alexandria saw the myth of Cain and Abel in purely dualistic terms with the opposing brothers representing aspects of the human soul. Predictably this concept

---

[35] See *Exodus 29:10-22* and *Leviticus 1: 1-17*.
[36] *Genesis 4:1-8*.
[37] *Genesis 4:3-15*.

depicts Cain as the *'first murderer'* and the representation of the Fall of Man and Original Sin. In Philo's view humanity has an innate capacity for violence and committing evil acts. In contrast to this primitive urge, Abel represents the human desire to good works that is in a constant struggle with the Cainite side of our psyches. It is no coincidence that Cain and his descendant and avatar Tubal-Cain as metal smiths are credited with forging weapons of warfare. In Philo's theory the story of Cain and Abel is illustrative of, or an allegory of, the psychic conflict within the human soul. However it is obvious from the biblical account that Cain and his descendants are also cultural exemplars acting as teachers to the human race and accelerating its evolution.

In the *Old Testament* it states that Cain left *'the presence of the Lord'* to live in the land of Nod, described as a place that was *'east of Eden'*. Although Adam and Eve and their offspring were supposed to be the first family, in Nod Cain married. His wife gave birth to Cain's first-born son Enoch, or Chanoch in Hebrew. When he had grown up Enoch was supposed to have been responsible for building the first city. Cain was also a cultural exemplar as he is credited with city building, being the first blacksmith and tamer of wild horses and inventing weights and measures.

Cain's descendants also carried on this civilising role as well. The sons and daughters of the patriarch Lamech, who was directly descended from Cain, were Jabal (Yaval), Jubal (Yuval), Tubal-Cain (Tuval Kayin) and Naamah (Nahamah). Jabal *'was the father [ancestor] of such as dwell in tents, and of such [who] have cattle'*; Jubal was *'the father of all such as handle the harp and organ'* (musicians); Tubal-Cain was *'an instructor in brass and iron'*; and their sister Naamah was a spinner and weaver.[38]

Lamech is described as semi-blind and there is a story he was out hunting one day with his beloved son Tubal-Cain, who appears to have been a step-son of the family. Suddenly they saw the figure of their ancestor Cain standing behind a tree or in a bush. He is clad in animal skins and wearing horns on his head. In his blindness Lamech mistook Cain for a king stag. Tubal-Cain however knew who he was a man, but despite this knowledge he still helped his father to aim the bow and fire the deadly arrow at their tribal ancestor. There are similarities between this story and the myth of Baldur, the god of light in Norse mythology, killed by his blind brother Holdur with a poisoned dart or arrow with the help of the fire god, Loki.

Cain fell dying, his life blood staining the earth. It was only when he spoke his last words that Lamech realised he was a man and became aware of the terrible mistake he had made. However Tubal-Cain cunningly consoled his father by reassuring him that because Cain had horns and was so covered in hair he was like a *'night*

---

[38] *Genesis 4: 19-22.*

goblin'. Therefore Lamech should feel no guilt for accidentally killing his ancestor as he looked like a creature from another world.

In the Traditional Craft it is taught that when Cain left behind his *'cloak of flesh'* he became the leader of the Hidden Company, the discarnate human guides and teachers of humankind. It is also said that, as the archetypal farmer and ploughman, Cain lives on as the corn spirit or the spirit of the grain that grows each year and is cut down in its prime to feed humankind. His mythical story is recorded in the popular folk story *Old John Barleycorn,* where Cain takes the mythic role of the sacrificed god or divine king. He marries Sovereignty or the goddess of the land and has to die at the end of his reign to ensure the fertility of the harvest.

In the account of Cain's death at the hands of his descendant Lamech it is said that the *'hairy one'* is hiding behind a tree and is concealed by its leaves or branches. This naturally evokes the image of the English folk character known as Jack-in-the-Green or the Green Man and the woodwoses – the so-called *'wild men'* or arboreal spirits believed to haunt woods and forests in medieval times. In pre-Reformation churches foliate masks, believed by some folklorists to represent the Green Man, can be seen with a human, feline or goblin face peering out from behind leaves, branches or flower tendrils. Cain has also been identified with St George, the patron saint of England, and in Islamic lore with the Sufi saint Al-Khidir or the *'Green One'*.

Some of these images of foliate masks replace the human face with a skull with tendrils or branches sprouting from the jaw and eye-sockets. These images are supposed to be Christian symbols of death and resurrection (reincarnation). However they have obvious links with the story of Cain and Abel and the fertility cycle of growth and harvest in agriculture. In modern traditional witchcraft the God is often seen as a dual–faced Janus type figure. He is the Green Man and Lord of the Greenwood in his summery aspect and the Lord of the Wild Hunt and the Wildwood in his winter form. In English folklore the Wild Hunt is sometimes known as Cain's Hunt. It is traditionally led by the first murderer masked in a stag's skull and with his black dog running alongside.

Lamech's daughter is called Naamah and she is supposed to have invented divination, invented spinning and weaving and is the patron of practitioners of those traditionally female crafts. As such she connects with pagan goddesses like Holda who are also associated with spinning and with witchcraft. On a symbolic level in the Traditional Craft weaving and spinning connect to the aspect of the witch goddess as Fate because she controls the web of wyrd or destiny.

Paul Huson has connected Naamah with the creation myth in Italian witch lore describing the seduction of the sun god Lucifer by his sister Diana, the moon goddess of hunting. In this dualistic myth, first recorded by the American folklorist Charles Godfrey Leland in the late nineteenth-century: *'In the beginning of the Great Darkness, Diana divided herself into two equal and opposite forces, night and day.'* Diana ruled the night as the silver crescent or orb of the moon, while her twin brother Lucifer commanded the fiery solar disc in the daytime. Shape-shifting into a cat, Diana seduced her brother and from their incestuous union was born the witch-goddess Aradia. She is supposed to have incarnated on Earth in human form, like the Watchers of biblical myth, to teach humanity the magical arts.[39]

Huson says there are Gnostic overtones in the Italian legend of Diana and Lucifer and these are reflected in the Kabbalistic tradition that Naamah seduced the fallen angel Shemyaza. He was known as Azael, Azrael or Azazel and was identified with Lucifer as the leader of the Watchers.[40] According to Huson, Naamah is an aspect of Lilith, the traditional consort of Lucifer. Azael is the Babylonian sun god Shamash in his underworld aspect as the Lord of Riches and artificer of metals. In fact Huson claims that Azael is the alter-ego of Naamah's brother Tubal-Cain, the biblical first blacksmith. He goes on to say that Azael or Azazel is one of the modern witch's gods.[41]

In Islamic lore it is Azazel who collects the dust from the four quarters of the world used by Yahweh to make the first man Adam. As the leader of the fallen angels Azazel is responsible for teaching humans how to forge weapons including swords, knives, breastplates and shields. He also makes known to them *'the metals [of the earth] and the art of working them.'*[42] In biblical times Azazel was a Semitic goat-god with a retinue of demons known in Hebrew as the *seirim* representing the satyrs of classical paganism. In the *Old Testament* there is a description of the sacrifice of the *'scapegoat'* to Azazel. The animal is selected by the high priest by the casting of lots and is abandoned in the wilderness to die. This unfortunate animal carries with it the sins of the Children of Israel. In that respect it symbolises the sacrificial god who dies to cleanse the sins of humanity.[43]

Naamah's name in Hebrew means *'pleasant'* and this is supposed to refer to her habit of singing *'pleasant songs'* to pagan idols. In the *Zohar* or *Book of Splendour* she is described as an angelic being who is the patron of prostitutes. As the Queen of Hell she is the consort of its king, Samael, a version of Lucifer as the serpent in Eden and the alleged father of Cain. Naamah is also said to have been one of the many wives of King Solomon and he was also helped by her brother Tubal-Cain to build his temple in Jerusalem.

---

[39] See *Aradia: Gospel of the Witches* by Charles Godfrey Leland.
[40] Huson, Paul. *Mastering Witchcraft: A Guide for Witches, Warlocks and Covens*, pp. 9-10.
[41] Ibid, p.10.
[42] See Canon, Charles. *The Book of Enoch*.
[43] *Leviticus 16*.

Vs.

The offspring of the union between Naamah and Samael was the bull-headed Asmodei or Asmodeus, possibly a demonised version of the Canaanite fertility and thunder god Baal. Nigel Jackson says that Asmodeus was the result of an incestuous union between Naamah and Tubal-Cain and is worshipped by some traditional witches under the name of Atho, allegedly derived from the Welsh *Arddhu* meaning the *'Dark One'*.[44]

In some Jewish sources Naamah is regarded as the alter-ego or possibly the sister or human incarnation of the ancient Sumerian bird goddess of the dark moon, Liliya, Lilitu or Lilith. Both are said to inhabit the Red Sea area and to have seduced Adam before the creation of Eve. Lilith is represented in ancient imagery as a naked woman with long hair, small horns or a horned cap or head-dress, and the feet and wings of an owl. In Sumeria Lilith was the leader of the Lilu, a race of female vampires that were the sexual predators of humans. Later in Hebrew demonology Lilith became a child-killer and she stole the semen from men while they were having erotic dreams or engaged in homosexual intercourse. She used these emissions to spawn demons or the Otherworldly race of elves, faeries and goblins. For this reason there are some traditional witches today who revere her as a form of the Queen of Elfhame or Faerie.

In Sumeria Lilith was associated with Ereshkigal, the elder sister of Inanna, and in Babylon with the goddess of love and war Ishtar as the *'Lady of the Evening Star'* (Venus). In Phoenicia and Canaan, where the Israelites settled after their escape from slavery in Egypt, she was Baalim, the *'Great Lady'*, and Astarte, the consort of Baal. Barbara Black Koltuv describes Lilith as an aspect of the Great Goddess and the dark side of the Shekinah or *'Bride of God'*, the female consort of Yahweh. Lilith the Younger, who is supposed to be her daughter or possibly her sister, is identified by Black Koltuv with *'Naamah, the maiden and seductress. Lilith, the Ancient One, is child killer, hag and snatcher, while Lilith herself is...the goddess of Life and Death.'*[45] In the Traditional Craft the witch goddess is dual-faced, having bright and dark aspects associated with the forces of life and death. She is also represented as a hag or a young woman, as either Diana or Hecate.

When the writer was a student of the Order of the Morning Star in the 1960s he was told a creation myth of Lucifer and Lilith by its founder, Madeline Montalban. She said they were emanations of the Cosmic Creator or Father-Mother God and manifested in the universe in a polarised dualistic form as male and female principles. In a lesson called *The Book of Lumiel* in Montalban's course on angelic magic, she described how Lucifer and the planetary archangels were created:

---

[44] Jackson, Nigel and Howard, Michael. *The Pillars of Tubal Cain*, pp. 161-2.
[45] Black Koltuv, Barbara. *The Book of Lilith*, p. 121.

Vs.

> *'God the Parent manifested himself in his Divine Form, which is a Body of Light. He was dual-natured, the perfection of male and female, the positive and negative poles which are needed for light. To create he brought forth first, before the Archangels, the Divine Mother part of himself, who is his twin and spouse eternally, his inner self, she who is God the Mother, or that magnetic force field called the Shekinah.'*

As stated above, Madeline Montalban regarded the Shekinah or *'Bride of God'* as the *'shining [feminine] force field of [the male] God'* through which he was able to create the universe. She taught that only a woman, and in fact only one who was an initiated priestess of the Mysteries, could work magically with the Shekinah. In fact she claimed: *'In magical studies and practice the female is held to be not only the equal of the male, but often the superior, since by her vibrations...she can more easily create the shining force field through which magic works, for this is a feminine power.'*

Lilith is represented in the *Zohar* as an aspect of the Shekinah and in fact she is described as ruling the Earth while the Bride of God is absent in Heaven. Barbara Black Koltuv says that *'Lilith and the Shekinah are essentially motherless forms of the feminine self. They arose with the coming of the patriarchy as the embodiment of the neglected [and] rejected aspects of the Great Goddess. Lilith is the part of the feminine that is experienced as seductive witch, outcast and shadow'.*[46] In common with Lilith the *Zohar* rather coyly says that the Shekinah *'rests'* on men when they are parted from their wives and she is also an exile who wanders in the wilderness.

In the *Zohar* it states that Lilith's hatred of Yahweh is based on her role as the *'lesser light'* (the moon) after the *'greater light'* of the sun represented by Lucifer. Kabbalists say that originally Lilith and Lucifer were one androgynous being who split in two to become separate entities. This reflects an ancient belief that originally Adam and Eve were once a single hermaphroditic being. Hence the biblical reference to Eve being created from Adam's spare rib: *'And Adam said, this is now bone of my bones, and flesh of my flesh; she shall be called Woman, because she was taken out of man. Therefore shall a man leave his father and mother, and shall cleave unto his wife; and they shall be one flesh.'*[47] In ancient pagan rites and medieval alchemy this is the concept of the *'sacred marriage'* and in Jungian psychology the *'conjunction of the opposites'* is the union of the *anima* and *animus*, the contrasexual male and female aspects of the human psyche.

---

[46] Black Koltuv, Barbara. *The Book of Lilith*, p. 118.
[47] *Genesis 2:23-24.*

Vs.

In those modern branches of traditional witchcraft that have a Luciferian mythos Lucifer and Lilith are seen as the archetypal witch god and witch goddess, the Lord and Lady. Cain is the ancestral patron spirit of the witch-blood, Tubal-Cain and Naamah are avatars representing the Divine Couple, and the *'Children of Cain'* are the spiritual descendants of the first murderer. There is a considerable amount of confusion and misunderstanding about the true nature of the *'witch blood'*. It does not refer to a physical descent from Cain or, as been fantastically claimed, a special type of DNA possessed by traditional witches. Instead in a spiritual sense it is the passing down through human incarnations of magical power, psychic gifts such as the Second Sight and occult knowledge.

Although traditional witchcraft is largely based on duotheism and apparently has a dualistic cosmic-view, the existence of two principles depicted as the witch god and witch goddess should not be seen as entirely dualistic. Many traditional witches also recognise the existence of a Supreme Creator who exists behind the duality of the God and Goddess. This nameless and unknowable force or energy cannot be imagined nor fully comprehended by humans while they are incarnated on the earthly plane. Therefore it can only be understood or approached in dualistic terms through the Divine Couple. However, ultimately the two are united and become the One as they were originally.

Bibliography
Arberry, A.J. (trans) *The Koran* (Oxford University Press 1983)
Black Koltuv, Barbara. *The Book of Lilith*. Nicholas-Hay, 1986.
Collon, Dominique. *Queen of the Night*. The British Museum Press, 2005.
Canon, Charles. *The Book of Enoch*. Oxford University Press, 1912.
Ginzberg, Louis. *The Legends of the Jews*. John Hopkins University Press USA 1998.
Graves, Robert and Patai, R. *Hebrew Myths: The Book of Genesis*. Cassel 1964.
Halevi, Shimon ben Z'ev. *Adam and the Kabbalistic Tree*. Gateway Books 1994.
Huson, Paul. *Mastering Witchcraft: A Guide for Witches, Warlocks and Covens*. Rupert Hart-Davies UK and G.P. Putnam USA 1970.
Jackson, Nigel and Howard, Michael. *The Pillars of Tubal Cain*. Capall Bann 2000.
Leland, Charles Godfrey. *Aradia, or the Gospel of Witches*. 1899 Phoenix Publishing 2002.
Montalban, Madeline. 'The Way to Occult Power', *Prediction Annual 1969*. Link House Publications 1969.
Patai, R. *The Hebrew Goddess*. Wayne University Press USA 1990.
Wise, M, Abegg, M. and Cook, E. (trans). *The Dead Sea Scrolls*. Harper Collins 1996.

Vs.

TOADS AND DIAMONDS

Portrayals of Good, Evil, Virtue and Wickedness in Fairy Tales

by Chrissy Derbyshire

In fairy tales, the concepts of good and evil are remarkably unproblematic. There are few ethical dilemmas in the land far, far away. Right and wrong are almost always clearly defined, and invariably in opposition. These ideas are made slightly more complicated by the fact that they operate on more than one level. *'Right'* can be conceptually separated into the absolute *'good'* and the conditional *'virtuous'*, *'wrong'* into the absolute *'evil'* and the conditional *'wicked'*. These labels are not set in stone in the text of the tales (which are, after all, mainly literary crystallisations of oral folktales), but they are terms which come to us intuitively when we read or remember a fairy story. We know from our childhood the figures associated with good and evil, virtue and wickedness in fairy tales. Princesses, princes, fairy godmothers and plucky youngest sons battle stepmothers, witches, beasts and cads: the beautiful vs. the bestial, the virtuous vs. the vain, and the canny vs. the complacent. This essay examines the various portrayals of right and wrong in fairy tales, and the ways in which the two interact.

Cinderella, Snow White and Sleeping Beauty are three characters whose stories are quite distinct in our minds. Cinderella's features the glass slipper, the pumpkin coach and the flight at midnight. Snow White faces the escape to the forest and the dwarves' house, the magic mirror, the deadly apple and the glass coffin. Sleeping Beauty's story is one of a wicked thirteenth fairy, a spinning wheel, an enchanted sleep and a forest of thorns. And yet, despite the huge variance in imagery in these three stories, each heroine (if they may be called such) has an identical function. They each fall under the archetype of the put-upon daughter – specifically, the put-upon princess – common in fairy tales. They are all initially beloved daughters of good breeding, beautiful and virtuous, who quickly fall prey to misfortune and, helpless on their own, require some form of saviour. I have chosen these characters to open my discussion, because they are so unequivocally associated with goodness in our minds. They are *'goodies'*. Of course they are. It is notable, then, that while Cinderella, Snow White and Sleeping Beauty are customarily

Vs.

described as *'virtuous'* or *'good and kind'*, we are provided with little evidence of their virtue. The label seems to be based solely on these characters' passive acceptance of their circumstances. Modern adaptations (no major film studios mentioned) offer largely gratuitous acts of kindness towards dwarves, fairies and cuddly woodland creatures in order to (barely) flesh out the characters. This is to little avail. *'Goodie'* or not, we are unlikely to aspire to the virtue of a fairy tale put-upon princess, in whom pliancy, beauty and goodness are one.

The unfortunate daughter is usually pitted against her polar opposite – that potent symbol of femininity corrupted, the wicked stepmother or witch. It is not without thought that I mention these two archetypes in the same breath. They are treated in a significantly similar way in fairy tales. Both are ruthless, and persecute children, especially girls. Both are clever and deceitful, often appearing virtuous (if only to their lustful, misguided husbands and their gullible young nemeses) before revealing murderous intent. They are not entirely interchangeable, however. Though a stepmother may also be a witch and vice versa, there are important qualities that the two do not necessarily share. Let us first examine the archetype of the wicked stepmother. The stepmother is a usurper. She has taken up residence in the true mother's home, usually too soon after her death, and installed her own cuckoo children (always unpleasant and usually ugly) in the family nest. She is jealous of her stepdaughter, envying either her beauty, or the rewards that she reaps from being a *'good girl'* which are denied to her own spoilt offspring. Fairy tale stepmothers generally neglect their stepdaughters, treating them as servants in their own homes and refusing to acknowledge their good name. Sometimes a stepmother will take this a step further, actually attempting to murder the good daughter to make way for herself and her own children. Thus is Snow White first strangled and then poisoned (her stepmother being a witch also), Vasilisa sent off to her supposed death at the hands of the fearsome Baba Yaga (a rare ambiguous witch figure, of whom more later), and the son in *'The Juniper Tree'* cooked up for his father's tea.

Yes, an alarming number of good children in fairy tales fall prey to, or narrowly escape, cannibalism. The cannibalistic urge is a vice associated with witches. *Snow White*'s witch-queen devours what she thinks is her stepdaughter's heart, while the witch in *Hansel and Gretel* lures innocent children with her gingerbread house before caging them and feeding them up until they are ready to roast in the oven. The Baba Yaga has a fence made from human bones, or bolts on her doors made of fingers. If the stepmother represents the childhood *'other'*, the invader who is not quite family, the witch is the imaginary *'other'* – the invader who is not quite human. We see the jealousy associated with the stepmother attributed to a witch in

Rapunzel. Here, the beautiful young girl is locked up in a tower when she reaches puberty, to ensure that she will not come into contact with the opposite sex. When the witch discovers that the prince has been climbing Rapunzel's long hair she shears it off close to the scalp, robbing her of the greatest symbol of female beauty. The fairy tale witch is generally old and ugly, sometimes to the extent of deformity. The witch in Hans Christian Anderson's *The Tinder Box* has a lower lip that *'[hangs] quite down on her breast'*, many witches are described as having noses that bend down and chins that bend up, so that they meet in the middle, and most of the Grimms' witches have red eyes. Most tellingly, the witch in a tale entitled *The Old Witch* appears as a *'creature with a fiery head'*. Witches are not just evil. They are godless. They are both part-human, part-beast, and as close to demons as we may find in tales habitually told to children.

Witches do not have a monopoly on magic use in fairy tales. Nor is magic considered wicked in itself. The mirror image of the witch is the good magic user – typically, the fairy godmother. To consider the practical differences between a witch and a fairy godmother helps us to gain an understanding of what we mean by *'good'* and *'evil'* in the context of a fairy tale. The major difference between the archetype of the witch and that of the fairy godmother lies in their interaction with the hero or, more usually, heroine, of the tale. In the simplest terms (and fairy tales rarely stray from the simplest terms) the fairy godmother is helpful to the heroine, while the witch hinders. We are given no clue as to the fairy godmother's motives for helping the heroine. She merely does so, because that is her archetypal function. The witch may have her own selfish reasons for her hindrance (usually either jealousy or the desire to eat the girl) but more often than not is cruel simply because she is intrinsically and non-specifically evil. Alongside the iconic archetypes of the witch and the fairy godmother, there exist stories (most of them comparatively obscure) which feature magic users whose virtue is ambiguous. This is unusual in fairy tales. Only these ambiguous magic users and the odd trickster figure (they are less prevalent in fairy tales than in the wider spectrum of the folktale) present any kind of moral food for thought. Probably the best known example of the ambiguous magic user is the figure of the wish-granter. In *The Arabian Nights*, this wish-granter is generally a genie. In western fairy tales, the genie is usually substituted for an ugly human (the hideous women in *The Three Spinsters*, the dwarfish Rumpelstiltskin) or a magical creature such as the great fish in *The Fisherman and His Wife*. These figures are amoral (as opposed to immoral) and allow the recipients of wishes or good counsel to use them as they will. The good are rewarded, and the wicked are punished. *The Pied Piper of Hamelin* is a particularly callous example of this. Very occasionally, as in *Vasilisa the Beautiful* or *The Tinder Box*, a witch figure may be ambiguous, but this is exceptionally rare. Indeed, in *The Tinder Box* the poor old semi-helpful witch is beheaded just as readily as if she were straight-down-the-line evil. It seems that, if your lower lip hangs down over your breast, there's no point pretending to be anything other than a witch.

Figure 5 - Red Riding Hood, from The Fairy Book

Wish-granting fish and other fortunate creatures represent only a small fraction of the various beasts and non-humans that populate the fairy tale landscape. In these stories, the great majority of creatures are evil. Probably the most common magical creature in the fairy tale is the giant, ogre or troll. These three are fundamentally interchangeable. Like all wicked beasts, their main function is to attempt to eat the protagonist of the tale. *'Fee, fie, foe, fum,'* rumbles the giant in *Jack and the Beanstalk*, *'I smell the blood of an Englishman. Be he alive or be he dead, I'll grind his bones to make my bread.'* This is an unusually sophisticated threat for a giant. Most cannot be bothered to grind bones into bread. The troll beneath the bridge in *The Three Billy Goats Gruff* simply gobbles the little goats up. When an ogre meets a human, the motive is hunger. When any wicked beast meets a weaker animal, the motive is just the same. But when a beast, particularly a wolf or fox, meets a young girl, the undercurrents shift in an even more sinister direction. These are beasts whose motive is lust. Many variations exist on the theme of a foxy gentleman wooing a naive young girl, and all the while plotting to kill her once they are married. Bluebeard is a type of Mr Fox, not strictly animal but not quite human either. It may seem tenuous to include *Little Red Riding Hood* in this category. We tend to assume that the *'never speak to strangers'* message of the tale has been tacked on at a later date, and that the wolf's original motive must have been simple hunger or straightforward wickedness. Here folklore has dealt us a rather neat and clever double bluff, for the earliest known version of the tale is so explicit in its sexual references that it may be unpalatable to the modern imagination. *'Take your clothes off, my child,'* says the wolf, *'and come into bed with me.'* When the girl asks where she should put each item of clothing, he answers, *'Throw it onto the fire, my child. You won't be needing it any longer.'*

With all this danger about, it pays to be resourceful. Indeed, it pays so well that the reward is frequently the rule of a kingdom, or at least the hand of the king's daughter. With the great and colourful variety of evil in fairy tales, it is easy to dismiss the good as bland and uninteresting. But, blazing a trail past the long line of static princesses and formulaic fairy godmothers, one type of character is out to change that view. These are the true heroes of the fairy tale – far more than any prince or woodcutter who turns up fortuitously at the end to save the day. They are youngest sons, devoted servants, or lowly workers. They are the canny ones, the brave ones, the loyal ones, the *Valiant Tailor* and the *Boy Who Couldn't Shiver*. They are people who, from humble beginnings, use genuine courage, wit and intelligence to win wealth and fame. Usually their stories consist of a series of seemingly impossible tasks, the fulfilment of which carries a title or a woman as a prize. If the woman has set the tasks herself, then the clever character often has the further function of cutting her down to size. The canny, humble one is rewarded with a beautiful woman's hand in marriage, while the proud woman is punished with a husband below her station. And so, after taking a winding route through the forest, we find ourselves back where we started: in fairy tales, the concepts of good and evil are remarkably unproblematic. There are few ethical dilemmas in the land far, far away. This is because the good (however unsubstantiated their supposed goodness may be) are almost always rewarded, and the evil almost always punished. A succinct illustration of this may be found in the tale entitled, *Toads and Diamonds*. In this tale, the good girl, the one who helps a fairy disguised as an old washerwoman, is given the gift that every time she opens her mouth, gold and diamonds will fall from it. Her jealous sister wants the same treatment, but for her wicked behaviour she is instead given a curse. Every time she opens her mouth, not diamonds but snakes and toads fall from it. The good girl gets diamonds. The bad girl gets toads. There are a great many good girl/bad girl tales, and both good and bad almost always get what they deserve.

But that is another story, and will be told another time.

Bibliography
Bettelheim, Bruno. *The Uses of Enchantment: The Meaning and Importance of Fairy Tales.* Penguin Books, 1991.
Pinkola Estés, Clarissa. *Women Who Run with the Wolves: Contacting the Power of the Wild Woman.* Rider, 1992.
Gilbert, Sandra M. and Gubar, Susan. *The Madwoman in the Attic: The Woman Writer and the Nineteenth Century Literary Imagination.* Yale University Press, 1979.
The Brothers Grimm. *The Complete Illustrated Stories of the Brothers Grimm.* Octopus Books Ltd., 1990.
Jordan, Rosan A. and Kalčik, Susan J. ed., *Women's Folklore, Women's Culture.* University of Philadelphia Press, 1993.
Tatar, Maria ed., *The Classic Fairy Tales.* Norton and Company Ltd., 1999.
Tatar, Maria. *The Hard Facts of the Grimms' Fairy Tales.* Princeton University Press, 1987.
von Franz, Marie Louise. *Shadow and Evil in Fairy Tales.* Shambhala Publications Inc., 1995.

Websites:
Hans Christian Andersen Fairy Tales and Stories, http://hca.gilead.org.il/.

Vs.

Constellations

Perseus and Andromeda Rite

A Stellar Beltane Rite to constellations Perseus and Andromeda, star-crossed lovers.

by Payam Nabarz

The following is an excerpt from: *Stellar Magic: A practical guide to the rites of the moon, planets, stars and constellations* by Payam Nabarz (Avalonia, 2009). www.stellarmagic.co.uk

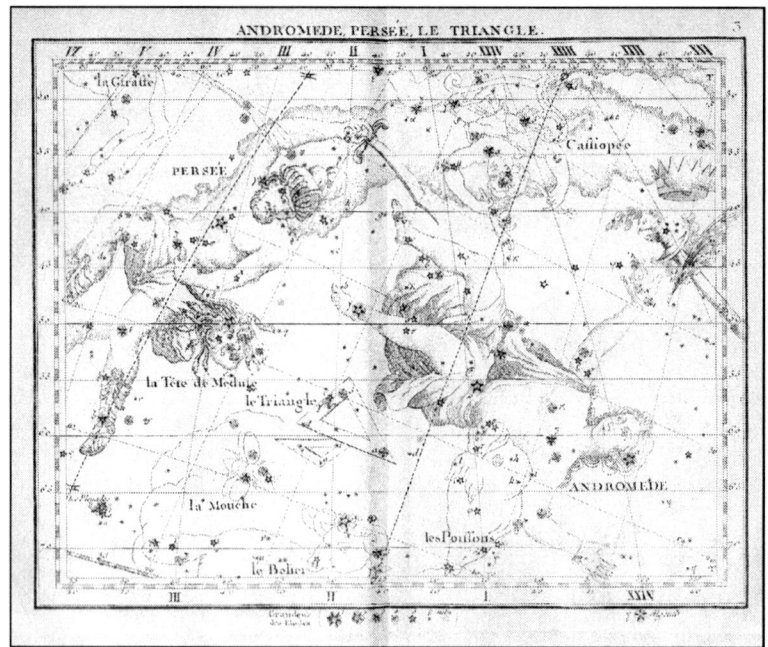

Figure 6 - Atlas Celeste de Flamstéed
'U.S. Naval Observatory Library'

Vs.

Introduction
'For I am divided for love's sake, for the chance of union.' –Nuit (Liber Al vel Legis)

This is a story which involves six constellations, Pegasus, Cetus, Cassiopeia, Cepheus, Perseus and Andromeda. According to Aratus' *Phaenomena* Queen Cassiopeia in Greek mythology was married to King Iasid Cepheus of Ethiopia and their daughter was Andromeda. They were akin to Zeus as they descended from Io. One day Cassiopeia announced that she was more beautiful than the Aegean Sea nymphs the Nereids. The sea nymphs Doris and Panope, on hearing this, complained to the sea god Poseidon, who decided to avenge the insult by sending floods to Cepheus' kingdom, followed by sending the Cetus a sea monster. To appease Poseidon and the sea monster, the court Oracles advised the king to sacrifice Andromeda to the monster. She was then chained to a rock on the cliffs by the sea. The hero Perseus was flying on the Pegasus across the sky having killed Medusa already and was carrying her head in his bag, when he came across Andromeda chained to the rock. He immediately fell in love with her and asked for her hand in marriage, to which she agreed. He also obtained King Cepheus' permission, which was given on the condition that Perseus could defeat the monster. Perseus accepted the challenge and flew on his horse Pegasus and attacked the monster. He succeeded in killing the monster by taking Medusa's head out of the bag and showing it to the sea monster. The monster, upon looking at Medusa's head, turned to stone. Perseus and Andromeda hence married and were given a kingdom of their own by Cepheus. Their first son was called Perses (Persian) and was said to be ancestor of the Persians.

When Andromeda and Perseus died they were placed among the stars, as well as all the main characters of the story. The constellation Perseus is still defending Andromeda from the constellation Cetus - the leviathan of the sky. Perseus' horse constellation Pegasus flies close to the constellation Andromeda who appears chained with her arms stretched across. Andromeda's parents King Cepheus and Queen Cassiopeia are also constellations and both sit on their thrones near their daughter. However, Cassiopeia as part of the punishment for her insult to the sea nymphs is sometimes turned upside-down while in her throne in the sky. She can easily be spotted as her constellation is in shape of W or E. The Cepheus constellation is next to the Cassiopeia constellation. The Pegasus constellation can be spotted by locating the *'Square of Pegasus'* next to the constellation Andromeda: they have a star in common. The Pegasus is flying upside down in the night sky. In addition to transporting Perseus, the Pegasus was according to Aratus' *Phaenomena* famed for stamping his foot at the summit of the Helicon causing water to emerge from where his foot had stricken the ground.

There are some beautiful modern poems that highlight the themes of the Perseus myth, for example *Perseus - The Triumph of Wit Over Suffering* by Sylvia Plath (1932-1963), and *Perseus* by Robert Hayden (1913-1980) in addition to the poems included here.

A Tale of lovers for Beltane, Perseus and Andromeda Rite

Omnia vincit amor - Love conquers all things.

The format of this rite is along the lines of a Bardic *Eisteddfod*, where great poems are recited. The rite here is set up as a group ceremony; however, it can be adapted for a couple or solo working.

Set up
- Location: a place with good visibility of the stars.
- Central fire lit but kept to a size not to affect the night vision too much.
- Time is determined using a Star-globe or Star-chart ensuring visibility of Perseus and Andromeda constellations.
- Clothing: sensible outdoor clothing & footwear.
- Food and drink to share.

A standard ritual opening can be used by the practitioners of the rite.

After the opening *Soror* 1 recites the following while others listen and meditate on the tale.

> Now Aeolus had with strong chains confined,
> And deep imprisoned every blustering wind,
> The rising Phospher with a purple light
> Did sluggish mortals to new toils invite.
> His feet again the valiant Perseus plumes,
> And his keen sabre in his hand resumes:
> Then nobly spurns the ground, and upwards springs,
> And cuts the liquid air with sounding wings.
> O'er various seas, and various lands he past,
> Until Aethiopia's shore appeared at last.
> Andromeda was there, doomed to atone
> By her own ruin follies not her own:
> And if injustice in a God can be,
> Such was the Libyan God's unjust decree.
> Chained to a rock she stood; young Perseus stayed
> His rapid flight, to view the beauteous maid.
> So sweet her frame, so exquisitely fine,
> She seemed a statue by a hand divine,
> Had not the wind her waving tresses showed,

Vs.

And down her cheeks the melting sorrows flowed.
Her faultless form the hero's bosom fires;
The more he looks, the more he still admires.
The' admirer almost had forgot to fly,
And swift descended fluttering from on high.
O! Virgin, worthy no such chains to prove,
But pleasing chains in the soft folds of love;
Thy country and thy name (he said) disclose,
And give a true rehearsal of thy woes.
A quick reply her bashfulness refused,
To the free converse of a man unused.
Her rising blushes had concealment found
From her spread hands, but that her hands were bound.
She acted to her full extent of power,
And bathed her face with a fresh, silent shower.
But by degrees in innocence grown bold,
Her name, her country, and her birth she told:
And how she suffered for her mother's pride,
Who with the Nereids once in beauty vied.
Part yet untold, the seas began to roar,
And mounting billows tumbled to the shore.
Above the waves a monster raised his head,
His body o'er the deep was widely spread:
Onward he flounced; aloud the virgin cries;
Each parent to her shrieks in shrieks replies:
But she had deepest cause to rend the skies.
Weeping, to her they cling; no sign appears
Of help, they only lend their helpless tears.
Too long you vent your sorrows, Perseus said,
Short is the hour, and swift the time of aid,
In me the son of thundering Jove behold,
Got in a kindly shower of fruitful gold.
Medusa's snaky head is now my prey,
And thro' the clouds I boldly wing my way.
If such desert be worthy of esteem,
And, if your daughter I from death redeem,
Shall she be mine? Shall it not then be thought,
A bride, so lovely, was too cheaply bought?
For her my arms I willingly employ,
If I may beauties, which I save, enjoy.
The parents eagerly the terms embrace:
For who would slight such terms in such a case?
Nor her alone they promise, but beside,
The dowry of a kingdom with the bride.
As well-rigged galleys, which slaves, sweating, row,
With their sharp beaks the whitened ocean plough;
So when the monster moved, still at his back

Vs.

The furrowed waters left a foamy track.
Now to the rock he was advanced so nigh,
Whirled from a sling a stone the space would fly.
Then bounding, upwards the brave Perseus sprung,
And in mid air on hovering pinions hung.
His shadow quickly floated on the main;
The monster could not his wild rage restrain,
But at the floating shadow leaped in vain.
As when Jove's bird, a speckled serpent spies,
Which in the shine of Phoebus basking lies,
Unseen, he souses down, and bears away,
Trussed from behind, the vainly-hissing prey.
To writhe his neck the labour naught avails,
Too deep the imperial talons pierce his scales.
Thus the winged hero now descends, now soars,
And at his pleasure the vast monster gores.
Full in his back, swift stooping from above,
The crooked sabre to its hilt he drove.
The monster raged, impatient of the pain,
First bounded high, and then sunk low again.
Now, like a savage boar, when chafed with wounds,
And bayed with opening mouths of hungry hounds,
He on the foe turns with collected might,
Who still eludes him with an airy flight;
And wheeling round, the scaly armour tries
Of his thick sides; his thinner tall now plies:
'Till from repeated strokes out gushed a flood,
And the waves reddened with the streaming blood.
At last the dropping wings, be foamed all over,
With flaggy heaviness their master bore:
A rock he spied, whose humble head was low,
Bare at an ebb, but covered at a flow.
A ridge hold, he, thither flying, gained,
And with one hand his bending weight sustained;
With the' other, vigorous blows he dealt around,
And the home-thrusts the expiring monster owned.
In deafening shouts the glad applauses rise,
And peal on peal runs rattling thro' the skies.[48]

---

[48] *The Metamorphoses of Ovid* translated into English verse under the direction of Sir Samuel Garth by John Dryden, Alexander Pope, Joseph Addison, William Congreve and other eminent hands, 1717.
Another translation available is:
The Metamorphoses of Ovid Vol. I, Books I-VII Translator: Henry Thomas Riley, 1893.
Other translations include: May M. Innes, Penguin Classics (1955, New Edition 2002) and David Raeburn translation, Penguin Classics; New Ed edition (2004).

Vs.

'For I am divided for love's sake, for the chance of union' –Nuit (Liber Al)

[Notes: The group at this stage is divided into two groups: men and women. Each group is standing on either side of the fire. After looking at the constellations the following poems are recited, the Fraters calling on Andromeda, the Sorors calling on Perseus. Men are calling upon their stellar lover Andromeda, while women are calling upon their stellar lover Perseus, inviting them to the circle.]

Frater 1 recites:
>*The smooth-worn coin and threadbare classic phrase*
>*Of Grecian myths that did beguile my youth,*
>*Beguile me not as in the olden days:*
>*I think more grief and beauty dwell with truth.*
>*Andromeda, in fetters by the sea,*
>*Star-pale with anguish till young Perseus came,*
>*Less moves me with her suffering than she,*
>*The slim girl figure fettered to dark shame,*
>*That nightly haunts the park, there, like a shade,*
>*Trailing her wretchedness from street to street.*
>*See where she passes -- neither wife nor maid;*
>*How all mere fiction crumbles at her feet!*
>*Here is woe's self, and not the mask of woe:*
>*A legend's shadow shall not move you so!*[49]

Soror 1 recites:
>*The saviour-youth the royal pair confess,*
>*And with heaved hands their daughter's bridegroom bless.*
>*The beauteous bride moves on, now loosed from chains,*
>*The cause, and sweet reward of all the hero's pains,*
>*Mean-time, on shore triumphant Perseus stood,*
>*And purged his hands, smeared with the monster's blood:*
>*Then in the windings of a sandy bed*
>*Composed Medusa's execrable head.*
>*But to prevent the roughness, leafs he threw,*
>*And young, green twigs, which soft in waters grew,*
>*There soft, and full of sap; but here, when laid,*
>*Touched by the head, that softness soon decayed.*
>*The wonted flexibility quite gone,*
>*The tender scions hardened into stone.*
>*Fresh, juicy twigs, surprised, the Nereid's brought,*
>*Fresh, juicy twigs the same contagion caught.*
>*The nymphs the petrifying seeds still keep,*
>*And propagate the wonder thro' the deep.*

---

[49] *Andromeda* by Thomas Bailey Aldrich, 1836-1907.

Vs.

*The pliant sprays of coral yet declare
Their stiffening Nature, when exposed to air.
Those sprays, which did, like bending osiers, move,
Snatched from their element, obdurate prove,
And shrubs beneath the waves grow stones above.*[50]

Frater 2 recites:
Andromeda (by Gerard Manley Hopkins 1844-1889)

*Now Time's Andromeda on this rock rude,
With not her either beauty's equal or
Her injury's, looks off by both horns of shore,
Her flower, her piece of being, doomed dragon's food.
Time past she has been attempted and pursued
By many blows and banes; but now hears roar
A wilder beast from West than all were, more
Rife in her wrongs, more lawless, and more lewd.
Her Perseus linger and leave her to her extremes?
Pillowy air he treads a time and hangs
His thoughts on her, forsaken that she seems,
All while her patience, morselled into pangs,
Mounts; then to alight disarming, no one dreams,
With Gorgon's gear and barebill, thongs and fangs.*[51]

Soror 2 recites:
*The great immortals grateful Perseus praised,
And to three Powers three turf altars raised.
To Hermes this; and that he did assign
To Pallas: the mid honours, Jove, were thine,
He hastes for Pallas a white cow to cull,
A calf for Hermes, but for Jove a bull.
Then seized the prize of his victorious fight,
Andromeda, and claimed the nuptial rite.
Andromeda alone he greatly sought,
The dowry kingdom was not worth his thought.
Pleased Hymen now his golden torch displays;
With rich oblations fragrant altars blaze,
Sweet wreaths of choicest flowers are hung on high,
And cloudless pleasure smiles in every eye.
The melting music melting thoughts inspires,
And warbling songsters aid the warbling lyres.
The palace opens wide in pompous state,
And by his peers surrounded, Cepheus sate.
A feast was served, fit for a king to give,*

---

[50] *Andromeda* by Gerard Manley Hopkins, 1844-1889.
[51] *Andromeda* by Gerard Manley Hopkins.

Vs.

> *And fit for God-like heroes to receive.*
> *The banquet ended, the gay, cheerful bowl*
> *Moved round, and brightened, and enlarged each soul.*
> *Then Perseus asked, what customs there obtained,*
> *And by what laws the people were restrained.*
> *Which told; the teller a like freedom takes,*
> *And to the warrior his petition makes,*
> *To know, what arts had won Medusa's snakes.*[52]

The spark is now kindled by each gender calling upon their appropriate constellation – men calling Perseus and women Andromeda. The men then *'draw down'* the energies of Perseus into themselves and the women *'draw down'* Andromeda into themselves.

The group can use music, chants, dance and any other technique (if it feels appropriate) to infuse itself with the Perseus and Andromeda current and to reach a trance state or heightened state of awareness. The goal is at least one person in each group will be giving an Oracle of Perseus and Andromeda in turn. If more than one person in the group is in trance, then continue to give Oracles in turn, until all have spoken. The Oracle may be interactive between Perseus and Andromeda, as they speak to each other as well as to the gathering.

If it feels appropriate perhaps each group will make a sigil representing their constellations. After the Oracles have been given the two sigils are united and tied together with a string and then if possible placed in the river (symbolic of the Milky Way) to float away to cosmic bliss. If you are not near a river during the rite, hold on to the sigil and float it later when you are able to get to a river or lake or sea.

When this has been completed the two gender groups become one circle again, and a simple circle dance to finish helps strengthen the unity of the two.

All should then sit down to meditate for a while on what has been said, some relevant music could be played to help with the meditation.

The group should give thanks to spirits of the place, and give final thanks to Cepheus, Cassiopeia, Perseus, Andromeda, Cetus and Pegasus, in whatever way the group sees fit.

A standard group closing should be used here to end the rite. This is followed by having something to eat and drink, then clearing the space.

---

[52] *The Metamorphoses of Ovid.*

Figure 7 - Hyginus - Poeticon Astronomicon, 'U.S. Naval Observatory Library'. Cassiopeia and Andromeda

The author would like to thank the U.S. Naval Observatory Library for their illustrations from their rare books.

Further reading:
The Metamorphoses of Ovid translated by M. Innes, Penguin Classics (1955, New Edition 2002)
Star Myths of the Greeks and Romans: A Sourcebook, by Theony Condos, Phanes Press, U.S, 1997.
Stellar Magic by Payam Nabarz, Avalonia, 2009
Sun, Moon & Stars by Sheena McGrath, Capall Bann, 2005.

Vs.

VODOU MARYAJ

by Sophia Fisher

The following definitions may be required prior to reading this piece; being necessarily short, they are incomplete. The tradition of Vodou itself has been introduced elsewhere in this and related Avalonia publications, and a basic knowledge of the religion and a few of its *Lwa* (spirits) will be assumed throughout.

First, the terms *Houngan*, *Mambo* or *Hounsi* refer to initiates of varying levels within Haitian Vodou (masculine, feminine and unisex respectively).

A *Lwa* is a *'spirit'* or *'angel'* of Vodou, viewed as an intermediary between ourselves and *Bondje* (God). The Lwa are not deities in their own right, although each has particular powers and attributes and is seen to exist in a very real, non-archetypal fashion. Meanwhile, possession (otherwise known as *'mounting'*) is that moment when a spirit ascends, descends or otherwise enters the body of a human being (the *'horse'*), whose personality is entirely replaced by that of the Lwa, so that he/she retains little or no memory of the spirit's ensuing behaviour.

The Lwa are *'served'* by people who may call themselves Serviteurs or Vodouisants: this refers to any devotee of the Vodou spirits, whether initiated or not. Such a person gives *Sevis* (the act of spiritual service or devotion) to the Lwa. Finally, a *Maryaj* is that contract of divine or spiritual marriage between a Lwa and human *serviteur* further expostulated below.

The concept of the Spiritual Spouse is in no way limited to Haitian Vodou; it is particularly widespread in other *'shamanic'* and *'indigenous'* cultures including *ole marapu* (*'spirit marriage'*) in southern Indonesia, the *ayami* or 'spirit-helper' of parts of Siberia, and practices of the Baule people on the Ivory Coast – to name but three. It is certainly a fascinating subject and worth exploring in its own right.

> *"Just as in many other religions, so in Voudoun there exists the mystic marriage between divinity and devotee. Such marriages may be requested, and even required, by the Spirits..."*[53]

---

[53] Odette Mennesson Rigaud, 'Notes on Two Marriages with Voudoun Loa, cited in full as 'Appendix A' in Maya Deren, *Divine Horsemen: The Living Gods of Haiti* (McPherson 1983)

Vs.

I would like to address the topic of Maryaj with a rather personal touch: my husband is engaged to be married to a certain female spirit connected with water. He wears her engagement ring on the ring finger of his right hand. When he marries her, a *'proper'* wedding ceremony will be conducted complete with cake, wedding dress and appropriate feasting; the Lwa will enter into possession and through her horse she will give her vows. In fact the ceremony will be just like a marriage between two human beings, except for one small fact: there is no possibility of divorce after a Maryaj!

Luckily for us this is a spirit that we have both honoured with genuine feeling for a number of years.

I say it is lucky because it has been known, as might be imagined, for jealousy to ensue when a Maryaj occurs. Normally this is on the part of the serviteur's human partner, however it can also be the spirit themselves who becomes envious, and I have heard (for example) of a man being forced to marry Ezili a few days before the wedding to his human lover in order to establish the *Lwa*'s precedence. Generally speaking, though, for as long as the serviteur keeps his/her vows, the spirit will have no problems *'sharing'*, though they might involve themselves rather heavily in the choice of earthly lover!

The spirit who chose my husband - and it was that way around, by the way - has acted as my mother, sister and confidante over many years, and I am genuinely happy to share him with her; it does not really feel like I will lose anything in the transaction. She is one of the first spirits that I ever *'met'* (in possession) and, with respect to the Lwa, my most-beloved. I look forward to their Maryaj with great excitement as it is going to be a beautiful affair.

How did she *'choose'* him? It was notable that she had given him a great deal of affection previously, always favouring him among the men (she frequently embraced him when mounting a horse, showing similar love for only one other male friend, who was one of her *petit*, or *'children'*). She also appeared to him in dreams. The penny only dropped, however, when my husband requested a reading with a Houngan who not only described these dreams in some detail, but additionally transmitted her message: she would like to marry you, will you accept? My husband's reaction was an instant yes.

Why do serviteurs marry the Lwa? For my husband, it is primarily romantic: he loves her! Yet this is not traditionally how one approaches the matter. A Maryaj to the Lwa is a transaction of vows. The human promises to devote a certain night each week or month to that Lwa. In return the Lwa will take care of his/her spouse in special ways. They will support each other in much the same way as husband and wife (or husband and husband, or wife and wife - see below) and the relationship between them will usually, although not always, take on a sensual nature.

Vs.

For the rest of his life, there will be a certain prescribed day during which, for 24 hours, my husband will not touch another human being in a way that could be deemed as *'sexual'*. Instead he devotes himself to the Lwa alone. As he is heterosexual, he will not flirt with or otherwise engage with another woman, even myself, his wife; he will not fantasise about other women or even sleep in our marital bed. If he were bisexual or gay the same would apply with appropriate changes to gender.

A Maryaj can take place between a Lwa and a human of any sexual preference, whether gay, straight, bi, trans ... but that does not mean that any Lwa will marry any human regardless of gender. Certain Lwa are known for marrying the opposite sex only. Interestingly, a common *'wife'* chosen by gay men is Ezili Freda: she may even honour the Maryaj by visiting them in dreams with the body of a man! Freda can also be persuaded to marry other women, but this is normally a difficult process; the classic choice for a gay woman being Ezili Dantor, patroness of lesbians.

Nor is Maryaj limited in the way of most Western countries to occur between two souls only. It is frequently the case that the presiding Houngan or Mambo suggests the serviteur marry more than one Lwa at the same time. If it is felt that the divine spouse will bring too much *'heat'* into the serviteur's life, it will be suggested that they marry someone *'cool'* to even themselves out: thus a woman marrying Ogou (a warrior spirit) may also wed Danbala (a spirit associated with coolness and peace). The opposite also applies: if a serviteur is marrying a very *'cool'* spirit they may also need to wed a *'hot'* Lwa. Ultimately, Vodou demands balance. Each situation is different because each serviteur's spiritual court (the Lwa we walk, mache, with) is totally unique. A well-trained Houngan or Mambo will be able to advise.

It interests me that, despite the physicality of the ceremony - in all respects, including financial loss, it is a *'real'* wedding - and despite certain seeming trivialities on the part of the vows - that a Lwa may become jealous, or angry, if not given their prescribed night may seem to Western eyes to be less than *'enlightened'* - the understanding we Vodouisants have that a Maryaj will somehow alter the serviteur (to either heat them up or cool them down) suggests a more *'subtle'* or *'mystical'* nature to the union. Namely, in a very real way this is nothing more or less than the *Hieros Gamos* (Divine Marriage) with a Vodou slant.

While much has been made of the sexual nature of the *Hieros Gamos* ritual (and, as has been alluded, sex does play a part in Maryaj; for the *Lwa* will visit his/her spouse in dreams upon the allotted night, and these dreams may take on a sexual nature) it is the internal harmonization of opposites that interests me more. The concept that marrying Ogou will heat a person up so much that she needs cooling down lets us know that on some level, the person has unified with or strengthened her own Ogou *'principle'* via that marriage. If one's Danbala principle – I flinch from the phrase *'one's inner Danbala'* - is given too much precedence a certain balance may be lost in the individual. This tells us that although the Lwa exist *'out there'*, the principle of the Lwa also exists *'in here'*: what lies without also exists within, as above so below.

So as well as literally marrying the Lwa (who are traditionally understood to – and routinely remind us that they do – exist independently as neither archetype nor universal aspect: there is no *'all Goddesses are one Goddess'* in Vodou!) one is also, and at the same time, committing a magickal inner transaction with one's Anima or Animus, unifying Inner and Outer; Samadhi, or spiritual completion begins to resonate.

The fact that the human spouse is potentially changed by Maryaj to such an extent that they require rebalancing – or, as is often true, that the serviteur enters spirit-marriage in order to bring certain energies into his/her life, strengthening powers that are lacking within themselves - means that this could not be more obvious, although such subtlety is hidden in plain sight by more worldly concerns: choosing a wedding party, feasting the Lwa with neither too much nor too little (for one must avoid slighting the other spirits as well as one's spiritual spouse) or the shocking price of wedding-cake! These trivialities have caused many a wedding-plan to seem little more than a row of red figures, a difficult diplomatic mission to ease the complaints of relatives. Yet at its core, Maryaj is a union of the deepest sort.

After all, what is a human wedding ceremony if not a re-enactment of this same all-prevailing myth - and why should it not exist with equal truth here in a marriage to the spirits?

Vodou Maryaj is (as might be imagined from some of the information above) not for everybody. But it is a powerful thing, and one of the most beautiful aspects of my beloved tradition, as far as I am concerned.

For those readers who might question the notion that humans should even deign to marry the gods at all, I leave you with a final point: as Vodouisants, we never forget that we are all Angels (Spirits) wearing human casing, and ultimately we have come from the same source as the Lwa. As related point, the first thing in most rituals during the Priye (a prayer-song used as precursor to Vodou ceremonies) is:

Nu tut se zangh-o, zangh anbara se mwen!
'We are all angels, angels embrace me!'

Also see: www.sirenabotanica.com

Vs.

RECOGNITION OF THE DIVINE

by Ellie Horne

> *"Creation itself cannot be brought within the comprehension unless space and time are removed from thought, but if these are removed, it can be comprehended. Remove them, if you can, or as much as you can, and keep in your mind an idea abstracted from space and time, and you will perceive there is no difference between the maximum and the minimum of space"*
> ~ Emanuel Swedenborg

When the world and heavens were created, devoid of any human input, conceptualisation or input they were perfect, they could be nothing else because they were, in their essence, divine. There was no bad there simply was, the beauty of creation in and of itself. Yet the mere creation of the oppositions of heaven and earth, night and day, one and other by definition is dualistic. So it seems that within that perfection already the seeds had been sown for man to eventually come to understand the world about him and within in a dualistic manner.

The reasons for the original fertilisation of those seeds that represented dualism and the dualistic transition, from being one with a divine to being separate from that source, are open to speculation. Yet the truth is that somewhere along the line we did become separated and from that moment forward man has been attempting to understand and to reunite with that source of creation.

Dualistic labels and concepts developed alongside the expansion of languages, ideas and thoughts from ancient civilisations who worshiped the sun and moon, traced the seasons and passages of life, the philosophical ideas of Plato featuring metaphysical dualism, involving the distinction between the material world of becoming and the immaterial world of being, through esoteric thinking of the Rosicrucian Chemical Wedding; of man and woman resulting in the regeneration of the soul and its attainment of divine union. It matters not. All spiritual systems have developed within a system of opposing energies. These creations of our mind have provided the backdrop for mankind to seek answers to the fundamental questions he has been struggling to answer about himself for thousands of years. Yet we have struggled with those concepts and theories within

Vs.

the realms of a self-created dualistic system, using a dualistic language, in a continuous attempt to transcend that same dualism we are locked into.

Neither religion nor philosophy is at fault for using dualistic concepts in an attempt to achieve transcendence. The truth is that it is impossible for us to interact in a world of relativity without resorting to the comfort and familiarity of labels and concepts of duality. Driven by the need to define and understand our world, we have developed spiritual ideas, beliefs and methods that enable us to better appreciate who we are and understand the world we live in. We have sought to explain the rising of the sun, the cycles of the moon and changing seasons through personification of objects, concepts and actions. That act of personification has allowed man to more readily accept the concept of a personal god or goddess in polytheism or a singular God within monotheism. Man also anthropomorphically personified those positive and negative emotions that drive us to the peaks and troughs of emotional experiences as human beings. Many mythologies throughout the world created anthropomorphic deities expressing human characteristics such as love, hatred and jealousy. We have imbued the gods, in human form or otherwise, with depictions of the powerful human traits we all experience, and we have worshipped the manifestation of the best, and worst, of those experiences through those created entities and symbolic images.

The myriad of gods, goddesses and deities that have emerged, the manifestation of the forces of good and evil, the emotional qualities of positive and negative, and differing ideas of human and divine have defined who we are as humans and by definition what the divine is as opposed to what our experience of being human is.

Over thousands of years these ideas have been contemplated and continuously clarified in attempts to find ways they could be used to understand the internal psyche and to guide us on a path that would allow us to touch the ultimate. All in an attempt to transcend the dualistic world of suffering that we recognised about us. It is not surprising given that as soon as man had labelled the duality he was driven to transcend it. The relationship that man developed with his spiritual guide, his god, became the path of transcendence, the '*Holy Grail*' within religion, spirituality and also philosophy. The personification of areas of our lives we related to was used as a pathway, a systematic method, to utilise on that journey.

Yet even wanting to transcend our experiences of the mundane, at this starting point there is a division. We are attempting to transcend from our human existence to a state of divinity, and because of this division we relate to the relative world of phenomena and existence in a state of increased confusion and it is this confused relative world that we are trying to break out of in a confused relative way. So where could this starting point of

Vs.

understanding both the divine and our relative world begin? How can we come to see our dualistic world as one? How can symbolic images, relative concepts and a limited language allow us to taste the divine?

> *"That which is Below corresponds to that which is Above, and that which is Above corresponds to that which is Below, to accomplish the miracles of the One Thing. And just as all things have come from this One Thing, through the meditation of One Mind, so do all created things originate from this One Thing, through Transformation."*
> ~ The Emerald Tablet

Many have declared that *The Emerald Tablet* contains the sum of all knowledge. It does indeed carry within it a profound spiritual message that transcends religions and ideologies and gives seekers markers on their journey to transform and transcend reality. To understand the message of *The Emerald Tablet* requires the use of the active imagination. Yet the active imagination itself has many manifestations whether it is the Kantian notion of the imagination that was without a homeland, Henry Corbin's analysis of the *mundus imaginalis*, the mind with ability to act upon Nature. It could be argued that they all have a role in the transcendence to touch the divine dependent on the practitioner and the practice undertaken.

As contemplation on the aspects of self and divine developed more theories on the practices required to taste that which was beyond duality were established. One such development that established the foundations of Hermeticism, *The Corpus Hermeticum*, is a collection of texts dating from the second and third centuries attributed to Hermes Trismegistus. These texts communicate through Hellenistic Gnosis rather than a single prescribed spiritual or religious viewpoint. In the *Corpus Hermeticum* Poimandres (Nous) taught Hermes that the mind becomes what it contemplates and that the knowledge of God can be obtained by contemplation of the universe.

But what characterises the universe is a complex web of analogical and dynamic relationships: relationships between the macrocosm and the microcosm. An important constituent of Gnosticism is metaphysical dualism, the notion that there exist two things, two types, and two substances. The body-mind dualism of Plato assumed the existence of two distinct principles of being in the universe, spirit and matter. The objective of the individual in attempting to transcend his *'earth bound'* consciousness was to elevate the consciousness beyond the matter to contemplate pure spiritual form. As if to reaffirm this, man's symbolism developed as a mirror of his own mind, and in our relative world that which has been created as one thing was distinct from another. Yet the *Corpus Hermeticum* postulates a theory that there is in the world an absence of dualism, simply because the world itself is of divine origin. Therefore once humans could read the symbols of creation they could know God directly, negating ontological dualism between God and his Creation.

In the modern world we have inherited a plethora of ideas, theories, speculation and experiential teachings. But it is now left to the spiritual seeker to pick between all of these writings and developments that have taken place over millennia. However we label or understand duality the recognition of its existence and the possibility of something spiritually beyond human existence as we recognise it is a first important step to a simple understanding that the separation of things means they are not joined up. It is only from this recognition that we start to search for ways to bring that separation together, to find unity, to experience both sides. In doing so we strive to understand what happens when there is no duality, what happens when we have transcended the *'this and other'* that leads to our continued attachment to the mundane world and the continued experience of our human negative emotions and experiences such as grasping, attachment jealousy and aversion.

> *"Behold you are become free. Do that which most pleaseth you. For behold, your own reason riseth up against my wisdom. Not content you are to be heirs, but you would be Lords, yea Gods, yea the Judgers of the heavens"* ~ *Spiritual Diaries of John Dee*

In that search for transcendence what we are seeking is to step outside of this dualistic world that we have created. The starting point we all have, no matter what spiritual path we are travelling, will be where we are, utilising the knowledge we have come to know and understand. Knowledge that we have tried and tested and accepted as the truth for ourselves, it is then that the iconography that we are spiritually and culturally comfortable with, teachings that have resonated with us or lit a spark of spirituality within us wanting to push us further forward to develop our understanding of ourselves and to seek something more. All of the dualistic supports can be used to move us toward the Holy Grail of becoming one with the divine as we understand it.

Despite many great thinkers and writers of our aeon who have attempted to show us how to move outside of duality the axiom holds fast. *I can only show you the way, the journey depends on yourself.* So when all is said and done the only way we are able to develop to transcend duality is alone and it is alone that we can experience what lies beyond the borders of the self imposed box that we create around our minds. We can practice within a group and share experiences but the self-experience can, by definition, only ever be experienced and accepted individually. It is by necessity that our

Vs.

journey starts on a path where we utilise the man created dualistic symbolism that has evolved and from which many have started to follow a spiritual path to lead us to a further spiritual goal beyond knowing to a goal of experiencing.

The external symbolic creations that can support our development have taken many forms, representations of deities and divine beings through art and poetry, the understanding of the world we have conceived about us represented through the creation of mandalas, or hidden meanings in the art of alchemy, all are representations of the dualism that we live within on a daily basis. All symbolism is linked to knowledge of the symbols, knowledge either imparted or self deduced. But even when we understand what these symbols represent we need to develop further.

> *"We build the bridge of intelligence, which is lacking in most of our contemporaries, and with the aid of this bridge, we transport ourselves to the other shore, where we may gather precious pearls that cannot be picked by those with no hands"*
> ~ *Pascal Beverly Randolph*

The step away from defining and acceptance using knowledge and the *mundus imaginalis* we have been looking for experiences beyond the mundane. The ultimate goal is the step to taste that which exists beyond the mundane play of our human existence. By understanding the experience of the divine means that we come to realise that the human experience and the divine experience need to be conceptualised as having reciprocal dependence on each other. It is when we are in prayer or practicing our spiritual path, when the magician is performing his art and sees the equality and the undivided nature of human existence and the ultimate, that we are able to taste the true essence of both. It is an essence that is complete but in itself is empty of any inherent existence. This is an important point. Because when that belief in inherent existence drops away so too does the belief in inherent existence of everything you see hear smell touch and taste. We see that our senses deceive us and our mind labels phenomena to convince us of its inherent reality. But this is a fallacy. So where then does this leave the dualistic world around us, and where does it leave the symbolism and iconography, the spiritual tools we have used on the journey on this path of understanding?

Moving beyond our relative world, beyond duality is a process not of rejecting dualistic concepts, images or teachings but of understanding that they are simply tools to be used in our own transformation. Metaphors, symbolism and ritual have combined in an attempt to give meaning to experiences that, by necessity, are ineffable.

Vs.

"Man is the son of his works; he is what he wills to be; he is the image of the God he makes; he is the realisation of his own ideal. Should that ideal lack basis, the whole edifice of his immortality collapses. Philosophy is not the ideal, but ought to serve as its foundation. The known is for us the measure of the unknown; by the visible we appreciate the invisible; sensations are to thoughts even as thoughts to aspirations" ~ Eliphas Levi

We started our journey attempting to understand the world we lived in, the emotions that we experienced on our journey within that world. This dualism drove us to dissatisfaction with the suffering that had been created about us and wanting to understand we have developed systems, images and practices to touch that which is beyond the physical self. Delving into our minds we have striven to touch the creator, the divine, that which is perfection and with effort, focus and time we have managed to experience that beyond words. The irony of the journey itself is that which we are seeking is always there; it does not appear from nothing, it is like peeling away the layers of the onion. As each layer is discarded and the baggage of daily life and emotions lifted we come to see that the duality we have existed in, the duality of our own creation was just that, self-created. At the moment of liberation, transcendence, feeling or tasting beyond the mundane, it is at this point that we understand that all of the regalia, created deities, gods, practices are just supports and have no inherent existence outside of our own minds. It is only at this point that duality falls away and we are truly liberated, and it is only at this point in that non dualistic existence we have tasted we can understand that we could never have touched a divine separate from ourselves, because we are the divine.

Vs.

THE DIVINE HUMAN

Nature/Shakti and Spirit/Shiva

by Rachel Donaldson

What is evolution? Simply put it is the process of change. How about if we consider the concept of evolution as discussed within the structure of Indian philosophy? It is the process of change relating to our consciousness – it is conscious evolution.

However, change usually requires some thought and effort and it is this concept which threads through many schools of Indian philosophy. One of the earliest sources of this concept comes from *samkhya* philosophy – an ancient school of Indian philosophy. Samkhya tells us that without thought (consciousness or spirit) and effort (life energy or nature) there can be no change, transformation or creation. In samkhya philosophy thought is *purusa* (spirit or consciousness) and effort is *prakrti* (nature or prana). It is this distinction between two complementary forces that enables transformation on a personal level to take place, and it is this interactive process between the two that will be explored here.

Samkhya philosophy

> "The union of the spirit with the nature is for contemplation of the nature; the union of the nature with the spirit is for liberation. The union of both is like that of a lame man with a blind man. The creation is brought about by that union"
> ~ Samkhya Karika

There is a story about two men travelling with difficulty in a caravan – one was lame and the other was blind. Their travelling caravan was attacked by robbers in the forest and the two men were deserted by their fellow travellers. The two men wandered about haphazardly for a while until they came across each other – they decided to join forces, the blind man carrying the lame man on his shoulders. The lame man told the blind man where to walk and together they found their way out of the situation. At the end they parted as their goal had been achieved. The lame man was *purusa*, having knowledge but inert; the blind man was *prakrti*, having the power of action but no knowledge – only by working together could they achieve their aim.

This quote and story come from the major text of samkhya philosophy the *Samkhya Karika*. The text was written around the 4th or 5th century by a man called Ishvara Krishna. He claimed to be descended from a great sage called Kapila through a succession of disciples. In his *Samkhya Karika* he writes 72 slokas which describe the concept of *purusa* and *prakrti* and their relationship. The Samkhya School attested that creation was manifest through these two eternal principles. It did not advocate a higher principle.

As samkhya discussed evolution of purusa and prakrti, so later Indian philosophers took the concept and added their own flavour or evolution of the philosophy itself. The influence of samkhya is felt through the *Upanishads*, the *Bhagavad Gita*, and Patanjali's yoga sutras and into saivism through the concept of Shiva (*purusa*) and Shakti (*prakrti*). A discussion of samkhya would not be complete without considering the impact on saivism, so at times it will be necessary to discuss purusa/prakrti and Shiva/Shakti, but in essence they reflect the same principles. It is also important to remember that samkhya had a profound effect on Buddhism and Jainism that is not discussed here due to space.

In the beginning

To properly understand how purusa and prakrti come together to create we must first understand where they come from.

Purusa is the individual soul, the spirit principle or consciousness and state of awareness in the human mind. We understand it as our consciousness and, in the tantric texts, it represents the male principle or Shiva:

> "Always dwelling within all beings is the Atman, the Purusha, the Self, a little flame in the heart." ~ Katha Upanishad part 6

In many of the later Vedanta and yoga texts, purusa is also called the *atman* – the individual spirit. Purusa is pure knowledge, it knows absolutely everything.

Prakrti is our individual life force, our energy or prana. It is the nature principle and, in the tantric texts, represents the female principle or Shakti:

> "There is nature, never-born, who with her three elements - light, fire and darkness – creates all things in nature" ~ Svetasvatara Upanishad Part 4.

For those who study yoga, prakrti will be most familiar as prana – our life force. Purusa and prakrti cannot exist or function without the other. Purusa is dormant, consciousness without active power, and prakrti is an active force without the knowledge to direct or will.

Vs.

They are independent forces that are interdependent on each other. United they bring creation, separated they bring dissolution. They are the mechanism that is responsible for everything in both the cosmic and individual dimensions.

In samkhya philosophy, before the union of creation, purusa and prakrti are totally separate and prakrti manifests the principles of nature (tattvas) without any nudging from purusa:

> "The revealed is like the evident one. It is linked with impurity, destruction and inequality. Other than that is better – proceeding from the right cognition of the Manifest, Unmanifest and the Knower." - Samkhya Karika II

The Manifest are the tattvas, the Unmanifest is prakrti and the Knower is purusa. Purusa is separate and not a part of manifesting creation, although as we see later it is considered the last tattva and must relate to prakrti positively for evolution to happen; however, if purusa withdraws then prakrti can evolve on her own, but it takes more time and tends to be undisciplined – purusa can guide towards evolution or indeed involution.

In the tantric texts of saivism, Shiva (purusa) and Shakti (prakrti) are not different but one. In the scheme of creation, be that manifest or potential, Shakti is the opposite polarity to Shiva – the midpoint between the two is the *bindu*, the point at which creation occurs. Tantra describes several bindus: *maha bindu* (the entire conscious creation), *para bindu* (the form of Ishwara or god), *sukshma bindu* (the individual mind) and *sthula bindu* (the gross bindu in the form of ovum and sperm). In maha bindu, Shiva and Shakti are in total equilibrium but when movement occurs in Shakti, the two split and emerge as separate entities. When the two reunite the manifestation of creation begins.

The journey to manifestation

Samkhya explains how prakrti evolves (separately from purusa) into the twenty-four tattvas which lead to the last (earth - prthvi) and the gross manifestation of matter. We already know in samakhya that purusa and prakrti were separate in the beginning so prakrti moves of its own will.

To start from the subtlest concept there is mula-prakrti (root-nature). This is nature in its most infinite and attributeless stage and it can only be comprehended by intuition. Within mula-prakrti the three qualities of nature exist in complete equilibrium – these are the attributes or gunas; sattva (purity); rajas (vibrancy) and tamas (inertia).

> "The Attributes are of the nature of pleasure, pain and delusion; they are adapted to illuminate, to activate and to restrain. They mutually suppress, support, produce, consort and exist" ~ Samkhya Karika XII

Vs.

The attributes or gunas are mutually supportive – they all bring about the existence of the other. Sattva is the source of rajas and tamas, rajas the source of sattva and tamas, and tamas the source of sattva and rajas.

Mula-prakrti then evolves into the phenomenal stage and the attributes/gunas lose equilibrium with each other, giving nature its turbulent aspect. The first manifestation of the phenomenal stage is *mahat* (the great principle/tattva). The mahat is the spontaneous and motivating aspect of nature, creating and destroying with no objective.

From mahat evolves the ego (*ahamkara*) and the five subtle elements (smell, taste, light, touch and sound). A further sixteen tattvas then emerge. The five gross elements – earth (prthvi), water (ap), fire (tej), air (vayu) and ether (akasa) emerge respectively from the five subtle elements - smell becomes earth, taste becomes water, light becomes fire, touch becomes air and sounds becomes ether. Manas (the mind) is formed, from which comes the organs of action (arms, legs, mouth, genital and excretory organs) and the senses of perception (ears, eyes, nose, tongue and skin). These make up the twenty four tattvas. The last and twenty fifth tattva which is purusa must interact positively with the other twenty four for the individual to experience true bliss.

Saivism uses the same fundamental basis as this but adds a further eleven principles which do not conflict with samkhya, only enrich. As we saw earlier, Saivism believes that Shiva and Shakti are always together in maha bindu until Shakti moves and the two become separate creating Shiva tattva and Shakti tattva – they then have to reunite in order for the thirty six principles to emerge. Shiva tattva is one and whole but Shakti tattva subdivides into five further tattvas, separate but remaining Shakti tattva. These subdivisions are *kaala* (time), *niyati* (space), *vidya* (knowledge), *raga* (passion) and *kala* (power).

When Shiva tattva and Shakti tattva reunite it creates the potential of *nada* (vibration) and the product is *sadashiva tattva* – Shakti is still unmanifest but a very subtle notion of existence arises. Shakti continues to move, becomes predominant and evolves into bindu Shakti (or Ishwara/para bindu) – this is the totality of Shakti.

Nowhere is the imagery of the full force of primordial Shakti better represented than in the goddess Kali. There are many representations of Kali, fierce and frightening, standing on the inert form of Shiva. This representation perfectly describes the emergence of primal Shakti.

Kali is generally shown as the south-facing black Kali – as everything is absorbed into blackness. She is garbed in space (niyati), she is full-breasted representing the power of creation, her dishevelled hair represents the fabric of space and time (kaala). She wears a garland of fifty heads representing the fifty letters in the Sanskrit alphabet, symbolising the repository of knowledge (vidya). The garland of human hands can also be seen as representing action and power (kala). Her demeanour is fierce, changeless, and represents limitless passion (ragas). Even the three attributes or gunas are found in her appearance – her white teeth symbolise sattva, her red tongue symbolises rajas and the activating quality of nature leading downwards to tamas. She stands above and on Shiva, but he is not dead or even unhappy – he is in a complete state of bliss. In these representations Kali is dominant and larger than Shiva representing her totality as she emerges into bindu Shakti:

> "Thou are the seed of the universe, and the supreme Maya. All this universe has been bewitched by thee" ~ Devi-Mahatmya

From bindu Shakti emerge the tattvas of creation and the journey to gross manifestation. Shakti moves through sudda vidya (illuminated wisdom) and then creates Maya, the force by which form is measured, Shakti tattva creates this Maya and illusion and the separation of form and consciousness:

> "With Maya, his power of wonder, he made all things, and by Maya the human soul is bound. There know that nature is Maya" ~ Svetasvatara Upanishad

The reference in the above quote to a *'he'* is interesting and is a good example of a higher principle creeping into Vedanta philosophy – a concept not advocated by samkhya. However, the reference to Maya is clear and the relationship with Shakti with the result of the bound human soul – separate and unaware of purusa or Shiva.

From this point forward the remaining tattvas are created along the same lines as samkhya discussed above. The last tattva is earth (prthvi) at which point the forms of the universe are separate and identifiable – including ourselves, the human form. So where does Shakti then go once the universe has been created? She withdraws and collapses back into the Shiva-Shakti tattva that produced it. In the human body this is at the lowest chakra *muladhara* – she is coiled like a serpent three and half times around the Shiva lingam, asleep but holding the key to spiritual potential. Dormant, she represents the instinctual part of our life but awakened our spiritual potential can be realised.

The journey back to Spirit

So we are created, we are in human form and the potential of spiritual evolution lies dormant in our earth centre – muladhara chakra. In order for our true potential to be realised we must awaken the dormant Shakti and allow her to reunite with Shiva in his highest abode at the *sahasrara* chakra or by taking the path to Samadhi.

But why should we care? What are the consequences to us as individuals if we do not strive to rejoin the polar forces of Shakti and Shiva?

> *"There are demon-haunted worlds, regions of utter darkness. Whoever, in life denies the Spirit falls into that darkness of death" ~ Isa Upanishad*

The human who has not realised their spiritual potential is likened to a chariot – out of control with the horses as the senses and the path as their object:

> *"He who has not right understanding and whose mind is never steady is not the ruler of his life, like a bad driver with wild horses" ~ Katha Upanishad, Part 3*

It is no coincidence that the tale of the *Bhagavad Gita* and Arjuna's struggle to take arms against himself (represented by his family) is told from the confines of a chariot with Krishna as the driver. Control of the senses and the mind leads us to back to purusa or Shiva and union with the universal consciousness – Samadhi.

> *"When the five senses and the mind are still, and reason itself rests in silence, then begins the Path supreme. This calm steadiness of the mind is called Yoga." ~ Katha Upanishad, Part 6*

So our purpose is to reawaken the Shakti potential in us but this time for involution back to Shiva or purusa. It is spiritual evolution as opposed to manifest evolution.

Interestingly, the path of Shiva through the Vedic tradition represents this journey. The origins of Shiva can be found in the *Vedas* starting as Pashupati or Rudra – a wild nature god and controller of our animal instincts. His origin appears to be Dravidian and then inherited by the Kapalikas – only after 200 BCE does he become Shiva and then the creator in the time of the *Upanishads*. So his historical emergence represents that of individual spiritual evolution from primal understanding to enlightenment.

Unlike the journey to Nature that follows a set path, there are many journeys one can make to reunite Shiva and Shakti. The overriding name of the journey is Yoga but the routes are many and varied. Some examples are:

Karma Yoga – the path of action which teaches us how to live in the spirit of self-integration

Jnana (Gyana) Yoga – the path of wisdom and knowledge which teaches us how to achieve a sense of inner integration on a mental level

Vs.

Hatha Yoga – described as the physical path. However, it is not a distinct path of Yoga at all but a branch of Raja Yoga

Raja Yoga – the path of meditation and the central teaching of yoga and at the heart of Samkhya philosophy

Yoga means *'Union'* – bringing back together that which was separate. It is the journey of self-discovery. For our purposes I will consider Raja and Hatha yoga as they reflect the practices of Samkhya and Tantra.

Raja means *'royal'*, it is considered the ultimate path and its aim (as with all yoga) is the union of Spirit with Nature to form super-consciousness. The path of Raja yoga takes us along eight limbs (with the intention that all eight limbs must be observed at the same time to achieve the goal – they are not steps along the way). The eight limbs are:

- Yama – moral and ethical restraint or social discipline
- Niyama – individual discipline
- Asana – the practice of yoga postures
- Pranayama – control of the breath
- Pratyahara – mind withdrawal from the senses
- Dharana – concentration
- Dyana – meditation
- Samadhi – the aim, super-consciousness and union with the divine

Hatha yoga prepares the individual for Raja yoga through physical practices, some which are similar to Raja Yoga such as asana and pranayama, and some that are not such as Shatkarma, which are practices of purification and cleansing. However, Hatha yoga does have one distinction in that it talks about tantric practices to unite Shiva and Shakti. These practices are concerned with energy or prana within the body and how they can be manipulated to allow Shiva and Shakti to unite in the ultimate energy centre in the body (or just outside it) at the crown in *sahasrara* chakra. You will not see the texts of Raja yoga discussing these practices as, at the time they were written, tantric practices had fallen out of favour and were considered to be base: so Patanjali never speaks of prana or chakras in his sutras. When the main text on Hatha yoga was written, the *Hatha Yoga Pradipika*, tantric practices had found favour once more and the text speaks of these. Interestingly, the name Raja yoga did not even exist before Hatha yoga – it was just a way of distinguishing the two paths.

We have already seen how the individual must follow the eight limbs to achieve the goal of Raja yoga. In Hatha (or tantric) yoga we work with the energy body. As we have seen at the end of the journey of nature, Shakti resides asleep in muladhara chakra and the potential of Shiva lies in sahasrara chakra – to achieve Samadhi or true bliss the two must be reunited.

Shakti resides as a serpent coiled three and half times around the Shiva lingam and represents the kundalini. The number of times the serpent is coiled is significant – the three coils represent the past, present and future; the three gunas and the three parts of the mantra AUM – speech, mind and breathe of life. The half coil represents the transcendent state. So all the universe and transcendence is experienced within the three and half coils of kundalini.

When Shakti as the kundalini is awakened the whole body experiences a transformation – overall this is positive but there can be some negative aspects (or distractions) experienced. Kundalini does not belong to the physical, astral or even mental body – it is in the causal body where time, space and object are meaningless.

In this causal body, the supreme awareness of Shiva resides in sahasrara chakra at the crown of the head – it is the seat of the womb of consciousness. Just below at the third eye is ajna chakra, which is the seat of intuitive knowledge. It sits at the very top of the spinal column and it is connected with both sahasrara and muladhara chakra via sushumna – the psychic passage that runs through the spinal column.

Along sushumna lie other chakras or vortices of energy. There are many other chakras in the body but for the purposes of uniting Shakti and Shiva the principle ones lie along sushumna. This begins with muladhara at the base of the spine (the residence of kundalini and the chakra where one goes beyond animal instinct and towards illumination); then respectively swadisthana (corresponds to the sacral plexus of nerves and controls the unconscious), manipura (located at the naval and controls digestion and assimilation), anahata (at the heart controlling the heart, the lungs and the diaphragm), vishuddi (at the throat controlling the thyroid) and leading onto ajna. In kundalini yoga there is a final point before sahasrara which is the bindu – the point where oneness first divides into many. Finally, the kundalini/ Shakti energy reaches Sahasrara chakra and union with Shiva is complete.

Reunion

In Raja yoga we focus our attention on the object of meditation. When Samadhi is reached that goal is reached but the objectivity dissolves – duality ceases. The mediator loses their individuality and experiences the absolute. The 'I' no longer exists and nature and spirit are one. In Raja yoga there are levels of Samadhi with *nirbikalpa* Samadhi as the highest – that being union with god. It is the summit of spiritual experience.

In tantric practice the highest goal is sahasrara chakra but it is the same experience as Samadhi. Shiva and Shakti unite and the individual experiences the death of the mundane – there is no dual awareness, the veil of Maya has been broken, and there is only single awareness.

The journey to nature and spirit is complete and the individual becomes the divine human – the polarities of Shiva and Shakti have been absorbed and intermingled.

> "A swelling glory within me began to envelop towns, continents, the earth, solar and stellar systems, tenuous nebulae, and floating universes. The entire cosmos, gently luminous, like a city seen afar at night, glimmered within the infinitude of my being"
> ~ Autobiography of a Yogi, ch. 14.

Bibliography
Danielou, Alan. *Gods of Love and Ecstasy,* Inner Traditions, 1992.
Iyengar, B.K.S. *Light on the Yoga Sutras of Patanjali*, Thorsons, 1993.
Mascaro, Juan trans. *The Upanishads*, Penguin Classics, 1965.
Mascaro, Juan trans. *The Bhagavad Gita*, Penguin Classics, 1962.
Mookerjee, Ajit. *Kali - The Feminine Force*, Thames and Hudson, 2001.
Muktibodhananda, Swami. *Hatha Yoga Pradipika*, Yoga Publication Trust, 2002.
Muktibodhananda, Swami. *Swara Yoga*, Bihar School of Yoga, 1999.
Niranjanananda Saraswati, Swami. *Prana, Pranayama, Prana Vidya*, 2002.
Satyananda Saraswati, Swami. *Kundalini Tantra*, Yoga Publications Trust, 2003.
Sturgess, Stephen. *The Yoga Book*, Watkins publishing, 2002.
Woodruffe, Sir John. *The Serpent Power*, Ganesh & Co, 2003.
Yogananda, Paramhansa. *Autobiography of a Yogi*, Sterling Publications, 2006.

Vs.

A Lantern to the Cave

Magickal methods for conscious and unconscious communion

by Guy Gaunt

As this essay is in an anthology called *Vs.* it is important to first look at what this word means. *'Versus'* can be defined as things in opposition, perhaps a battle; or, contending forces. It implies duality. Within the present context, the duality in question is two-fold but, in essence, related – that of the conscious and the unconscious, of dreaming and waking. Within practical magick these are two of the most important states of consciousness, and facilitating and improving their interaction is often one of magick's primary aims. To tap into the unconscious, dreaming state, whether whilst actually asleep or not, and drawing upon the inspiration, wisdom and various forces of change embodied within are fundamental to many paths and practices. Some even go so far as to suggest that the subconscious is the greatest magician of all and that without the aid of the subconscious there can be no magick.

Within the confines of these pages I will limit myself to techniques inspired by the magician and artist Austin Osman Spare (1886-1956) with whose work I feel a close affinity. I will also try to confine myself to a model of the subconscious/conscious that is prevalent in some modern day psychology and psychotherapeutic schools of thought, e.g. Freudian, Jungian and Rogerian. However, it is worth noting that in some schools of thought the subconscious plays a greater role in therapy and a model of the mind than in others. I hope that an examination of these concepts will lead the practitioner beyond the boundaries of any limited beliefs, into the vast array of magickal and mystical schools of thought, and onwards towards that limitless and transcendental truth behind the world of appearances.

As the terms conscious and unconscious are so prevalent there is little need to elaborate on their meaning. It has, however, been pointed out that the use of the terms *'subconscious'* and *'unconscious'* is misleading. The 'subconscious' implies something below or lesser whereas unconscious implies something unknown or hidden from normal consciousness. Neither of these words is particularly valid as this area of consciousness is neither below nor particularly hidden. Within this essay I shall use the two terms interchangeably. Jan Fries, who wrote the excellent book *Visual Magick*, uses the term *'deep mind'*, which is perhaps more suitable.

From a mystical standpoint the unconscious comes before the conscious, followed finally by the world of appearances. The divine dreams the universe into existence and mankind dreams his or her own fragment of that universe. Sometimes our divine heritage is forgotten, the sun sets into the darkness of the underworld, and we must struggle to awaken from our slumbers, to the brilliant dazzling sun at its zenith. This reversal of the senses, the understanding that the dream came before the material, that the dream is behind the material, is very important to those of a more mystical nature.

As a side note: addressing issues of the conscious/ unconscious duality often leads into questions regarding the body/mind duality. This divide is present within modern day psychology but certainly wasn't prevalent in all systems of psycho-spiritual thought. For example, the chakra systems of India see the body and mind as an interconnected whole. Also some psychological methods, such as Reichian therapy, see a more holistic connection between the body and mind. Habitual thought patterns manifest as tensions and stresses within the body and vice versa. For instance, if you undergo physical exercise, these tensions go away and you feel much better mentally and emotionally.

When the concept of the unconscious is expanded to address the waking and dreaming state it could be suggested that a four-fold nature appears. Things are either unconscious or conscious in both the dreaming and waking states. It may be useful, rather than have an either/or scenario, to see various strata of consciousness, ranging from deep primal states to surface states of conscious. This is appropriate in the theories of Austin Spare, especially within the practical arena of atavistic resurgence, in which the evocation of various powers attributed to animals pulls the unconscious strata of genetic memory to the conscious forefront.

Having said this, when you begin to engage in practical work that seeks to access the unconscious consciously a *'versus'* situation certainly arises. This may be because you are making the model conscious, believing in the duality of the model, and therefore pitting yourself against yourself. However, after much practise the issue begins to dissolve. The boundaries between the conscious and unconscious become thinner. A clear line of communication between the two states of consciousness develops.

There are a number of ways to facilitate this communication between the conscious and unconscious minds. I believe that it was Austin Spare who catalogued some of these techniques although I am sure that they are evident in older magickal and spiritual practises as well. There are a number of ways to access and work with the unconscious depending on the goals of the magician. The

ways in which the unconscious and conscious interact can be categorised as follows:
- Communication from the conscious to subconscious.
- Communication from the subconscious to conscious whilst awake.
- Communication from the unconscious whilst asleep.

In the first category we find the practice of magickal sigils, the internalization of symbols, the use of affirmations, trance states and willed forgetfulness in which the purpose or goal of the magickal working is deliberately forgotten or removed from the conscious awareness of the magickian, allowing it to root itself more firmly in the magickal reality.

The second category contains phenomena such as daydreaming and visions, or skrying in crystal balls and dark mirrors; pathworking also finds its place here as it can be viewed as a form of willed daydream. In these techniques the inner workings of the subconscious and their meanings find their way to conscious awareness and understanding in the magickian's life.

The third category is interesting in that there are dreams that are remembered in the waking state and lucid dreaming, where you are present within the dream and able to act as if awake to a greater or lesser degree. The one tends to lead onto the other as part of you becomes aware that you are dreaming of what you want to dream and snaps into a state of awareness. Sometimes this becomes even more intricate as there are more areas of consciousness revealed. You become aware that you are asleep and dreaming but also that you are watching yourself.

From here dreams become portals to the higher planes, gateways through which the spirits can gain access to our world. They also lead away from the world of appearances, from the labyrinth of illusions that surround us, through the inner dreamscapes and outwards to the infinite worlds within the divine imagination. Also, this process can be reversed, that which is dreamt can be brought down onto the physical plane. That which is made of fantasy and fiction can be made flesh.

As to actual practical methods of communication there are many. It could be said that all true magickal techniques seek to create this current of communion. Before we begin you may well ask: why would you want to do this? And this is a perfectly legitimate question. Modern magickal practitioners do this for many reasons: for simple results magick; to draw upon inspiration; to find wisdom; to contact various states of consciousness personified as spirits, elementals, angels, gods etc.; and perhaps, ultimately, to achieve enlightenment.

Firstly, let us examine the methods of creating communication from the conscious to unconscious mind. The most common method, and most effective, is through the use of sigils. The technique of sigilisation was refined by Austin Spare around the turn of the 20th century, although it certainly existed before him in the ancient grimoires, such as the *Goetia*, and in orders such as the Golden Dawn. Spare's method of sigils is much more capable of personalisation than these others and can be seen as stripping away the religious and mystical connotations and getting to the essence of the process. The method is extremely simple. As so many are aware of this technique I'm not going to go into too much detail. You simply take a *'statement of intent'*, knock out the repeating letters, and combine them into an image or glyph. The statement of intent can be anything and can fulfil the aim of any of the magickal goals outlined above. You could create a sigil for simple results magick, such as *'I want to find a beautiful house'*, fire it into the unconscious, into the land of dreams, and await the outcome. Alternatively you could create a sigil embodying the wish 'I want to understand the movement of the stars in the heavens' and wait for the unconscious to supply such Gnostic wisdom. As a final example, you could create a sigil of an entity, one that you create yourself or wish to contact, and again await the results. Less specific aims can be chosen for experimental or explorative purposes.

Once you have a sigil you can perfect it as much as you like. Simplifying it down until you have an image that is appealing to your sense of art and beauty. If you wish you can colour it, with traditional colours from one of the various systems of symbolism, or according to your own intuition – which is arguably the more potent method. It is interesting to notice that over time certain similarities will recur in the shape of your sigils. Certain motifs or designs will become apparent. These are interesting for a number of reasons: these reoccurring designs often approach a personal symbol of something more universal, such as a phallus, or an egg; sometimes they signify something important, a certain reoccurring desire, becoming the basis for a personal *'alphabet of desire'*; or they are the sigil of some spirit, subconscious automata or elemental.

The interesting part of sigilisation, within the current context, is how to overcome the conscious vs. unconscious dichotomy. For sigilisation to work, according to Austin Spare and borne out by practical experience, the desired intent must be made unconscious; in other words, forgotten about completely. There are many ways to do this, ecstasy and vacuity being the most commonly employed methods.

The ecstatic approach can involve holding the sigil in the mind's eye, or gazing upon the sigil, allowing the lines of power to be absorbed, whilst having sex, running, dancing, drumming and so on. In fact any method of exhaustion can be used and is once again up to the magician. Of course exploring other methods, ones that you find difficult or alien, can be beneficial. If doing something like drumming, or dancing, it is valuable to do these spontaneously and record the outcome. These methods can lead to various forms – stances and rhythms in the examples above – that can be used in further magickal work; once again evolving a personal sorcerous practise and style.

Vacuity often follows ecstatic techniques or can be sought through inhibitory techniques such as meditation, or by idly drawing the sigil whilst engaging in other activities. Some common methods come under the heading of death postures. Spare uses this term in a specific sense but it has been expanded upon over the decade since his death. The original technique is to stare into your eyes in a mirror until your mind goes blank. As a precursor one would stand on tip-toe with your hand tensed behind your back, and essentially asphyxiate yourself until you almost black out. Also included under this category is the method of holding your breath until your mind blanks out, and sensory deprivation techniques such as wearing a hoodwink and earplugs submerged in a bath with a pipe to breathe through. Each to their own.

It is in trying to forget the sigil, or rather the desire attached to the sigil, that the conflict becomes apparent. Spare wrote that it was the duality of desire that leads to failure, not just in magick but also in life in general: if you want something you invent a million reasons as to why it should not be yours. It is the circumvention of this process that is the aim of sigilisation. The best way around this is to draw many sigils, in advance, and forget entirely what they are for.

It is this dynamic of sigilisation that makes apparent the first conflicts between the unconscious and the conscious. You want something consciously but your unconscious reacts against this and works against you. This dynamic function occurs no matter how good the outcome of the wish or thought you propose even if it is for the good of your entire being. It happens daily in every moment and portrays the inherent duality of everyday wills, desires and beliefs. It is only with the gentle methods of self-trickery described above that it can be overcome.

If you believe that this is just mystical and magical nonsense dreamt up by a strange artist then you have only to look at the modern methods of affirmation to see a similarity. Affirmation involves taking a sentence, such as *'I must, I must, I must improve my bust'*, and repeating it umpteen times daily until a result occurs. Spare's technique expands upon and, in my opinion, improves the methods of affirmation. This isn't to say that affirmations are useless, but that they may take longer. Affirmations seem, and this is purely intuitional on my part, to work in a slightly different way. They work from the point of view of the conscious mind programming the unconscious through repetition. They also don't have the magickal scope of sigils. However some strategies in the design of

Vs.

affirmations can be used to great effect in the practise of creating sigils: always make intents positive, for instance.

To establish communication between the subconscious and unconscious whilst awake also involves many techniques and is arguably easier. It is here that the conscious vs. unconscious becomes less of a battle and becomes more of a harmony. Perhaps because of this, these techniques can be used extensively in order to strengthen communication and make dream-work more possible. It is these methods that help you to trust your unconscious mind, and ultimately yourself – invoking the glorious state of self-love – and to let your unconscious know that you are prepared to listen to what it has to say. These techniques start to open the door, as it were.

I see the techniques of subconscious and conscious communion as two-fold: the techniques of automatic art, including both drawing and writing, and that of divination, including techniques using divination tools and those receiving direct understanding such as augury. It is perhaps through the second technique, of seeing oracle in everyday events, that you begin to realise that your unconscious is closer than you think and ever-present.

Automatic art and writing have been explored by many and have been proven to be useful tools for various purposes. They have been used for therapeutic goals, for example. In magick these techniques are undertaken for slightly different purposes, overlapping at points, and diverging completely at others.

Taking automatic drawing first: the hand is freed from any habitual styles of drawing or ways of moving by sketching this way and that way, and drawing squiggles and shapes without any purpose or preconceived image in mind. The aim here is to unlearn any habits that have been developed through writing or, if you've had any training as an artist, any artistic techniques. This is similar to how various art colleges teach their students to draw.

During these practises the automatic artist will come up against another barrier and find two parts of their being at odds: the hand and its learnt behaviour, and the desire for spontaneity and automatism. Your desire to draw automatically is at odds with the control of your conscious mind. If the practise is continued then eventually these limitations are overcome and drawing becomes automatic. This isn't to say that the hand drifts across the paper and draws wonderful pictures without any conscious awareness, but instead that there is a unity between the Hand, the Eye and the image you want to draw, in its entirety, which is held in the mind.

Some people find it easier to combine techniques such as meditating on the hand until it disappears or becomes a *'void'*, or gazing on a sigil drawn on the back of the hand. Some people like to imagine a spirit inhabiting their hand and taking over. This gives the magician some control over the nature of the work produced by being able to change the type of entity inhabiting the hand.

Vs.

In automatic writing a similar process occurs, although there is a different quality in that which surfaces. The best way to practise is to start writing a story and then to just let the story flow; to write what you see within the imagination and intensify the inner experience through the words on the paper – rather like a stream of consciousness. Eventually, once again, the inner vision, the narrator inside, and the hand become one. Another automatic writing method yielding slightly different results, yet equally as useful, is to write random words, albeit curiously related words, in a fashion similar to the well-known psychotherapeutic technique.

Once again, automatic writing can be developed by invoking various entities either into the hand, or into the practitioner and then engaging in the practise. Again sigils can be drawn onto the back of the hand, or onto the top of the piece of paper. It can also be helpful to begin by writing an invocation out and, once in *'character'*, continuing with the writing. The normal process of identification, as used in invocation, can then be used i.e. moving from the perspective of worshipper to worshipped, from *'thou'* to *'I'*.

As mentioned above, once the knack of automatic drawing or writing is acquired the conscious vs. unconscious dynamic is easily overcome. The results often seem peculiar and feel as if some other part of *'you'* is doing the writing or drawing whilst *'you'* are observing.

Augury and the use of oracles are equally as fascinating and again simply require training. There is a constant stream of information coming from the unconscious mind and often this is ignored. The trick with these techniques is to make you aware of this process and to gradually open the door. It has been said that we are constantly dreaming even while we are awake and this certainly seems true in practise.

With divination tools, such as tarot cards or runes, it is simply a matter of allowing stories to grow spontaneously within the mind featuring the cards or symbols. The aim is to access the dreaming process, the one that is constantly going on in the background, and lightly alter and specify the course of that dreaming through the use of the symbols on the cards, or stones etc. If you are doing a *'reading'* for someone else then you have to also feature him or her in the narrative. Whilst doing this other impressions, or visions, will arise in consciousness and these you must weave into the story.

Direct divination, or seeing oracles in everyday events, is also possible. Here also you tune into the ever-present dream and allow it to speak to you inspired by the objects that you see. Specific oracles can be found by using sigilic formulae. For example, you may ask a question, create a sigil, and then wander the streets looking for *'signs'*; this can be done in countryside or city: it matters little the actual location. For example you may see three crows sat on a fence and see them as you and two work colleagues figuratively *'sat on the*

Vs.

fence' over some issue. Alternatively you may see some graffiti that says *'your ass is grass and I'm a lawn-mower'* and realise you need to take a break and do some gardening.

It is often in this way that spirits communicate with us. You may work with a particular entity, see it as one of your famulus, and then receive a message in some luminous liminal moment when the conscious and unconscious align. These messages can truly take any form whatsoever – they can be snatches of conversations, arrangements of dropped forks upon the ground, a dog and cat fighting and so on. Within certain Gnostic states anything can become adorned with importance and meaning.

A word of warning though: the extent to which you open the doorway between the worlds of the conscious and unconscious should be seriously considered. It is all very well to make an oath to see everything as a direct message from God to you personally, but it isn't so good if all you can hear is God shouting at you day in and day out, as some people in mental health trusts will more than happily tell you.

And then we come to dreams.

Spare wrote about *The Witches' Sabbat*, the dream prototype of ritual itself, and this has been mentioned by more recent writers as well such as Kenneth Grant, Andrew Chumbley and Nigel Jackson. It has also been mentioned in academic works such as Carlo Ginzberg's *Ecstasies: Deciphering the Witches' Sabbat* and Hans Peter Duerr *Dreamtime: Concerning the Boundary between Wilderness and Civilisation*. Dream control itself has also been the focus of doctor and psychologists such as Dr. Deidre Bennett who wrote the paper *The "Committee of Sleep": A study of Dream Incubation in Problem Solving*. There are also millions of books on lucid dreaming, dream symbolism and so on.

The power of dreams cannot be underestimated and can be seen as the fount of all wisdom. They provide an undiscovered country, world, or even universe that can be explored. There is a chance for great adventure and access to your own personal inner creativity and genius. When harmonised with the conscious mind, the dreaming mind begins to reveal powerful secrets.

In the past people would go into temples and sleep in special chambers in order to receive prophetic dreams and/or healing. There was a reverence towards dreams that can be much learnt from today. Unlike other forms of conscious/unconscious communication dreams seem to provide direct, vivid access to the hidden depth of our being. Indeed, some traditions, such as Vodoun, still teach the importance of dreams, as it is in dreams that the spirits of Vodoun – the lwa – speak to their serviteurs.

Unfortunately, when you start looking into your dreams the conscious vs. unconscious dynamic becomes stronger than ever before. It seems as if the barrier between dreaming and waking is far greater than that between conscious and unconscious. Luckily the aforementioned practises can help dissolve the barrier between the two states of consciousness and facilitate dream recollection and control.

For any dream explorer the primary aim and the thing of most importance is to bring the dreams into conscious awareness as much as possible. Trying to remember dreams is like trying to find a black moth, in a pitch-black room, with a single match. One method of doing this - a tried and tested (almost to the point of cliché) method - is to keep a dream diary. The more you record your dreams the more you remember. It is as if you send a message to your dream-self and say 'hey, you out there!' It is like passing a lantern down to someone in a cave. Another method is to simply tell someone your dreams upon awakening, even yourself out loud if necessary. I find dreams so bizarrely interesting that the excitement of telling someone my dreams often uncovers more of the dream than I thought I could remember. You may notice something strange in the recollection of a dream: that they appear easier to remember backwards starting from the most recent event and retreating back into the slumber of sleep - just as some witches walk backwards from ritual spaces, so must the dream-traveller walks backwards into dream.

Another method to help with dream recollection is to pretend that you are dreaming whilst you are awake. No, this isn't a call to run naked down the high street. Rather you ask yourself at various points throughout the day: *'Am I awake or am I dreaming right now?'* Eventually this will lead to you asking the same question in your dream-state. This can lead to a lucid dream where you are able to interact with your dream as if you were awake.

At this point I must touch briefly upon sleep paralysis as it is a common occurrence and can be a scary experience if you don't know what is going on. Sleep paralysis occurs when you become conscious whilst asleep, but instead of partaking in the dream you find yourself floating in a void unable to move. Often you are disorientated, confused and scared. Many believe that this is the cause of so-called alien abductions. It may also manifest as you waking but being unable to move (hence *'paralysis'*, with a dream-state occurring) thus, people who experience sleep paralysis may report seeing figures in the room with them, and feeling presences around or on them. These hallucinations (for hallucinations are simply the dream-state process of REM occurring during waking moments) usually become negative and terrifying because the person experiencing them perceives the state of sleep paralysis as such.

It is possible that you may drift out of your dream-state into the state of sleep paralysis. In this situation there really is only one thing that you can do, and that is to relax and go with it. I have found that you either drift back into dream, either lucid or normal, or that you slowly wake up.

Vs.

Beyond dream recollection there are many ways of inspiring the content of dream and dreaming for specific purposes. The simplest is simply to think of something that you want to do in your dream whilst you are falling asleep. This can be enhanced by drawing sigils for various dream goals and concentrating on them. Another method is to run through a pre-designed pathworking whilst slowly drifting off.

You can also use various objects, such as talismans and hag-stones, which you either hold or place around your neck. These are particularly effective. It seems that these serve to not only remind you that you have an intention to dream of something specific but also as a hindrance to normal sleep - rolling over and having a hag-stone sticking in your chest may put you in the liminal state between sleeping and waking.

A final method can be the assumption of certain postures whilst falling asleep. These can be *'god postures'* or just unusual postures that you have dreamed up (pun intended) for the purpose. I have difficulties falling asleep on my back so I find that by simply assuming this *'posture'* I remember my dreams better or fall into lucid states more often.

All of these techniques can be encased within ritual practises either of a traditional type of a non-traditional type such as drawing a sigil on yourself or simply unmaking and remaking the bed.

Here, the duality between conscious and subconscious/unconscious is very clear in the description of the practices; however through enacting them on a frequent and regular basis the dichotomy begins to disappear both on an intellectual and an intuitive level, allowing the magician to come one step closer to the unity that is desired.

Bibliography and Further Reading
Bennett, Dierdre (Dr.) *The "Committee of Sleep": A study of Dream Incubation in Problem Solving.* In *Dreaming*, Vol. 3, No. 2, 1993.
Bertiaux, Michael. *The Voudon Gnostic Workbook.* Weiser Books, 2007.
Bertiaux, Michael. *The Cosmic Meditation.* Holmes Pub. Group, 2007.
Bertiaux, Michael. *Vudu Cartography.* Fulgur Ltd., 2010.
Carroll, Peter J. *Liber Null & Psychonaut.* Weiser Books, 1987.
Carroll, Peter J. *Liber Kaos.* Weiser Books, 1992.
Chumbley, Andrew. *The Azoetia: a grimoire of the Sabbatic craft.* Xoanon Publishers, 1992.
Duerr, Hans Peter. *Dreamtime: Concerning the Boundary between Wilderness and Civilisation.* Blackwell Publishers, 1987.
Erickson, Milton H. *My Voice Will Go With You.* W.W. Norton and Company, 1991.
Freud, Sigmund. *On Dreams.* Cosimo Classics, 2010.
Ginzberg, Carlo. *Ecstasies: Deciphering the Witches' Sabbath.* University of Chicago Press, 2004.
Grant, Kenneth. *The Magical Revival.* Starfire Publishing, 2010.

Vs.

Grant, Kenneth. *Cults of the Shadow*. Skoob Books, 1995.
Grant, Kenneth. *Aleister Crowley and the Hidden God*. Skoob Books, 1993.
Jackson, Nigel. *The Call of the Horned Piper*. Capall Bann, 2001
Jackson, Nigel. *The Masks of Misrule*. Capall Bann, 1996
Jung, Carl. *Man and His Symbols*. Dell, 1968.
Spare, Austin Osman. *The Writings of Austin Osman Spare: Anathema of Zos, The Book of Pleasure, and The Focus of Life*. NuVision Publications, LLC, 2007.

Vs.

SUN AND MOON

An artist's perspective on polarity and its role in the Tarot

by Emily Carding

> *"You are sunlight and I moon, joined by the gods of fortune, midnight and high noon, sharing the sky..."* ~ *Miss Saigon*

As the above quote from a wildly popular musical demonstrates, polarity is an aspect of magical awareness and practice that is not just for the elite few but is a readily understood daily part of all our lives. Whereas in many cases key concepts such as this can be tied up in complicated imagery and symbols, this quote also neatly shows that the symbolism of the polarity of Sun and Moon can be appreciated easily on a very basic level.

As soon as children start to seek understanding of the world around them they pair things into opposites. Night and day, along with the most visibly obvious celestial bodies that inhabit them, must be one of the very first that we recognise, along with male and female. Polarity as a magickal reality has more depth and complexity than simply opposites, yet the sun and moon still serve as potent and easily accessible symbols with which to express and explore the subject. I have been painting visionary art now for about fifteen years on and off, with an intense focus over the last five years, and I have always been compelled to paint the sun and moon together, day skies mingling into night, like an eternal search for balance and unity. When I came to paint my first Tarot, it seemed natural that this theme should continue, as one of my aims was to express the meanings and journey through the cards in a way that would be instinctively accessible without a prior knowledge of esoteric symbolism. Through exploring the images in this way I have increased my own understanding of the journey towards unity that is represented in the Tarot, and I would like to share some of that with you here.

But what exactly do these most familiar of symbols represent? As the all-illuminating force that brings us the power of day, the Sun is an active revealing force. The Sun shows the surface of life and events in all its glorious detail, and at its peak may dispel deception and shadows. Science, logic and clear thinking therefore are ruled by the Sun. This cosmic force represents the innocent glory of all that is as it seems and in the western world is commonly perceived as a representation of male divinity. The Moon, on the other hand, is a changeable, shifting and mysterious presence. Although the Moon may reveal much, it is difficult to be sure of what you perceive by her light. Just as the Moon influences the tides of the oceans, so she holds sway over the element of water within us, the tides of intuition and emotion. The realm of the Moon is an underworld landscape of hidden dreams, magick and illusion. The Moon and the various stages of her monthly cycle can therefore be seen to represent the mysteries and the feminine divine.

The Sun and Moon, or Sol and Luna, are key symbols in alchemical practice, as personifications of the male and female opposing forces that must be combined together so that *"...a perfect light is begotten between them, which there is no light like through the whole world".*[54] Carl Jung interprets this goal on a psychological level as the *'individuation'* of a personality and also noted the significance of the Major Arcana of the Tarot as a journey towards this process. On a spiritual level this can be seen as the journey towards realisation of potential and the transcendent self.

It is easy to see how the Sun at various times of day, the Moon's different stages and the combination, (or indeed absence), of the two may convey much meaning when looked at with the eye of symbolic awareness. It is difficult to find true balance between two extremes however, without a third unifying quality. This can be found within another cosmic force- the stars. The stars symbolise the purity of spirit and the divine source, which lies in the elusive realm beyond all polarity, the ultimate home for which the soul is fated to always strive. As we are paring down to the bare minimum of symbolism, the stars can be seen as the light of the unified soul, in some cases as a glimpsed potential or in others as the realised goal of perfection.

These three forces perform an alchemical dance through the trumps of the Tarot, but the symbolism of most established decks refers to the Sun and Moon in only a handful of cards, preferring more complex esoteric imagery. The *Tarot of the Sidhe* is a collection of images that I created through direct inspiration from Otherworldly forces over a year and a day between November 2005 and 2006 with the intention of providing an intuitive system that required no previous knowledge of esoteric symbolism. As a result of the unusual creative process, I discovered (and indeed continue to discover) new depths to the Tarot imagery over time. This cosmic dance between Sun, Moon and Stars and the journey towards harmony is one of those insights, and though there are many other symbols present on the cards, it is interesting to see the journey through the Major Arcana in the context of these symbols alone and see what

---

[54] *Rosary of Philosophers*, Magnum Opus Hermetic Sourceworks p.34.

Vs.

Figure 8 - XVIII The Moon from
The Tarot of the Sidhe by Emily Carding

understanding of the cards it may bring. Our journey starts in the void of the card numbered '0', the Fool...

Behind the wildly leaping figure of the Fool, a rising sun marks the beginning of this journey, the golden rays reaching to the edges of the frame and casting the awakening light of dawn over the blossoming landscape. Here is a sign of new beginnings and a call to adventure as old as the world itself. Each rising sun of each new day is a story waiting to be told, and so it is with the Fool. As the Sun represents the conscious mind, the rising sun can easily be seen to represent a newly born awareness of the world, filled with innocence and wonder. The Sun is positioned directly behind the heart chakra of the leaping figure, drawing attention to the need for an open heart to embrace the child-like qualities of the card.

As we move on to the Magician it is still the solar power that dominates, but now it is a full and fiery mature sun of experience. This sun seems to blend with the fire that the magician holds in his hands, reflecting the element of fire and its qualities in the macrocosm of the surrounding landscape. Hovering above the ocean appearing to be in the last moments before setting, the circle of the sun is still complete, showing the mastery of the conscious mind through the fiery qualities of action and Will, but hinting at the further wisdom to come through sinking into the waters of intuition.

This leads us neatly into our first primarily lunar card, the High Priestess. It is a crescent moon that is featured, which she has assimilated into herself, her hair taking on its shape. However the sun's presence is still hinted at in the colours of the sky behind her, showing the last vestiges of the sunset. Without needing to look at the other symbols of the card, this gives us many clues as to her nature. The crescent as opposed to the full moon hints at mysteries still to be revealed, showing enough of itself to belie its presence, but leaving much to still be discovered. The last golden light of the sun sinking behind the hills is a hint to the liminal nature of the High Priestess, how she guards the veil between worlds. The solar, conscious mind is not completely absent, but is taking a lesser role in favour of the intuitive subconscious powers of the Moon. This is also the first card in which the Stars are present, showing that this card may hold part of the key to revealing the divine balance.

The Empress, fitting for such a feminine card, is also primarily lunar, although this is partially balanced by the golden solar landscape that can be seen within the folds of her dress, symbolising her nurturing and bountiful qualities. This card is dominated by the full moon, its shape reflected in the hair and heavily pregnant belly of the Empress herself. The full moon expresses the feminine divine energy at the height of her power and can also be seen as symbolising fertility, creativity and motherhood. Patience is rewarded as work may reach its fruition when the moon is full. Here the

Figure 9 - XIX The Sun from
The Tarot of the Sidhe by Emily Carding.

mystery of the feminine power is revealed in her glory, in contrast to the mysterious crescent of the preceding card.

The Emperor provides a fitting polar opposite for the Empress, bursting with solar energy! Although the sun itself cannot be seen, the figure of the Emperor appears to form a fiery sun from his own being, with his head being the source of an enormous crowning solar burst. Here we find the power of the conscious mind and the masculine force of active will at its most intense. The stars are present in both the Emperor and Empress, but only as a background pattern of spiralling energy. This can be seen as a hint of the potential that the two powers hold were they to unite.

In the next card on our journey, the Elder, (Hierophant), neither sun nor moon are seen directly, but it is clearly a solar card as it is a brightly illuminated daytime scene. From this we can glean that the emphasis is again masculine, but in a less forceful way, and that the learning offered is that of the conscious, active principle. To take this further, which may perhaps be stretching a point but it's an interesting thought nevertheless, the Elder is presented as an intermediary to the wisdom of the solar power, just as the High Priestess can be seen as an intermediary to the lunar power.

The Lovers shows the first appearance of the sun and moon together, but rather than being in their proper place, they are being held by nature spirits in the branches of two opposing trees, as though they were toys, tools, or objects of curiosity. The celestial spheres being thus placed in the hands of sentient beings speaks of the element of conscious choice and even manipulation which may be involved in bringing together the male and female polarities in this key alchemical card. Although they are being brought together and appear at an equal level of power within the card, even in symmetrical positions, they are still separate entities at this stage.

As we move into the Chariot, the sun and moon are brought together in a very different way. A solar eclipse forms the dramatic backdrop for the victorious figure of this card, the sun's beautiful corona being shown in full glory through the intervention of the moon directly between our viewpoint, (not necessarily the Earth in this case) and the sun's fiery sphere. A solar eclipse is a primal wonder, the visual spectacle that results from the sun and moon appearing to be the same size in the sky. Symbolically this is a powerful coming together of two opposing forces, and though they are not truly united, they work together to reveal something powerful and stunning. *'Corona'* means *'crown'*, an appropriate symbol for a card whose core meaning is victory! It is also possible to look at this image from a different angle and see it not as an eclipse, but as the Sol Niger, or alchemical black sun. This would bring a new depth of meaning to the card, the victory over the dark night of the soul, or shadow self, a key point in the journey towards individuation. The spiralling pattern of the stars is also revealed, giving a glimpse of the goal ahead.

Appropriately, Justice is divided equally down the middle of the card, into solar and lunar halves, the bright midday sun and dark crescent moon being held in perfect balance and their proper place within the cosmos. However, just as their place within the sky is ever shifting, so the clear-headedness that may come from the conscious and subconscious being brought into balance in this way is a temporary state and not the true balance of the spiritual goal.

This balance shifts into the natural retreat of the Hermit card. Here the deep red sun is setting behind the hill, bringing long shadows and a time of cognitive reflection.

It is hard to say whether the sun pictured in the Wheel of Fortune is rising or setting- perhaps somehow it is both, symbolising that all things must rise and fall in their time. In terms of the greater context of the journey, it would seem to be rising in power, as Strength is unashamedly and magnificently solar, the whole card being coloured in reds and golds and the rays of the burning sun reaching to all corners of the card. All shadows are dispelled and the active will and conscious mind holds sway over any darker impulses.

However, all things must shift in time, and the descent into darkness must be made. Neither sun nor moon are visible in the Hanged Man, but the stars can be seen in the darkness above his head. The Hanged Man must make the conscious choice to release to that darkness in order to reach his spiritual goal of the perfected self as symbolised by the stars.

The darkness that he falls into is represented by the Death card, dominated by a rising new moon. In the darkness of the new moon, the beauty of the stars, and hence the soul's truth, can be seen most clearly. The power of the new moon is in the gift of new beginnings. Out of the darkness is born a new cycle and a new level of perception. The dark side of the intuitive feminine self is powerful within this card, offering the initiatory gateway towards transformation.

Beyond that gateway dwells the healing and unifying realm of Temperance, in which a fiery winter solstice sun grows in reawakened power within the great lunar angel, framed by the full moon. The flaming rays of the solar orb appear to be melting the moon's ice, bringing forth life-giving water. Now the two energies are really starting to learn how to bring something new into the world through their collaboration, the intuitive female side nurturing the masculine active side into his potential as a balanced half of a whole, rather than a dominating force.

It can be difficult to maintain focus on the spiritual goal, however, as is shown in the next card, Pan, (the Devil). Perhaps it is because of the indulgence in the offerings of the physical realm that neither sun nor moon appears in the image, but the male and female polarities are certainly enjoying each other's company! However, the spiral patterns of the stars can be seen subtly towards the base of the card, hinting that indulgence can sometimes be the way forward to liberation, and that perhaps the goal is not that far from sight after all.

However the path of indulgence leads to the necessary purging and breaking away from habits and patterns, which is the painful process behind the Tower card. There is neither sun nor moon to be seen in this card, but little is left in the way of the starry void that may hold the greatest treasure. Once all material attachment is scorched away by the light of the soul, we are left with the bright hope and divine optimism of the Star.

The sequence of the last five cards of the major arcana is the climax of our journey. The Star card features the septagram in place of the third eye, symbolising the realisation that divinity dwells within as well as without. This relationship with the divine is another form of polarity, the concept reaching beyond solar and lunar, male and female, but into microcosm and macrocosm, the relationship between ourselves and the outer universe as a whole. It is the experience of the self as divine being that enables the complete experience of the polarities through the next few cards in the sequence and the ability to achieve the spirit's goal.

In this context, the Moon card demonstrates the mastery of the subconscious and underworld realm. All phases of the moon are visible in the sky, showing the experience and knowledge of all aspects of the inner world. In the reflected world, the moon is shattered- the illusory aspects of the lunar realm no longer hold sway.

Once the underworld initiation of the Moon is passed, then the spiral dance of the Sun follows. The Sun is pictured here at the peak of attainment, the centre of the cosmic dance of wholeness that all who are ready are invited to join. Within the sun itself is the labyrinth-like Glyph of the Sidhe, a gateway to other worlds, but also to the core self. The dance of life is an expression of the pure joy that is felt when the self is truly at one.

Sun, moon and stars are notable in their absence from the Judgement card, in which the Sidhe beings teach us to sing our truth to the universe. This song is borne from the trials and experiences of all the other cards, and acts as a bridge, or perhaps more appropriately, a staircase to the attainment of the World. It is a card of acknowledgement and evolution to new levels of awareness. Finally the Grail of our quest is attained, the final card of the Major Arcana: The World.

As is fitting, all three cosmic forces are pictured on the World card. The sun and moon come together in the above and below to form a complete circle, the symbol of completion, and the stars can be seen through the branches of the world tree as they reach into the underworld. It is an image of balance and wholeness, representing the achievement of potential and the beauty of perfected symmetry. This card shows us that the whole is indeed greater than the sum of our parts, but the Major Arcana as a whole has taught us that each lesson is as valuable as a bright gem in the crown of our unified soul.

It is tempting when interpreting symbolic art, and particularly when reading the intricate images of the Tarot, to focus on the figures and easily identifiable props and action. But through this procession of images, a deeper journey has taken place, one that can be observed through the ancient dance of sun, moon and stars, and one which may lead to the greatest treasure of all.

"I am the answer to all questions, I am the rainbow and the crock of gold. I am the journey and the destination, I am the key to all doors. All places are united within me, my branches reach every star and dark corner of bones and dust. I am all, I am nothing, I am the ceaseless renewing spiral of existence and the void from which it is born.

The great web binds all worlds within and is woven between my roots. I am whole, I am complete, I am sun and moon and stars in one.

The great tree has given its runic secrets and from them the Fool has made his name.

My path runs deep, eternal, winding to the infinite centre of all being. At the tips of my branches are the roots of another, at the depth of my roots, you will find more branches. Deeper and deeper, higher and higher, we end as we begin..." ~ The World, *Tarot of the Sidhe*.

Bibliography
Rosary of Philosophers, Magnum Opus Hermetic Sourceworks, Glasgow, 2006
Tarot of the Sidhe, Emily Carding, Schiffer Books 2011

For more information, as well as colour images of the *Tarot of the Sidhe* see at www.childofavalon.com

Vs.

SIR GAWAIN AND THE GREEN KNIGHT

The Self and the Other as sacred doubles in Arthurian mythology

by Katherine Sutherland

The long medieval poem *Sir Gawain and the Green Knight*, written by an unknown poet in the late 14th century, is a magical text that strongly resists the reader's urge to decode it in simplistic terms. A great sense of loss is felt when reading a critical interpretation that relies on reductionist strategies; equating the Green Knight to a simple fiend, and the narrative rendered as Christian allegory, removing the tale's mystery and allowing a rational response. The poem is loaded with symbolism, such as its use of details regarding dress, physical appearances, plants, and colours. However, in medieval times, symbols could embrace a wide variety of meanings, which could be interpreted only in their given context. This poem, therefore, encompasses a multitude of modes of meaning, rather than providing the reader with a static list of signs and their equivalents, and thus, provokes a variety of responses within the symbolic shorthand used. It is possible for the modern reader of this magical text to impose his / her own set of signs, and consequently reach a personal understanding of the poem through relating the *'Self'* and the *'Other'* to the characters of *Sir Gawain and the Green Knight*.

In the Arthurian court of Camelot, everything is safe as the turning of the wheel and Christmas are being celebrated. At the heart of the microcosm, all is well and the court exists in a happy and restful state of equilibrium. Disruption occurs when the macrocosm interrupts this pleasing state of affairs. The Green Knight, a terrible figure, crashes into the great hall, clad in green, mounted on a green steed; even his skin is green. The Green Knight carries a huge axe, and a bough of holly as a sign of peace. The macrocosm challenges the microcosm thus: the Green Knight will play the *'Christmas Game'* with any willing knight, the game involving an exchange of blows, the first to be delivered upon the Green Knight himself using his own gigantic axe. When Gawain steps forward in place of Arthur and decapitates the Knight, the reader's relief is short lived, as the Green Knight collects his head and reminds Gawain of the promise he has made: to journey to meet his adversary in the Green Chapel to receive a return blow in a year's time.

If the Arthurian court here represents the Self, then the intrusion of the Green Knight can be read as representing all Otherness. The Christmas court is a place of comfort and stability and the great crashing intruder can be likened to the experience of the practitioner who, in experiencing challenges on the path, is forced to step outside of his or her magical comfort zone. If magical practice is a quest for understanding the Self and the Other, then surely the tale of Sir Gawain and his encounter with the Green Knight can reveal a great deal about this process of confrontation, fear and acceptance, which can lead to eventual transformation and initiation. As a challenger, the Green Knight's colours and holly bough proclaim him as a champion of winter, the harshest of seasons; and thus the old champion of Otherness, a champion who waits for magical movement from the cold, still times, to the energetic of the coming of spring. This dynamic is aptly illustrated by John Matthews, in his *Gawain Knight of the Goddess: Restoring an Archetype*.[55]

Here, the notion of the battle between summer and winter can be equated to the inner turmoils of the developing practitioner. The seeker here, Sir Gawain, 'knows' how to find the Green Chapel or the place of the Other, not because he is told, but perhaps due to long associations with the cult of the Green Man, or the fertile Self, and the battle for the energies of Spring.[56] As in keeping with Western traditions, Gawain's journey to ritual combat with his otherworldly Other is oriented thus: the North is the place of winter and the defender, the South is the place of summer and the challenger.

As Gawain sets out on his quest for the Green Chapel, the time in the poem moves forward to Michaelmas, the time of the harvest. After much feasting, Gawain rides out with the device of the pentacle upon his shield: read by some as representative of the five wounds of Christ. In magical terms, the importance of this symbol should not be missed in that it may represent the elemental and spiritual balance, not only of Camelot, but of Gawain himself as the seeker. Apparently feeling no fear, Gawain and his horse Gringolet ride North, until on Christmas Eve he reaches a place of rest and sanctuary, a moated castle, where a generous Lord houses him. Here Gawain meets another challenge, the distractions of a beautiful Lady and by wrinkled countenance of her dowager companion. After three days and nights of revelling, Gawain states that he must leave, yet his host seems reluctant to let him do so. Gawain remains in the castle, whilst the Lord goes out hunting, and at the attempts of the

---

[55] Matthews, John, *Gawain, Knight of the Goddess: Restoring an Archetype*, Aquarian Press, London, 1990, p. 75.
[56] For more thoughts on this 'knowing', see Spiers, John, *Medieval English Poetry*, Faber and Faber, London, 1957.

Lady to seduce him Gawain will accept no more than a single kiss. On the Lord's return from the hunt, he offers his spoils in exchange for anything Gawain has won that day. The same procedure follows on the two successive days, with Gawain being given first two, then three kisses by the Lady. In maintaining his chivalric attitude and magical integrity, Gawain's only indiscretion is to accept a green baldric from the Lady, which she assures will protect him from all harm.

On the fourth day, the Lord sends Gawain onwards to his test in the Green Chapel. Gawain, as an individual seeker, resists the services of a guide and reaches a strange landscape around which ring the sounds of a great axe being sharpened against a whetstone. The Green Knight appears and holds Gawain to his challenge, Gawain has sought the Other and found him. The Green Knight, in preparing to make his fatal blow twice fakes his stroke and mocks Gawain's courage as he flinches each time the stroke is taken. This can be read as the safety net of this magical narrative, the blow of the Other can only be taken when the Self is fully prepared and the time is right! On the third stroke, the Knight hones his blade and Gawain is nicked upon the neck; Gawain springs up from his knees, stating that he has kept his part of their magical agreement. The Green Knight now reveals that he is in fact the generous Lord who gave him shelter at the castle. His shape as the Green Knight is a result of enchantment by the Loathly Lady at the castle, who is in fact the Goddess Morgan, who sought to test the integrity of the Arthurian court; the microcosm called into the macrocosm to prove its worth, the Self sent on a journey to Otherness to find self knowledge.

In the poem, Gawain's Self is saved from being overcome by his Other by the gift of a magical token, which is given by a woman. In receiving feminine gifts, Gawain's integrity is tested; as are the chivalric attitudes of the court towards the divine feminine, however she may choose to appear. In being a rightful champion, Gawain succeeds and wins the beheading game, proving his magical worth as an earthly representative of the divine, through trials and tests of temptation. Although the poem may be regarded as Christian in origin, it is interesting to note that Gawain functions as a magical figure, who in his quest for the Other bridges the worlds of organised religion and nature. As E.S. Dick states, Gawain is:

"...the perfect knight who is not perfect enough to settle in either of the two ideal worlds, too human and too superhuman at the same time."[57]

---

[57] Dick, E. S. *The German Gawein: Diu Crône and Wigolais*, in *Interpretations*, vol. 15, no. 2, pp 11-17.

Gawain in this sense represents the magical ideal, as he is truly a Green Knight of Camelot. He is not the boisterous manifestation of the macrocosm that crashes in wielding an axe, but a man who serves his own principles of nature in the guise in which he finds them manifest. The image of the pentacle of Gawain's shield thus represents harmony and unity of spirit; the Self and the Other reconciled.

Gawain is an exemplary figure in that he survives an otherworldly challenge in which the rules governing the ordinary world of the microcosm of the self are suspended. In setting forth from the microcosm of Camelot on his quest, Gawain is honoured more than any symbol, as an active individual striving and seeking. In being individualised in the poem, Gawain allows us to identify with him and to recognize our own strengths and weaknesses as we too quest for the unknown Other in our own Green Chapel. What follows here is a poetic working of the author's own such journey and work with the archetypical challenger figure of the Green Knight.

The Green Knight's Counsel (a poetic dialogue)

Green Knight:
Come into the Green Chapel
where I will tell a story,
of times that have long past,
and this land's ancient glory.
Step with me now
to the Chapel in the Green,
where this tale will be unwound,
and you will witness things unseen.

My bargain in simple
I will take your head,
as you will take mine
in the promise which led
you to travel here to me
across the ragged miles,
of times of men and tides
and all which beguiles.

I knelt at your feet at the Christmas court
when green bedecked the halls
with the watchful tinne and gort,
in strode I, clad all in green,
the most curious thing
that had ever been seen.

Vs.

*Your will was strong,
and in hand you took your sword,
as an honest protector,
of your rightful Lord.
I knelt at your feet,
and yet I was not slain,
three blows rained down upon me,
and yet I rose ~ the same.*

*I proved to you my honour
and I challenged yours,
to come to me and test it now
at the great new year's doors.*

*Now you have come, so enter
it is your traveller's right,
to sit with me and rest a while,
as a well-journeyed weary Knight.
But will you keep the promise?
The deal that we made?
To submit your neck unto my sword,
my green enchanted blade?*

*Seeker:
Oh Green Knight I come to you,
and I do not fear your fires,
I seek to worship in the green,
to fulfil my just desires.
When you came unto the court
I found you strange and gory,
now I long to sit with you
and hear your aged story.
I am sure that you have much to tell
about this loathy place,
I will rest me here and tarry
within your sacred space.*

*Green Knight:
But first good Knight, I must know
are you to be found worthy?
Only the strongest serve me well,
and become my noble clergy.
How can I test you and your will?
Will you bow your head,
and swear your truthfulness to me,
or will the snows run red?*

Vs.

Seeker:
Green Man I swear my pledge to you
I swear it loud and strong,
I have carried out my word,
and ridden far and long.
I am not the bravest of the Knights,
I rarely shine in battle,
I am a protector of the lands
and the livestock and the cattle.
Yet I kneel and swear my life to you,
for I have no other choice,
I bow my head ready for your blows
and seek the truth of my voice.

Green Knight:
Very well good Knight, your time has come
I reach for my magical blade,
know as I strike I will know your truth,
and your choices will be made.
You cannot turn away from me now,
you have used up your only chance,
to flee into the unknowingness,
away from nature's dance.
You choose to live in tune with me
the dying and rising Lord,
and I will test your mettle now,
with my trusty sword.

Narrator:
And in the Chapel in the green,
the young Knight knelt there waiting;
not sure about the trial to come,
or what the Green Knight was stating.
And yet he knelt upon the cold earth,
pledged in word and duty,
to take the trials of the winter lord
in all his powerful beauty.

Before he knew, the blade was ringing,
slicing fine the air,
and all of nature seemed to be singing
with the young Knight's dare.
The blade fell fast upon his neck,
but he did not feel a thing;
he dared not look at the powerful Lord
who did this dreadful thing.

Vs.

*The blade rained down upon him more,
two more blows, in total three,
then it ceased and he rose up,
not a drop of blood to see.
The Knight was beaming ear to ear,
a curious bright green smile,
"You have done well" his strong voice boomed,
"yet that is not the final trial."
The young Knight on knees, remained perplexed,
he thought he'd won his glory,
but the interesting part was yet to come
in this fateful story.*

Green Knight:
Good Knight, you here your word have proved
you have come with will strong and true,
but now you must lose your head to me,
it's something you must do.

Seeker:
But good Green Knight, I am confused,
I think you are mistaken,
you have tried, and failed, to slice my head,
your three blows you have taken,
I will submit to one more trial,
if it will give you ease,
and so I kneel awaiting your will,
you may test me as you please.

Narrator:
With those fated words, another blow fell,
and the young Knight's head did roll,
upon the ground, to the Green Knight's feet
and he placed it upon a pole,
from whence it spoke of many things,
the past and the future bright,
and the young Knight learnt from himself,
in the place of otherworldly might.

To speak the truth, and wield the sword,
to be faithful to his word,
when to whisper and when to shout;
how always to be heard.
When the head had spoken
of all it had to say,
the Green Knight planted back
on the young Knight's neck,

Vs.

where it remains to this very day.

*So armed with his sword of truth,
and his shield of spirit and beauty,
the Knight rode back to the land of men,
to fulfil his sacred duty.
Carrying his lesson with him,
deep within his soul,
of the Chapel Green and it's worthy Lord,
to whom he owes his role.*

*Yet the lesson does not end here;
at a curve in the green path,
for the Green Knight waits for all who dare,
at the great Green Chapel's hearth.*

*Do not approach him lightly,
he likes to see your fears,
and cut them free with words of truth
across the winding years.
Yet within his challenging counsel,
great beauty shines through the gory,
and maps a way for all to walk
the green path of this land's glory.*

Bibliography
Arthur, Ross. *Medieval Sign Theory and Sir Gawain and the Green Knight*, University of Toronto Press, Toronto, 1987.
Dick, E. S. *The German Gawein: Diu Crône and Wigolais*, in *Interpretations*, vol. 15, no. 2, pp 11-17.
Matthews, John, *Gawain, Knight of the Goddess: Restoring an Archetype*, Aquarian Press, London, 1990, p. 75.
Spiers, John, *Medieval English Poetry*, Faber and Faber, London, 1957.

Vs.

THE MOMENTUM OF POLARITY

The Battle of Calan Mai

by Gareth Gerrard

"The wheel is come full circle: I am here."[58]

A central liturgical motif of the modern Pagan sabbatical cycle is the seasonal battle between the Oak King of the light half of the year and the Holly King of the dark half. They constitute two aspects of a single whole, reflecting a basic solar duality, and their struggles for dominion over each other attain a polar climax at each of the solstices. The third protagonist in this linear enmity is the land, personified by various aspects of the Goddess, who then implicitly bestows sovereignty upon the biannual victor. Although the central dynamic is universal in Northern European mythology, this particular telling as part of an overarching seasonal narrative is a relatively modern construct, gaining prominence in the second half of the 20th century.

There are several variations of the story, the most common being that the Oak King of the waxing light is *'killed'* by the Holly King of the waning light at midsummer, which is paradoxically when the former is at the peak of his powers.[59] The corollary being that from that point onwards, as the sun progresses from its zenith, his power wanes accordingly and so *'sows the seeds of his defeat'*. At the winter solstice, the Oak King is then *'born again'* as *'the Child of Promise'*; the Holly King, being an evergreen and therefore metaphorically eternal, does not explicitly fall to the hand of his renewed twin, but the God of the waxing light is proclaimed triumphant nevertheless.[60]

Although both Frazer[61] and Graves[62] make mention of biannual seasonal battles, the former obliquely and the latter syncretically, some arguably more compelling antecedents are to be found with the Cymric myths. Often collectively known as the *Mabinogi* and codified

---

[58] Shakespeare, W., *King Lear*, Act V, scene III.
[59] Farrar, J. & S., *Eight Sabbats for Witches*, p. 94.
[60] *Ibid*; p145.
[61] Frazer, *Golden Bough*.
[62] Graves, *The White Goddess*.

between the mid 13th and early 15th centuries, the *Black Book of Carmarthen*, the *White Book of Rhydderch* and the *Red Book of Hergest* draw upon earlier works such as those of Taliesin and Aneirin to form a series of thematically congruent tales that represent the extant totality of early Welsh heroic literary tradition.[63]

Motifs mirroring that of the Oak and Holly kings, namely a struggle between seasonally identifiable protagonists over sovereignty of the land (either explicitly or via a female proxy) can be found within several narrative streams in the Cymric mythos, both as a major theme and as a seeming addendum to the central story. Prominent among the former category are the tales concerning Pwyll, Gwawl and Rhiannon from *Pwyll, Prince of Dyfed*; Lleu, Gronw and Blodeuwedd from *Math, Son of Mathonwy*; and most notably that of Gwynn ap Nudd, Gwyrthyr and Creiddylad from *Culhwch ac Olwen*. The annual battle between Arawn and Hafgan over sovereignty of Annwfn (also from *Pwyll, Prince of Dyfed*) is an example of the latter.

Triads are a leitmotif in Celtic mythology in general and within the Cymric mythos in particular, so it should come as no surprise that the basic duality of the antagonistics should be set within the context of the third party over whom they fight. In the first part of the First Branch of the Mabinogi, (*Pwyll, Prince of Dyfed*), the titular prince meets Arawn, Lord of Annwfn (the Cymric underworld). Here we learn that Arawn is engaged in a yearly battle with his rival, another king called Hafgan, for control over all Annwfn. Although the two antagonists are both underworld entities, a clue to a seasonal association is given in that Hafgan translates as *'summer white'*, and although the etymology of Arawn is more complex, the fact that they are due to meet in single combat one year later indicates a cyclical encounter. The intercession of Pwyll, who in accordance with Arawn's instructions and whilst magically transformed into Arawn's likeness, dispatches Hafgan with a single blow at the appointed time, thus allowing Arawn to unite their kingdoms.

In the second part of the First Branch, Pwyll must overcome Gwawl ap Clud for the hand of Rhiannon.[64] MacKillop defines Gwawl as having a possible meaning of *'light'* and, as established through his involvement with Arawn, Pwyll carries the epithet, Pen Annwfn, denoting an overt underworld correlation.[65] Rhiannon is betrothed, apparently against her will, to Gwawl, and having fallen in love with Pwyll invites him to contest against him for her affections. Pwyll agrees and is told to attend her father's court one year's hence. Here again we see the interval of one year between the initial and subsequent narrative action, strengthening the solar association of the protagonists. In addition, Rhiannon is one of the Cymric

---

[63] MacKillop J., *Dictionary of Celtic Mythology*, p. 276.
[64] Gantz, J, *The Mabinogion*; pp. 51–59.
[65] MacKillop, *Dictionary of Celtic Mythology*; p. 326.

characters most strongly associated with an established deity, and indeed many of the motifs in this tale underpin this association. Rhiannon derives from Rigatona (Great Queen) and is also associated with the pan Celtic horse goddess Epona; the former associated with sovereignty and the later with fertility.

However, Pwyll's actions illustrate that his name (meaning deep or wise) is quite certainly a sardonic device: at the feast for his and Rhiannon's betrothal he offers Gwawl, posing as a suppliant, anything within his ability to give (at which point Rhiannon utters a verbal facepalm!) and of course, he chooses Rhiannon. Not just her, but also the preparations for the upcoming wedding feast. Luckily for Pwyll, Rhiannon has ample wits for the both of them and hatches a plan to foil Gwawl without Pwyll injuring his honour in front of the assembled dignitaries. She gives him an enchanted bag, which is to be filled with food at the wedding feast, and of course, the bag will never become full, directly echoing the bag of plenty that is associated with Epona.

Again, a hiatus of one year is set before resumption of the next phase of the narrative, the nuptials of Rhiannon and Gwawl. Pwyll, as instructed by his wiser half to be, has hidden his men in a nearby orchard and is dressed in rags. When the party is well under way, but before the consummation, he makes his entrance, and in a reversal of the earlier instalment, pretends to a suppliant and requests enough food to fill his little bag. Gwawl, flushed with munificence gladly accedes, and orders servants to fill the bag. As expected, no matter how much food is placed in the bag, it never becomes full, and Pwyll explains that it requires a nobleman to press the food down with both feet. Rhiannon volunteers Gwawl, *'Champion, Rise at once!'* and with this he is caught in their trap. As he treads down the food, Pwyll quickly lifts the bag over Gwawl's head and pulls it tight. He then blows his horn to summon his men and throws off his rags. As his men enter, they strike the man in the bag having been told that it is a *'badger in the bag.'* Gwawl pleads for his life and is released on condition that he never seeks revenge or reparation. Pwyll and Rhiannon are then joined and return to Dyfed.

Although the cyclical seasonal motif here is not explicit, the role reversals at the two wedding feasts, both spaced a year apart and both concerning the same sovereignty-associated bride, is certainly suggestive of a deeper continuum. Moreover, we see that the spoils of the contest, far from being a passive participant, is mistress of her own fate who actively engineers her desired outcome.

The Oak King/Holly King dynamic is however, explicitly cyclical, playing out an eternal and fundamentally primordial theme of life, death and subsequent rebirth. The next example from the Cymric mythos is perhaps the closest thematically to this, in that the protagonists eternally replay their battle at an appointed date.

Vs.

Gwynn ap Nudd is arguably one of the better known entities from Welsh mythology, and although his influence is diluted over time, from God of the Dead and psychopomp in the *Black Book of Carmarthen*[66] to King of the Faery in later tales,[67] he is a powerful and enduring presence in modern Paganism.

In poem 33 from the *Black Book of Carmarthen*, he identifies himself to the poem's other protagonist, Gwydneu Garanhir with the stanza:

> *"Round-hoofed is my horse, the torment of battle,*
> *Whilst I am called Gwyn, the son of Nudd,*
> *The lover of Creurdilad, the daughter of Lludd."*[68]

This last line is important because it links to an earlier tale from *Culhwch ac Olwen*, one of the so-called Native Tales from the *Mabinogi*, in which the three protagonists make an appearance, albeit fleetingly. In the tale, Culhwch has been cursed by his stepmother to never know a woman until he has won the hand of Olwen, daughter of a formidable giant called Ysbaddaden. In order to do this, Culhwch is told to enlist the help of King Arthur, and in so doing they travel to the castle of Ysbaddaden, where the wily giant gives Culhwch a list of forty seemingly impossible tasks to complete before he will agree to any marriage. Young and impetuous, he agrees and, with the help of Arthur and a bewildering cast of ancillary characters, sets about their accomplishment.

Many of the tasks are compound tasks that must be achieved in order to attain a final object or accomplishment. One of these groups of tasks involves the hunting and capturing of a ferocious mythical boar called Twrch Trwyth in order to retrieve a comb and razor that lie between its ears. One of the heroes who must be enlisted to achieve this is Gwynn ap Nudd, of whom Ysbaddaden says, *'God has put the spirit of the demons of Annwfn in him, lest the world be destroyed. He will not be spared from there.'*[69] Although his name means fair or blessed, from this and the *Black Book of Carmarthen* texts we can surmise that Gwynn has a reputation as a hunter and warrior of exceptional ferocity (and is even described in the *Triads* as a great magician and astrologer!)[70]

Later in the tale we learn that Creiddylad daughter of Lludd Llaw Eraint (Lludd of the silver hand), described as the *'most majestic maiden there ever was in the Three Islands of Britain and her Three Adjacent Islands'*,[71] has eloped with Gwythyr fab Greidawl (Victor, son of Scorcher). However, before they could consummate she was

---
[66] Skene, W., *The Four Ancient Books of Wales*, p. 295.
[67] Jones, G., *Welsh Legends and Folk Tales*, pp.159-168.
[68] Skene, W., *The Four Ancient Books of Wales*, p. 293.
[69] Davies, Sioned, *The Mabinogion*; p. 199.
[70] MacCulloch, JA., *The Religion of the Ancient Celts*; p. 115.
[71] Davies, Sioned, *The Mabinogion*; p. 189.

forcibly abducted by Gwynn ap Nudd. Gwythyr then raises an army against him but it is Gwynn who triumphs and he takes many of Gwythyr's host as prisoner and even causes one to lose his sanity by forcing him to eat his slain father's heart. Arthur, upon hearing of these occurrences, travels *'into the North'*, and summons Gwynn to him. He brokers a truce, forcing the two rivals to agree to his terms and releases the hostages.

It is here that the narrative continues its tangential excursion into what is probably a fragment of an older tale and imprints the seasonal / sovereignty motif onto the protagonists. Arthur, as arbiter and narrative catalyst, imposes his judgement that Gwynn and Gwythyr are to engage in single combat every Calan Mai (May Day) until Doomsday, whilst Creiddylad remains with her father, and the victor of the encounter on Doomsday will have her hand.

Calan Mai (May Day; Beltane in the Irish), has long been associated with marriage, fecundity and supranatural occurrence, and is diametric to the festival of Calan Gaeaf (Hallowe'en; Samhain), which denotes the beginning of winter. In the modern Pagan telling of the Oak and Holly kings, the time of their principle encounter is midsummer at the solstice, with the inference that the corresponding diametric is the winter solstice. Although discordant with the Welsh myth, by using the summer solstice, the point where the sun is literally at its strongest, the solar association of the Oak King is further reinforced, and because of the temporal nature of this juncture, the implication that a turning point has been reached that will see his power wane as the year progresses. In addition, by aligning the Holly King with the winter solstice, the narrative taps into a wealth of folkloric associations, including the parallel dynamic between John the Baptist and Jesus Christ, which as noted by several commentators is echoed in the traditional seasonal song, *'The Holly and the Ivy'*.[72] [73]

It is interesting to note that Lludd, the father of Creiddylad, is a cognate of Nudd, Gwynn's father (Nudd Llaw Ereint becoming Lludd via alliterative assimilation), making the two would-be lovers siblings. This is not necessarily a hindrance to their union since, as shown in classical mythology, the incest taboo so prevalent and universal in human sexual interactions does not apply to those of deities. However, this might be an indication on why whoever codified this narrative used a differential theonym to denote the parentage of Creiddylad, especially since the extant texts have largely euphemerised the subject divinities. Nudd/Lludd is a significant figure within the Cymric texts, not least because he appears to be derived from the British god of healing, Nodens, to whom a 3rd

---

[72] Graves, R., *The White Goddess*; p. 180.
[73] Nichols, M., *Eight Sabbats of Witchcraft*; p. 21.

century BCE shrine was erected at Lydney Park on the banks of the Severn.[74]

Gwynn, in spite of his name, represents the dark-half of the year (i.e., the *'Holly King'*) by virtue of his chthonian role; whereas Gwythyr's solar association (*'Oak King'*) is explicit via his patronym. Doomsday can be read as either, *'forever'* or *'until the end of the World'*; either way the decisive victory is deferred to such a point in time that renders the outcome irrelevant to current proceedings. Thus, the battle becomes cyclical and essentially eternal, with the two combatants locked into a struggle for determination over the fate of the land's fecundity. Creiddylad, the embodiment of fertile potential forcibly abducted, becomes the Cymric Persephone, whose cyclical association with the Underworld signals the end of the period of growth and abundance precipitated by the onset of winter and in her return, the herald of the spring.

The Persephone comparison is further validated by the reference from the *Black Book of Carmarthen*, where Gwynn describes himself as, *'the lover of Creurdilad,'* which, as it is written may denote some form of reciprocation in their relationship. This suggests that either they were lovers before she eloped with Gwyrthyr or, as with Persephone, she came to accept her role as chthonic consort. In addition, the Latin form of her name is Cordelia, and it has been postulated that she was the inspiration for Geoffrey of Monmouth's Queen Cordelia and subsequently Cordelia in Shakespeare's *King Lear*.

There are other examples of the seasonal polar dynamic within the Cymric texts, most notably in the Fourth Branch concerning Lleu Llaw Gyffes and Gronw Pebyr's slaying of each other over the flower-maiden Blodeuwedd, which is particularly rich in allegorical imagery. However, even though Lleu, through the aid of his patron/father Gwydion, is renewed following his betrayal and death, the momentum of their enmity is concluded with the death of Gronw and transformation of Blodeuwedd into an owl. Only the Gwynn - Gwyrthr - Creiddylad narrative maintains the propulsion of continuation that resonates with the eternal struggle between the Oak and the Holly.

Bibliography & Further Reading
Davies, Sioned, *The Mabinogion*. Oxford, 2007
Farrar, Janet & Stuart. *Eight Sabbats for Witches*; Robert Hale Ltd, 1992
Frazer, James. *Golden Bough*. Wordsworth Reference, 1993
Gantz, Jeffrey, *The Mabinogion*. Penguin, 1976
Graves, Robert, *The White Goddess*. Faber & Faber, 1971
Jones, G., *Welsh Legends and Folk Tales*. Puffin Books, 1979.
Jones, Gwyn. *Welsh Legends and Folk Tales*. Oxford University Press, 1st Edition, 1957

---

[74] MacKillop, *Dictionary of Celtic Mythology*; pp.306-308.

Vs.

MacCulloch, J.A.M. *The Religion of the Ancient Celts.* Constable, 1911
MacKillop James. *Dictionary of Celtic Mythology.* Oxford, 1998
Nichols, Mike. *Eight Sabbats of Witchcraft.*
Rolleston, T.W. *Celtic Myths and Legends.* Senate, 1995.
Shakespeare, William. *King Lear.* BiblioLife, 2008
Skene, W., *The Four Ancient Books of Wales.* Forgotten Books, 2007.

Vs.

MARASSA DOSSOU-DOSA

The Divine Twins and Duality in Vodou

by Kim Huggens

> This paper is dedicated to Richard Meijir and his beautiful Bat-Marassa.

In researching this paper it became clear very quickly that the Marassa are notable for their comparable absence in the available literature as opposed to that about the other lwa (spirits) of the Vodou religion. The loquacious Karen McCarthy Brown in her *Mama Lola: A Vodou Priestess in Brooklyn* mentions them only in passing as the sacred twins of the Vodou religion. The work of folklorist and anthropologist Zora Neale Hurston merely lists the Marassa alongside a number of other spirits in a description of the order in which the spirits are called upon in a ceremony.[75] Even Maya Deren's classic *Divine Horsemen: The Living Gods of Haiti* gives the Marassa only three pages, and discusses them briefly outside the context of any other lwa – many of which are each given their own chapter. It occurred to me that very few authors, whether they were Vodou practitioners themselves or not, had devoted much wordage to these twin child spirits, and if they had they did so briefly, or by considering them as separate in some way to the other spirits.

Perhaps this is due to the fact that the secrets of the sacred twins are better taught in a ceremonial context and best understood through their service and songs; perhaps it is because (as is so often the case in Vodou) in the simplest of images – in this case twin children – is contained a great many cosmological and philosophical concepts. The simple-complex nature of the Marassa thus demonstrates not only the Vodou understanding of the universe around us, but also the nature of creation, magic, relationships, and self-awareness. In the twin faces of the Marassa the Vodouisant is given an image of the Self and Other, the I and Not I, the Is and the Is Not.

In this paper I wish to examine the Marassa on a dual level: firstly, as the visceral, immanent spirits that are served, danced for,

---

[75] Zora Neale Hurston, *Tell My Horse: Voodoo and Life in Haiti and Jamaica.*

and sung for by so many Vodou practitioners around the world, and lastly as a concept embodying Vodou's cosmological principles.

Although the Marassa are discussed here in a general manner as one spirit, it should be noted that – like many other lwa – the Marassa are actually a great number of spirits – all twins. Thus, there are Marassa Bois (Marassa of the Woods), Marassa Macaque (like the monkey of the same name),[76] Marassa Blanc (white Marassa), Marassa Caille (Marassa of the Home) and more.[77] They are found in every rite of Vodou, however most commonly they are depicted in their Rada (*'cool'*) aspect as the Sts. Cosmas and Damian,[78] and in their Petwo (*'hot'*) aspects as the Three Virtues of Faith, Hope, and Charity. It is generally considered a bad idea to serve the Marassa using the image of the Three Virtues instead of that of Sts. Cosmas and Damian, for in the words of Kenaz Filan:
> "*The twins can be a handful. There's no reason to further complicate your life by calling on the triplets!*"[79]

The Divine Parent-Children and Affirmation of Cosmic Unity in the Creation Process

In many traditions it is believed that the world and all its inhabitants were created either by a single power, such as the Egyptian Ra in his orgasmic moment of self-actualization or the God of the Old Testament when he breathed Life over the chaotic womb-waters of the earth, or by a divine parent-couple whose romantic union brought about a series of lesser deities that became the Gods of that culture - such as Chronos and Rhea of the Greeks. In these mythologies the duality exists also as a polarity of one opposite with another - in this case, chaos and order, and male and female. In the Vodou tradition, however, the creation of life and the universe comes not from a union of cosmic phallus and cosmic yoni that were once separate, but rather from the interplay between One Thing and The Other Thing in the form of siblings - twins, in fact - called the Marassa. Thus, Maya Deren writes:
> "*The concept of the Marassa contains, first, the notion of the segmentation of some original cosmic totality.*"[80]

---

[76] Marassa Macaque may have their origin in the tale told by Harold Courlander in *Tales of the Yoruba, Gods and Heroes,* retold by Sallie Ann Glassman in *The New Orleans Voodoo Tarot,* pp.51-2, in which the first human twins are born after a pair of mischievous monkeys entered a woman's womb to punish her husband for terrorizing them and driving them from his land.

[77] Harold Courlander, *Gods of the Haitian Mountains,* pp. 367, in *The Journal of Negro History,* vol. 29, no. 3, (Jul., 1944)), pp. 339-372.

[78] Herskowitz, Melville J., *African Gods and Catholic Saints in New World Belief,* pp. 638.

[79] Kenaz Filan, *The Haitian Vodou Handbook,* p. 83.

[80] Maya Deren, *Divine Horsemen: the Living Gods of Haiti,* p. 38.

These Marassa are not specifically one gender or another, in fact they are often considered to be both male; however in a similar African Diaspora religion from the Yoruba tribe of Africa the divine twins – called Ibeji - are usually male and female. This opposite gender depiction can be found in Vodou, however: Glassman in her *New Orleans Voodoo Tarot* depicts the Marassa as male and female with their legs and arms intertwined.[81] In some instances the Marassa are depicted as both female, as in Milo Bigaud's 1990 painting *'Marassa'*, in which two red-skirted women are shown with straw hats and freshly picked red roses, in a fecund rose garden (the women in this depiction seem to be younger women, maybe 14-15 years of age, so not children as some of the more traditional depictions show.)[82]

Naturally, however, the fact that the Marassa are the first segmentation from cosmic totality, means that they give rise to all the world's dualities, including that of male and female:

> *"But the Marassa, as the first cosmic totality, may also be thought of as intersected on the vertical axis as well as the horizontal one. The intersection on the vertical axis would yield two halves of which each rests partly in the physical and partly in the metaphysical world. This is the segmentation of the first androgynous cosmic whole which yielded the differentiation: male and female. Thus the Marassa are the parents of the race, and this progenitive function gives them, in fact, their major importance."*[83]

However, the child-like nature of the Marassa supports the idea that the Marassa themselves are not male and/or female at all, but rather that the fact that they are the initial abstraction from unity gives all other life the dual nature that leads to creation.

Nobody knows where the twins came from. Beyond them is only Bondye - God - who is not given much capacity for interaction in the universe beyond creating it, and whilst Bondye is usually discussed in Christian terms as *'He'*, this assignment of gender is merely for ease of dialogue. Presumably the Marassa came from Bondye, but certainly they were not born or created. They were just there, and have always been there, and are here now; Louis Martinie describes them as *'the moment before'*.[84] However, some Vodou traditions hold that the Sts. Clare and Nicholas are representative of the Mother and Father of the Marassa; female and male respectively, they relate to the West African Fon twin sky deities Mawu-Lisa: Mawu, the female representing the moon (linked with Saint Clare because of the moon-

---

[81] Sallie Ann Glassman and Louis Martinie, *The New Orleans Voodoo Tarot*, pp. 50-1.
[82] For this painting, see http://www.indigoarts.com/gallery_bigaud2.html
[83] Maya Deren, *Divine Horsemen: the Living Gods of Haiti*, pp. 39-40.
[84] Louis Martinie, *Cultus Marassa*, online at
  http://w3.iac.net/~moonweb/archives/LM/Marassa1.html

shaped crest she bears in her images) and the male the sun (linked with Saint Nicholas because of the golden coins he gifted in his story).[85] I believe that this is less literal than it sounds: Mawu-Lisa are not considered to be the creator of the Marassa in Vodou; instead it seems that this teaching refers to the fact that the concept and worship of Mawu-Lisa in West Africa, the land of origin for so many Vodou spirits and rituals, has given birth, figuratively, to an idea of twin spirits in a fundamental role in the Vodou cosmos.

Thus, the Marassa are the Universe and all of its interactions and interplays; they are both one, and two, and also three. As one they work together in a singularity - they do not have two individual names but rather one title; as two they are One Thing and Another Thing, Is and Is Not, Existence and Non-Existence; as three they form the basis of what Maya Deren termed the *'affirmation of cosmic unity'* - one *and* one make three, two *and* two make five, with the *and* (the unity) forming the extra digit in the equation.[86] Similarly, when two interplaying forces or states of being interact, they generally create a third state from themselves. So, when a couple create a child, the child becomes three from the one and one; when thought and voice unite, they create words; when two dots are drawn on a piece of paper, a line is formed between the two. Glassman reflects this in the fact that she chooses to depict the Marassa on the Lovers card of the *New Orleans Voodoo Tarot* – a card signifying unity between two to create a third, as well as the statement *"I am divided for love's sake, for the chance of union."*[87] So the Marassa are at once a couple of spirits that are served by Vodou practitioners, as well as the representatives of the cosmic process of creation, and the continuing process of manifestation that takes place on every level of existence. Louie Martinie writes:

> *"They are the first manifestation of duality; they were not so much created, as being, in themselves, creation (i.e. love). The twins are the first emanation from complete abstraction. Therefore, in their nature is the seed of the initial abstraction."*[88]

It is interesting to note that to reflect this understanding and cosmological view, the Marassa are most often properly titled Marassa-Dossou-Dossa, a term used in reference to the child that is born after a set of twins - the third sibling. This third child is said to

---

[85] In Patrick Bellegarde-Smith, ed., *Fragments of Bone: Neo-African Religions in the New World*, p.19. Herskowitz also suggests that the link between St. Nicholas and the Marassa is due to the image of him raising three children from the dead. See Melville J. Herskowitz, *African Gods and Catholic Saints in New World Belief*, p. 638.
[86] Maya Deren, *Divine Horsemen: the Living Gods of Haiti*, p. 41.
[87] *Liber al vel Legis* (The Book of the Law) 1.29.
[88] Louis Martinie, *Cultus Marassa*, 1986. Online at http://w3.iac.net/~moonweb/archives/LM/Marassa1.html

not only own his or her own magical power, but also that of the twins that came before it. To demonstrate this, the Marassa are indeed sometimes depicted as a set of twins, but very commonly as a set of triplets (but which are only ever referred to as twins, never as triplets.)

Yet logically it is understood that whilst one and one make three, two equals zero and zero equals two. So, these twin spirits - seen as identical twins rather than non-identical, and served exactly the same as each other down to the last grain of rice, and only ever called upon together - are a reminder that underneath the seeming duality of the world there is only unity, and when there is one there is also the understanding that there is a *'not one'* - zero.

It may also be noted that in the *veve* (sacred symbol that is drawn in cornmeal or a similar substance on the floor of the hounfor – temple – to call down a spirit) of the Marassa this principle of creation is depicted in the two eggs that are found entwined in the image. From the egg comes potential, and it is also a symbol associated with the number zero due to its shape. (See Fig. 10)

Given that the Marassa are intimately connected with the process of creation and genesis, usually viewed as a fertile act in most cultures, it may seem odd that they are viewed and depicted as young children, usually no older than five or six years. In possession too they display the features and behaviours of young children - they may cry, throw tantrums, pull at a woman's skirts to get attention, and babble incoherently. This manifestation as children rather than as fertile adults may simply indicate the fact that a child is the third product created by the union of one and one in biological creation, so instead of focusing on the duality of the process of creation, the Vodou worldview focuses on its product. As such, the Marassa are the special patron spirits of children from unusual births, including twins and triplets; they are also fond of any child, and in a Vodou ceremony no adults may eat of the food offered first to the Marassa - it is all distributed among the children. Only when the human children are satisfied is it considered that the Marassa have eaten their fill of the offerings.

That the creation of the Universe is an act given to the Marassa also highlights the fact that the Vodou religion has no single creation myth like Christianity – from which it draws much of its ritual practice and context – but can be seen instead as viewing creation as a continual process rather than an act that occurred in the past. This is an important distinction to make for it places the lwa, humans, and the world around us in an ever-evolving and ever-changing milieu with which we can engage; our wills, desires, and actions interacting with everything else. This seems a far healthier attitude to hold towards our immediate environment than that of one viewing the world as a dead rock, upon which we force our wills – an act that is rather more like a pneumatic drill hammering its way through a concrete pavement than that of a tree swaying in the wind.

The Other Side of the Mirror – Marassa as 'Self' and 'Other'

> *"Twins are sacred because they are living representations of the balancing forces found throughout Vodou belief. Together, they represent both the human and the divine, the mortal and the immortal. They form a connection between the physical world and the world of the spirits, and they live in both worlds. Some practitioners of Vodou believe that they are even more powerful than the lwa because of the union they symbolise."*[89]

Everybody can be seen as having a twin: this is the face that stares back at us when we look in a reflective surface. The act of looking in a mirror and recognizing that the face on the other side is not the Self, but something Other (as Freud said, *'ce n'est pas une pipe'*)[90], is a sign of consciousness. This mirror is an extremely important symbol in Vodou, as it is said that all the lwa live on the other side of the mirror – the back side of reality.[91] But the Marassa, as self-reflecting twin spirits, straddle this mirror and the thin sheet of glass that separates our world from that of the spirits. As the spirits that straddle the mirror they can be seen as manifesting the other spirits into this side of the mirror - hence they are the spirits served almost first in traditional Vodou reglemen, only after Papa Legba, the opener of the way. When Vodouisants sing for the Marassa near the start of a ceremony[92] they sing to acknowledge the twins as an absolutely necessary part of the Vodou universe - the genitive force in nature as well as the creation of duality that enables a relationship between human and lwa to be formed, or even the relationship between any One Thing and any Other Thing. When we look in the mirror we see our reflection, but it is not quite the same as what somebody looking at us without the mirror would see. Thus, the mirror shows us the Other, and when we recognize the possibility of this Other we also begin an awareness of the possibility of the

---

[89] Shannon R. Turlington. *Do you do Voodoo? The Real Religion Behind Zombies and Voodoo Dolls.*
[90] "This is not a pipe." In other words, the image of something is not the thing in itself.
[91] For more on the Other Side of the Mirror, see Kim Huggens, *The Admiral, the Siren and the Whale: Water Spirits in the Vodou Tradition*, in *From a Drop of Water*, pp. 47-66.
[92] It should be stated that Papa Legba and the Marassa are sung for not at the very start of a ceremony, as is often incorrectly assumed by many Western practitioners of Vodou, for what precedes the service of the spirits in a Vodou *sevis* is the traditional prayers called the Priye, consisting of a series of hymns, Catholic prayers, prayers to saints, the Catholic creed, Our Fathers, Hail Maries, and more.

unity with the Other as a means of transcending duality. Thus, from the human reflection in the mirror the lwa and all spirits come.

It is this recognition of the *'Other'* and the *'Self'* in the form of the spirit twins that can be found in some traditional ceremonial songs for the Marassa. One song says:

Genzye-o, Marassa layo,	You have eyes, you Marassa
Genzye-o	You have eyes,
Genzye-o, Marassa layo,	You have eyes, you Marassa
Genzye-o	You have eyes
Genzye-o, genzye Marassa	You have eyes, you have eyes Marassa
Pou nou gade ouvre	to look at them open.[93]

Another says:
Marassa Dosou Dosa	Marassa Dosou Dosa
Mwen yanvalou mwen	I'm calling you now
Dosou Marassa	Dosou Marassa
O mwen gen ge pou mwen gade-yo	I have eyes to look at them
Bondye devan, Lesen deye	God first, the saints after[94]

Very few songs for any other lwa mention the importance of eyes - why the Marassa? In discussing this with a friend it was posited that each of the two Marassa children represent an eye - one left eye, one right eye. You need both eyes to see the world clearly. The third Marassa child could represent the 'third eye', or the spiritual eye through which we perceive the universe's spiritual identity and interact with the spirit world. The importance of eyes is also reflected in the concept of looking at one's reflection in the mirror, and the first instance of recognition in children that what they see around them is separate to themselves - the first seed from abstraction, the recognition of a Not I vs. an I. Thus, the *'eyes'* and the *'seeing'* of the Marassa refer directly to their representation of the Other Side of the Mirror and the Self and *'Other'* relationship.

This state of reflection and otherness is depicted in the veve used for the Marassa (see Fig 7) since one can see within it the sacred

---

[93] Song taught by Houngan Hector Salva of Sosyete Gade Nou Leve; all translation errors and interpretation are my own.
[94] Taught by Houngan Hector Salva of Sosyete Gade Nou Leve; all translation errors and interpretation are my own.

crossroads (also an important symbol in the Vodou religion);[95] if one were to draw the veve of the Marassa on a sheet of paper, then fold it in the centre horizontally, one would find the central fold line acting as an intersection between a diagram mirror-imaged; this would also be the case were one to fold the diagram in half again. Even the title 'Marassa' hints at the state of the twins as reflections of each other:

> "The Creole word for twins, marasa, is derived from the Kikongo word mabassa, which means "those who come divided", or the one who comes as two."[96]

Figure 10 - Veve of the Marassa

It is within this mirror that the Vodouisant is presented an image not only of the self, but also everything else, and thus the Marassa spirits that enable the capacity of reflection in the universe are responsible for one of the most fundamental processes of consciousness:

---

[95] It is notable that the veve of the Marassa bears a striking resemblance to that of Papa Legba, the lwa who stands at every threshold and every crossroads – the crossroad image in the case of the Marassa's veve is in a triplicity, however, rather than as a single crossroads.
[96] Patrick Bellegarde-Smith, ed., *Fragments of Bone: Neo-African Religions in the New World*, p.14.

"For the Haitian, the metaphysical world of Les Invisibles is not a vague, mystical notion; it is a world within a cosmic mirror, peopled by the immortal reflections of all those who have ever confronted it."[97]

The First Children are the First Ancestors

It is often said that the Marassa are the first children, which certainly fits with the idea that they are the first abstraction from the original cosmic unity. As such, the first children must also be the first to die, and therefore must be the first ancestors. This puts the Marassa in a significant position in the Vodou world, since they are both young and ancient, innocent and wise, alive and dead. In this sense, the Marassa can be considered to not only demonstrate duality, but also to contain within themselves the crossroad of paradox, of being two opposing states of existence simultaneously.

Marassa as the Self

In a painting by the modern Haitian artist Guidel Presume, entitled *'Les Trois Marassa'* (1999)[98] these spirits are shown in a rather menacing light: three white-clad, black-faced spirits, standing over a tomb and a bowl of blood. The artist here identifies them as presiding over the post-mortem splitting of the individual's soul into its constituent parts - the *gros bon ange* (Big Good Angel), *ti bon ange* (Little Good Angel) and the flesh. While the flesh is given to the earth (depicted in the painting as a hand coming from the red earth) the *gros bon ange* and the *ti bon ange* remain on the metaphysical plane. Although there is no room here to discuss Vodou beliefs about the nature of the soul and the afterlife, this link with the individual's splitting after death and the Marassa is reminiscent of the sacred twins and the splitting of zero into two discussed above. Thus, the Marassa may be seen as not only representative of the recognition of the Self and the *'Other'* (in reference to the world around us and the realization that there is a Not I) but also as representative of the recognition that there are many aspects of one individual, and that these constituent parts are to be balanced and united in life.

The human being is also made up of a dual nature that allows for us to both live and work in a mundane context, as well as communicate with a spiritual world. This dual nature manifests itself in the image of Marassa as the reflection in the mirror, as we are reminded that there is a reflection of ourselves that is always on the other side of that mirror. In the Western Mystery Tradition it may be analogous to the maxim *'As above, so below'*. Maya Deren writes:

---

[97] Maya Deren, *Divine Horsemen: The Living Gods of Haiti*, p. 34.
[98] To see this painting, go to http://faculty.goucher.edu/mbell/lestrois.html.

Vs.

> *"The worship of the Marassa, the Divine Twins, is a celebration of man's twinned nature: half matter, half metaphysical; half mortal, half immortal; half human, half divine."*[99]

As well as this fundamental dual nature of the human being, it is believed that any given individual has a *'court'* or *'entourage'* of spirits that walk with them throughout life – some stay for life, others only for a given time. In a Western context we might call them spirit guides or patron deities, although the relationship with these spirits in Vodou is far more visceral and reciprocal. In one's court one may have any number of spirits, including a main spirit called a *met-tet*, or *'Master of the Head'*, which is more closely guarded and entwined with a person's power and spiritual strength. Due to the nature of the lwa as clearly defined personalities, with their own likes and dislikes, attitudes, and ways of talking, a person could have in their court a number of lwa that conflict with each other or represent forces and processes that rarely come into contact with each other. A Vodouisant is required to balance these separate spirits in their life and in their personality to create a more advanced state of awareness and being on an everyday level. For me, the ultimate aim of this balancing act is to align all the spirits that walk with me to a higher purpose, to walk the same, united road. When we sing for the Marassa in a Vodou service, we acknowledge the existence of different parts of the self, and therefore the necessity to continually balance the many aspects of God within us.[100]

This manifold nature of existence and humanity, created by the first duality in the Marassa, is also found in the nature of the lwa. There are said to be many nations (sometimes called divisions) of spirits which each have their own personality. For instance, in the Nago nation we find warriors and spirits concerned with the application of power; the Ghede family hosts all the dead spirits, who are usually raucous in nature, fun-loving, rude, yet retain all wisdom. Thus, in a Vodouisant's court we may have a number of Rada spirits, some Nago, Petwo, Ghede, and more! So a Petwo spirit may manifest itself in our temper, a Rada spirit in our obsession with housework or appearance, a Nago spirit with our desire to be a political ambassador, and a Ghede spirit in our awful jokes and love of rum. In life, and in Vodou service, these spirits and the aspects of our personality that they relate to must be balanced. This is not to say that they must be given equal weight and attention – balance does not always require equality.

---

[99] Maya Deren, *Divine Horsemen: The Living Gods of Haiti*, p.38.
[100] Some readers may think this means I view the lwa as merely aspects of one's psychology. This is not the case; the lwa live in one's blood and in one's energy and everyday life – the possibility of their actual existence is not in conflict with viewing them as aspects of the self.

Vs.

Cosmic Balance, not Cosmic Competition

One thing that becomes very clear from the service given to the Marassa is that the Vodou concept of duality is not one of polarity and competition, as is the case in many other religions (such as God and Satan, Moon Goddess and Sun God) but instead one of balance and interaction. The twin forces of the universe embodied in the figures of the Marassa are not in competition with each other; they do not fight over a third figure in the mythology; one does not rule one half of the year whilst the other rules the second half; one is not light/sun/summer and the other dark/moon/winter. It might even be incorrect to state, as I have done above, that one *'Is'* and the other *'Is Not'*, because this also implies competition.

What is given to one Marassa twin is always given to the other. This is vital in their service. When the Marassa are served in any Vodou ceremony, their offerings are placed in a special container that has two or three joined bowls/bottles. Equal amounts of food must be placed in each container, and the Marassa will always eat together. Once again, this demonstrates the fact that there is not a cosmic polarity or competition here between one state of being and another – if this were the case, it would be more appropriate to serve the Marassa with one bowl full and another empty, or with one bowl containing all the sweet foods and another all the savoury. Instead, there is cosmic balance: both states of being, both sides of the universe, must be given equal consideration, equal care, and equal attention.

The fact that the Marassa are not given two separate names but instead go by their one title suggests that we might approach different sides of the universe as being representative of a cosmic unity, a common divine source. Even in possession these twin spirits often only *'mount'* (possess) one *'horse'* (Vodouisant) although it is common for individual spirits to mount multiple horses simultaneously. The Marassa remind us that all comes from God, the Ultimate; in this, all separate and disparate aspects of the self and the universe are in balance – not because all are born equal or because all things are equally good, but because all and everybody contains the same seed of divinity, the same common origin in the source. This is the balance that the Marassa teach us, and they invite us to look at the world and people around us from this perspective.

Divine Power vs. Human Impotence in Vodou - a new look at the Self/Other relationship

In many traditions it is understood that there is a divide between the nature of the Divine (e.g. Gods, spirits, archetypes) and the nature of the human realm, the gap between which can only be bridged by a series of trials, tests, and mystical efforts, and the differences between the two are understood as part of the defining point of the relationship between human and divine. In Vodou the distinction between Divine and human is less clear cut. Humans are not viewed as impotent in comparison with the spirits, and humans don't petition Gods to effect change in the world nor do they rely upon spirits for aid and succour. In Vodou the court of spirits that walk with us throughout our lives, some of which we are born with and inherit from our bloodline and parents, live in our blood (or in our life-force), and very much rely upon our service to them for their own wellbeing and vitality. Without service, they cannot speak to us; without our recognition they are not given life and personage. Without our working with them they cannot hope to rise up closer to God along with our own minds and souls. Yet without the lwa Vodou practitioners might as well be banging their heads against a brick wall.

This is not to say that the lwa are the impotent ones in this relationship; rather, the human and spirit partner are better off for the relationship, and work in a symbiotic fashion. This symbiosis and the results of it can be seen today in the case of the deforestation of Haiti: the spirit who lives in forests, and rules over trees, is called Gran Bwa (*'Big Wood'* – also suggestive of a phallus). Barely a decade ago Gran Bwa was a very popular lwa, served and danced for all over Haiti. Now that the forests are dwindling and the civilized areas of Haiti becoming more urban, Gran Bwa is served less and less. Some houngans and mambos believe that in certain areas where he is not served, Gran Bwa is effectively dead. This manifests in the practitioners' lives, as it can be noted that in urban societies and cities there are fewer Vodouisants who have Gran Bwa in their *'court'* than those in rural areas. So, the environment dictates the concerns of a community; the community expresses these concerns in religion; the religious practices for a spirit lessen, and the energy or idea of that spirit decreases in the community's collective mind.

Vodou is not a religion in which the Gods are talked about or at: they are talked to and with; it is not a religion in which the divide between human and divine is such that we may only talk with the Gods in a ceremonial or religious setting - they walk with us in our daily, everyday mundane world. Although it is believed that the lwa live on the *'Other Side of the Mirror'*, or beneath the waters of Ginen, and thus there is a distinction made between the spirit realm and the human realm, it is understood that the two worlds are juxtaposed upon each other – there is no *'veil between the worlds'* here, merely the necessity for a change in perception.

In many traditions it is viewed that the Gods or spirits function as the *'Other'* in a psycho-spiritual personal mythology of awakening. Whilst this can be applied to Vodou, it is more traditional to view the lwa not as an *'Other'* but rather as both an extension and retraction of the self. Thus, the lwa are ourselves in spirit, but also deeper essences of the self. They are not yearned for as a Sufi mystic might yearn for union with the Beloved (God), because the unity is already present – they walk with us already. Instead, we look to gain a greater communication with them, to listen to them with increased clarity and understanding.

Children will be Children: Marassa as Mischievous Spirits

Although in the modern practice of Vodou the Marassa are considered, as above, to represent a great many philosophical concepts and to give the spiritual context for a Vodouisant's life and work, the Vodou as practiced in Haiti treats the Marassa, even in a ritual context, as mischievous spirits – at best – or as malicious spirits – at worst. In 1946, George Eaton Simpson recorded the following songs for the Marassa, having attended a ceremony for a dead houngan:

Jumeaux-yo, mere mange	Twins, here is the food
Nape ba ou.	That we give you.
Jumeaux gangnin l'habitude	Twins, you are accustomed
Quand yo ba yo,	After you have received food from us
Yo dit yo pas mange!	To say you have not eaten!
Jumeaux-marassa, Diable rhele.	Twins-Marassa, the Devil cries.
Dossi! Dossi-dossa! Diable rhele!	Dossi! Dossi-dossa! The Devil cries!
Credo, manman-jumeaux.	Credo, Mother of Twins.
Diable rhele!	The Devil cries!
Moin dit: Manman-jumeaux,	I say: Mother of Twins
Ban-moin sall'-la, souple!	Please leave us this room!
Marassa-jumeaux, Ban-moin salle, souple!	Twins-Marassa, Please leave us this room![101]

Here the Marassa are first offered food, though it is acknowledged that they may be greedy – like children offered their favourite foods – and demand more; it seems that they are not

---
[101] George Eaton Simpson, *Four Vodun Ceremonies*, in *The Journal of American Folklore*, vol. 59, no. 232, (Apr.-Jun. 1946), pp. 154-167.

inclined to leave the ceremony however, and become mischievous, thus the singers and houngan attempt to remove them from the ceremony, begging them to leave the room so that it may be continued without further disturbance. This preoccupation with removing the Marassa may be due to the fact that their service must be so exact, as mentioned above: the same amount of foods given to each twin, for instance. Such an act, in a busy ritual context, can be difficult to maintain for an extended period of time, thus making the window of opportunity for error wider.

Marilyn Houlberg has suggested a happy medium between the two views of the Marassa as important cosmic spirits and mischievous, malicious spirits:

> *"Marasa eat during a ceremony, then hide behind the door;*
> *Then they come out and say they haven't eaten.*
> *They hide behind the door on purpose,*
> *They know that they are so important that they can cause*
> *Their ceremony to be done all over again."*[102]

What the participants in a ceremony may perceive as trouble-making – hiding behind doors and people, asking for more food after they've been given some already – the Marassa perceive as ensuring the ceremony is not spoiled. When they hide from sight, they show that they represent a fundamental truth of the universe that if considered and faced directly can cause difficulty in the mind of the thinker. When they demand more food, they are ensuring that the correct offerings are given in enough quantity, giving the Vodouisant the opportunity to ensure this as well.

Conclusion

For anybody viewing the Vodou religion as primitive, the existence of the Marassa in its philosophy proves shocking. The understanding surrounding these twin spirits demonstrates a deeply held awareness of the self, the relation of humans to spirits and to God, and the interaction of dual states of being in the creation of the universe. That the belief in the Marassa enables a view that holds creation to be a continual process, in which Is and Not Is, One Thing and Another Thing eternally act and react, shows the Vodou religion's more complex cosmology. It would seem, however, that the religion does prefer to leave the practitioner to discover these ideas and concepts through the deceptively simple names, songs, and symbols of the spirits. Simple and complex, revealed and hidden – the mysteries of the Marassa hold manifold paradoxes that really aren't paradoxical at all.

---

[102] In Patrick Bellegarde-Smith, ed., *Fragments of Bone: Neo-African Religions in the New World*, p. 13.

Bibliography

Bellegarde-Smith, Patrick, ed., *Fragments of Bone: Neo-African Religions in the New World*. University of Illinois Press, 2005.
Courlander, Harold, *Gods of the Haitian Mountains*, in *The Journal of Negro History*, vol. 29, no. 3. (Jul., 1944), pp. 339-372.
Crowley, Aleister, *The Book of the Law*. Samuel Weiser, 1976.
Deren, Maya, *Divine Horsemen: The Living Gods and Haiti*. Thames and Hudson, 1953.
Filan, Kenaz, *The Haitian Vodou Handbook: Protocols for Riding with the Lwa*. Destiny Books, 2007.
Glassman, Sallie Ann and Martinie, Louis, *The New Orleans Voodoo Tarot*. Destiny Books, 1992.
Herzkowitz, Melville J., *African Gods and Catholic Saints in New World Belief*, in *American Anthropologist*, New Series, vol. 39, no. 4, Part1 (Oct – Dec, 1937), pp. 635-643.
Huggens, Kim, ed., *From a Drop of Water: A Collection of Magickal Reflections on the Nature, Creatures, Uses and Symbolism of Water*. Avalonia, 2009.
Hurbon, Laennec, *Voodoo: Truth and Fantasy*. Thames and Hudson, 1995.
Hurston, Zora Neale, *Tell My Horse: Voodoo and Life in Haiti and Jamaica*. Harper and Row, 1990.
Karade, Baba Ifa, *The Handbook of Yoruba Religious Concepts*. Weiser Books, 1994.
Martinie, Louis, *Cultus Marassa*, 1986. Online at http://w3.iac.net/~moonweb/archives/LM/Marassa1.html
McCarthy Brown, Karen, *Mama Lola: A Vodou Priestess in Brooklyn*. University of California Press, 1991.
Michel, Claudine, and Bellegarde-Smith, Patrick, eds., *Vodou in Haitian Life and Culture: Invisible Powers*. Palgrave Macmillan, 2006.
Murphy, Joseph M., *Working the Spirit: Ceremonies of the African Diaspora*. Beacon Press, 1994.
Olupona, Jacob K., ed., *African Traditional Religions in Contemporary Society*. Paragon House, 1991.
Simpson, George Eaton, *Four Vodun Ceremonies*, in *The Journal of American Folklore*, vol. 59, no.232, (Apr-Jun, 1946), pp. 154-167.
Turlington, Shannon R, *Do you do Voodoo? The Real Religion Behind Zombies and Voodoo Dolls*. South Street Press, 1999.

Vs.

BROTHERS AT ARMS

The Smith and the Soldier

by Magin Rose

There is little evidence of fraternal love between the Olympian war-god Ares and the smith-god Hephaestus.[103] Ares is the destructive fire, the destroyer of cities, strong, fast and fierce in battle; lame Hephaestus is gentle and kind, embodying the creative fire of the forge and the technical skill of the craftsman. Their animosity is best known through the love-triangle created when Hephaestus marries Aphrodite. In this myth Ares (Aphrodite's favoured lover), is one of the Olympians who tries to convince Hephaestus to release Hera (our protagonist's mother and Queen of Heaven) from the throne in which he has trapped her; eventually Hephaestus relents and is given the hand of Aphrodite in marriage as reward. The consequences of this marriage are described by Homer:

> "...the minstrel struck the chords in prelude to his sweet lay and sang of the love of Ares and Aphrodite of the fair crown, how first they lay together in the house of Hephaestus secretly; and Ares gave her many gifts, and shamed the bed of the lord Hephaestus... And when Hephaestus heard the grievous tale, he went his way to his smithy, pondering evil in the deep of his heart."[104]

Despite their dysfunctional filial relationship, the sons of Hera and Zeus have a great deal in common (besides Aphrodite): the smith creates the weapons of the soldier; both have a tempestuous relationship with their parents; and both are subjugated in some way to their younger sibling Athena. I will be arguing that, in the Classical Hellenic culture through which we know them best, Ares and Hephaestus are simultaneously set in opposition to each other and *'othered'* within the Olympian family. The archaeological, historical and mythical evidence paint a picture of two gods who are both celebrated and despised, emulated and ridiculed, exulted and

---

[103] I will be using the Latin spelling 'Hephaestus' throughout rather than 'Hephaistos' – this is just a matter of personal preference.
[104] Homer, (800BCE) *Odyssey* 8.266-274.

repressed by their celestial family and earthly worshippers. Almost all pantheons work within a framework that sets Order and Chaos against each other, each struggling for the upper hand; but in my view it is the liminal, and often flawed, deities, who are the most fascinating. Ares and Hephaestus are particularly flawed – one thoroughly disliked, adulterous and bloodthirsty, the other ugly, lame and sexually frustrated. It is these imperfect gods, however, who get their hands dirty; they are both the Olympian first line of defence and the embodiment of that territory where the powers of Order and Chaos intermingle as they struggle. In this paper I suggest that Ares and Hephaestus may be flawed, but it is their flaws that make them powerful and thus necessary and valuable to their prettier and more proper Olympian family.

My own inclinations have led me to work more with Hephaestus than Ares; through the myths I always felt a greater sympathy for the kindly and inventive smith than for the angry and passionate warrior. My work for *Vs.* has led me to re-evaluate this and to see their relationship more as a careful balance, maintained and mediated by those closest to them: Zeus, Hera, Athena and Aphrodite. At the end of this exploration of the parallels and animosities between Hephaestus and Ares, I offer you my own counter-myth, forged in response to my growing love for these star-crossed brothers.

Origins and cult

> *"Ares insatiable in battle, blazing like the light of burning fire in his armour and standing in his chariots, and his running horses trampled and dented the ground with their hooves . . . And all the grove and the altar . . . were lighted up by the dread god, Ares, himself and his armour, and the shining from his eyes was like fire . . . Manslaughtering Ares screaming aloud, courses all over the sacred grove."*[105]

The roots for both Ares and Hephaestus pre-dated Classical Hellenic culture and both brothers were said to originate, and reside, outside Greece. Ares (the name literally meaning *'war'*), was believed to be (or to be the ancestor of), Thrax, founder of Thrace, the region covering the North-East of Greece and European part of Turkey. The boundaries and peoples of Thrace were loosely defined; they were unlikely to have self-identified as *'Thracian'* but may have been perceived as a group as early as the Bronze Age. They were certainly established by the Iron Age and were considered bloodthirsty and savage by the outside world and thus more suited to the wild,

---

[105] White (8-7th century BCE), *Shield of Heracles*.

Vs.

barbarous Ares than the civilized Greeks.[106] Thrace was the cradle for heroes including Orpheus and Spartacus, and home to legendary kings such as Ares' giant son Diomedes, owner of the man-eating horses stolen by Hercules. Diomedes' horses were controlled by being tied to a bronze manger, which is interesting when we note Ares cult title *'Ares Hippios' (of horses)* and the connection between Ares, Hephaestus, bronze and control which will recur later.

Diomedes was not the only one of Ares' children to suffer at the hands of Hercules (mortal son of Zeus and so Ares and Hephaestus's half brother). The Amazonian Queen, Hippolyta, was widely considered to be a daughter of Ares and, although she willingly gave her girdle to Hercules (which he needed for his ninth quest), many tales have Hera subsequently instigating her death at his hands.[107] *The Shield of Heracles*[108] describes the death of Cycnus, Ares' bloodthirsty son, who was believed to have wanted to construct a temple in honour of his father made entirely of human skulls. In *The Shield* Cycnus and Ares are riding through a sanctuary of Apollo and are attacked by Hercules (other accounts have Cycnus instigating the conflict or Hercules attacking to stop the skull temple.)[109] Cycnus's death is interesting from our point of view because Hercules is assisted by Hephaestus (who makes some of his armour in bronze as well as his shield) and by Athena (who instigates the conflict). Athena also instructs Hercules to leave Cycnus's body and immediately attack Ares (who ends up wounded but not killed):

> *"And Cycnus fell as an oak falls or a lofty pine that is stricken by the lurid thunderbolt of Zeus; even so he fell, and his armour adorned with bronze clashed about him. Then the stout-hearted son of Zeus let him be, and himself watched for the onset of manslaying Ares: fiercely he stared, like a lion who has come upon a body and full eagerly rips the hide with his strong claws and takes away the sweet life with all speed: his dark heart is filled with rage and his eyes glare fiercely, while he tears up the earth with his paws and lashes his flanks and shoulders with his tail so that no one dares to face him and go near to give battle. Even so, the son of Amphitryon, unsated of battle, stood eagerly face to face with Ares, nursing courage in his heart. And Ares drew near him with grief in his heart; and they both sprang at one another with a cry."*[110]

---

[106] Walter Burkert, *Greek Religion*, pp. 169.
[107] http://en.wikipedia.org/wiki/Hippolyta
[108] Hesiod, *The Shield of Heracles*.
[109] http://www.theoi.com/Heros/KyknosItonios.html
[110] Hesiod, *The Shield of Heracles* 424-436.

Vs.

Despite the muddled accounts of how these conflicts occur, there definitely seems to be a common pattern of Zeus's favoured son proving himself by defeating Ares and his children and being tutored by Athena and assisted by Hephaestus in his tasks. The scene of Cycnus's death suggests a transference of power: first willingly from Zeus to Hercules; and then unwillingly, from grief stricken Ares to Hercules (whose fierceness and demeanour are reminiscent of Ares' normal mien).

> *"Ares, to gory strife he speedeth, wroth with foes, when maddeneth his heart, and grim his frown is, and his eyes flash levin-flame around him, and his face is clothed with glory of beauty terror-blent, as on he rusheth: quail the very gods."* [111]

Ares had a temple in the Agora of Athens, famous for having been re-situated brick by brick by the Romans, perhaps as part of the effective Roman *'integration'* policy, but also interesting in that it raised the status of Ares/Mars by placing him within the city. At one point it was thought that the temple had originally been a temple to Ares situated in Acharnai, but it is now thought more likely to have started life as a temple to Athena Pallenis in Stavro[112] as an empty foundation matching the Athenian temple was subsequently found there. Interestingly the size and layout of this temple matches that of Hephaestus's temple in the Agora, perhaps a coincidence, but possibly an architectural allusion to the balance Athena brings by sharing the aspects of her two brothers and also dominating them in her own city. Pausanias reported that Ares' temple contained two statues of Aphrodite, one of Ares and one of Athena; even in civilized Athens, the bond of passion between Ares and Aphrodite proves more enduring that that of Aphrodite and her husband Hephaestus.[113] It is also worth noting that, despite the enhancement of her seductive powers which the girdle Hephaestus crafts for her bestows upon Aphrodite, the love goddess is never referred to as *'Aphrodite Hephaestia'*. She does, however, bear the title Aphrodite Areia (of War), perhaps homage to her occasional appearance in battle but I would think it a more likely reference to her ability to inspire battle (note that in the *Iliad* she makes a rather unconvincing appearance on the battle-field,[114] she was also the instigator of the whole affair as she gifted the already married Helen to Paris and so started the Trojan Wars).

---

[111] Quintus Smyrnaeus, *Fall of Troy* 7. 400 ff.
[112] Spawforth, *The Complete Greek Temples,* p. 136.
[113] Pausanias, *Description of Greece* 1.84.
[114] Homer, (800BCE) *Iliad*, Book V.

Vs.

The Roman veneration of Mars went on to emphasise the war-god's connections with Thrace as a number of self-made, military emperors originated from that region. This, coupled with the lack of archaeological evidence for his worship in Classical Greece itself, might suggest that Ares was a fairly minor deity in the Hellenic pantheon and cult. However, we do know of cult activity in both northern and southern Greece, as well as Thrace, which suggests otherwise. As might be expected, sacrifices to Ares were particularly common during times of war, which might explain the lack of permanent temples to him as few cultures can sustain war in perpetuity. As already discussed, Hippolyta was Ares' daughter and the Amazons his worshippers;[115] Aeschylus describes the founding of the Athenian tribunal court upon the hill where once the Amazons built a citadel to rival Athens and made sacrifices there to Ares. The hill became known as Ares Hill and it is interesting to note the Athenian diversion of the power of the warrior-god's sanctuary into a function of civic authority and judgement.[116] As well as Ares Hill and his temple within Athens, I have also mentioned Ares' connection with Athena through their joint horse cult at Olympia, which is an important signifier of the shared aspects of this God and Goddess balancing out some of the more hostile aspects of their relationship.

In Thrace a temple to Ares stood in Bistonia (said to have been built by his son Diomedes), which was believed to house Ares' shield[117] and Herodotus told of the worship of Ares by the Scythians (inhabiting the territory to the north-east of Greece and Thrace), who sacrificed horses, cattle and the blood and limbs of prisoners to the God upon mounds topped with a sword (thought to be the embodiment of Ares).[118] While we might take the blood-curdling legends of Thrace and Scythia as exaggerated tales designed to 'other' Ares by recognising his power but keeping safely at a distance, there is certainly archaeological evidence of the Scythian sword-mounds.[119] Putting aside the aspects of these cults less palatable to the modern mind, the worship of Ares as a sword suggests to me that Ares was more a god of the fighting man than of the state function of war (which was more Athena's provenance). If Ares is the sword, then he gives power to the wielder (the soldier), who, in turn, is wielded by his leader. In this sense Ares becomes a destructive force that must be wielded effectively.

In a no less macabre story set in Arcadia in Southern Greece, Ares was said to sustain the lifeless body of his lover so that she might continue to suckle their newborn child, his cult title

---

[115] Aeschylus, *Eumenides*.
[116] Aeschylus, *Eumenides*.
[117] http://wapedia.mobi/en/Thracians
[118] E.V Cerneko, *The Scythians 700-300 BCE*, pp. 13-14.
[119] E.V Cerneko, *The Scythians 700-300 BCE*, p. 14.

'abundant' came from this myth.[120] Gender exclusive rites for Ares were also performed; the logic of male-only rites for a god of war might seem self evident, but he also gains his title *'feasted by women'* from a battle in the Lakonian War where the women formed an additional ambush force and succeeded in driving away the enemy.[121] If we consider these tales in conjunction with Ares' fierce Amazonian warrior-women, and Aphrodite's adultery, we might begin to form the idea of a special relationship between Ares and women - one that allows women to be driven by passion and break the laws of society and nature in order to achieve their desired ends.

Ares also had a strong association with dragons. His spring at Thebes had a dragon sentry[122] which the city's founder, Cadmus, killed (under instruction from Athena) in order to grow an army from its teeth; in a similar tale, the Golden Fleece (from Jason and the Argonauts) was guarded by the Colchian dragon in a grove sacred to Ares – the dragon was slain by Jason and its teeth used to grow an army. Now isn't the time to enter into a long discussion of the symbolism of the dragon – but their associations with underworld forces, life/death/rebirth, and the testing of warriors are worth considering in relation to Ares.

Pausanias described a statue of Ares kept in chains by the Spartans so his power would not leave the city,[123] and the image of Ares in chains is discussed by Burkert who takes the myth in the *Iliad* where Ares is chained in a brazen barrel for thirteen months as an indication of a *'festival of licence'* (e.g. a free-for-all) taking place on the thirteenth month when Ares is freed.[124] In both of these examples the act of constraining the God appears to be about maintaining and harnessing his power (not suppressing it). We might see Ares as the *'big-gun'*, wheeled out in times of need and otherwise kept under lock and key. Burkert's festival of license might indicate a precursor to the Roman Saturnalia and Bacchanalia where people let down their hair and broke social taboos. Masked frolics and role disruption might not be Ares' cup of tea, but who could be a more appropriate patron for the modern games of football and rugby than the fierce god of the fighting man? The passion and dedication of many football fans speaks of a tribal identity and a sense of unity that is both powerful and tangible, conversely, the fear Ares inspired in enemies and leaders alike might be akin to that experienced by an outsider trapped within the surging crowd or an authority figure trying to control it.

---

[120] Pausanias, *Description of Greece* 8.44.7.
[121] Pausanias, *Description of Greece* 8.48.47.
[122] Pausanias, *Description of Greece* 9.10.5.
[123] Pausanias, *Description of Greece*, 3.15.7.
[124] Walter Burkert, *Greek Religion*, p. 168.

Vs.

Now, man-eating horses, temples of skulls, milk-giving corpses and armies of the dead paint a somewhat ghoulish picture, but there is a tantalising motif of *'life in death'* to these Ares legends which fits very neatly with a modern pagan worldview of the cycles of life, death and re-birth. This may well be my own, imposed, view but I find it compelling and full of possibilities for a more complex vision of Ares.

My research unearthed many comments lamenting the lack of information about Ares cults and I cannot help but wonder if perhaps this warrior-god of the fighting man was done a disservice by the *'civilized'* Greek poets, artists and men of letters. Burkert explains that the Greeks relied on Hesiod and, even more so, on Homer, to bring authority and spiritual unity to their profusion of traditions.[125] It is from them that the familiar versions of the Olympic pantheon stem. In their work, and that of their successors, Ares is often (but not always) characterised in the negative; he is *'Blood stained'*, *'murderous'* and *'violent'* but also *'Swift'*, *'Mighty'*, *'Bronze'*, *'He who rallies the fighting men'* and, sometimes, he provides the antidote to his own nature, giving people the courage and boldness to avoid conflict:

> *"Ares, exceeding in strength, chariot-rider, golden-helmed, doughty in heart, shield-bearer, Saviour of cities, harnessed in bronze, strong of arm, unwearying, mighty with the spear, O defence of Olympus, father of warlike Victory, ally of Themis, stern governor of the rebellious, leader of righteous men, sceptred King of manliness, who whirl your fiery sphere among the planets in their sevenfold courses through the aether wherein your blazing steeds ever bear you above the third firmament of heaven; hear me, helper of men, giver of dauntless youth! Shed down a kindly ray from above upon my life, and strength of war, that I may be able to drive away bitter cowardice from my head and crush down the deceitful impulses of my soul. Restrain also the keen fury of my heart which provokes me to tread the ways of blood-curdling strife. Rather, O blessed one, give you me boldness to abide within the harmless laws of peace, avoiding strife and hatred and the violent fiends of death."*[126]

In Ares we get a sense of a powerful and yet difficult to control force. Sometimes he is depicted as able to control his own nature, but more commonly there is a complex web of controlling elements which surround and direct him (e.g. his parents, Athena, Hephaestus, objects of Bronze, chains forged by men). We might go

---

[125] Walter Burkert, *Greek Religion,* p. 120.
[126] *Homeric Hymn to Ares* (Trans: White).

as far as to say that the God of War (as we know only too well from the lessons of history) is the most vulnerable of all the Olympians to manipulation by those in power.

The worship of Hephaestus is believed to have originated in Lemnos, an island in the northerly part of the Aegean Sea between Greece and Turkey. Hephaestus fell to Lemnos from Heaven and was cared for there - Homer declares that Hephaestus loved the island more than any place on Earth.[127] The smith-god was the patron of fire and it was only later that he became associated with volcanoes (his Roman successor, Vulcan, developed the volcano association further). As a volcano god we don't find any references to destructive, chthonic energy, rather, volcanoes are seen as the chimneys of Hephaestus's underground forges. In particular he was believed to have workshops at Mount Etna (where he and the Cyclops made the thunderbolts for Zeus),[128] Mount Olympus and Lemnos, as well as in his bronze house bedecked with stars[129] at Olympus.

For Hephaestus, the symbol of fire, and particularly creative and beneficial fire, is much more important than the volcano. When fire is stolen from Heaven, it is described to Hephaestus as *'Your own flower, flashing fire, source of all arts'*[130] and, importantly, Zeus is enraged by its loss and devises a particularly cruel punishment for the thief which Hephaestus is forced to enact. Hephaestus's fire is described as *'weariless'*,[131] the strength of Hephaestus,[132] the breath of Hephaestus,[133] and is found in cooking fires,[134] hearths,[135] sacred fires,[136] forges,[137] volcanoes,[138] magical fires[139] and pyres.[140] Apart from the volcano fire, these fires are *'useful fires'* of great benefit to mankind; unlike the power of Ares which has to be contained, these fires are pervasive and welcomed everywhere. In his play *Birds*, Aristophanes has one of his characters place all the weapons next to the fire of Hephaestus for protection;[141] it isn't specified what exactly is being protected but we might speculate that Ares' power is being tempered by Hephaestus's protective gentleness. Hephaestus's gentleness and weakness are often the subject of

---

[127] Homer, (800 BCE) *Odyssey* 8. 267ff.
[128] Euripides, *Cyclops 296*.
[129] Homer (800BCE) *Iliad, Book 18*.
[130] Aeschylus, *Prometheus Bound*, 7.
[131] Homer, (800BCE) *Iliad*, 17.88.
[132] Hesiod, *The Theogony of Hesiod*, 864 and White, *Homeric Hymn 4 to Hermes* 115.
[133] Quintus Smyrnaeus, *Fall of Troy* 4.440 and 13.70.
[134] Homer (800BCE) *Iliad .2426* and *9.476.*
[135] Quintus Smyrnaeus, *Fall of Troy* 4.440.
[136] Homer (800BCE) *Iliad 23.33*.
[137] Hesiod, *The Theogony of Hesiod*, 864.
[138] Hesiod, *The Theogony of Hesiod*, 864.
[139] Seneca, (1CE), *Medea 824*.
[140] Homer, (800BCE) *Odyssey* 23.71.
[141] Aristophanes, *Birds 436*.

ridicule (as will be discussed below), but they also provide safety and protection; a particularly important function in this regard is the protection of the hearth fire – the sacred fire of the virgin Goddess Hestia. Every city and every home had a hearth fire which was considered the altar of Hestia, and Burkert speaks of *'ancient sexual taboos surrounding the hearth; it is the daughters of the household who tend the hearth fire, a fire which is also experienced as a phallic force'*.[142] I have found some intriguing suggestions that, in his earliest form, dwarf-like statues of Hephaestus were placed around the hearth fire to protect it,[143] but sadly I have yet to uncover evidence to support these claims. Nevertheless one can't imagine the passionate Ares being allowed anywhere near the virgin goddess and her shrines, but a lame and impotent fire god would the perfect protector and it is undoubtedly the case that, as the embodiment of fire, Hephaestus would be the most likely *'phallic force'* for the virgin hearth.

Hephaestus and Ares are directly contrasted with each other in the tale of Aphrodite's adultery. Virile, passionate and underhand Ares is caught in the act with Aphrodite by a net cunningly contrived by cuckolded and vengeful Hephaestus.[144] At first glance Ares might be considered the loser in this encounter and the Gods certainly laugh at his expense – but essentially Hephaestus has provided evidence of his wife's dissatisfaction with him and her preference for manly Ares. Soon the laughter turns to humorous agreement that any of the Gods would trade places with Ares. Another, equally humiliating, incident swiftly follows:

> "Athene went to Hephaistos because she wanted to make some weapons. But he, deserted by Aphrodite, let himself become aroused by Athene, and started chasing her as she ran from him. When he caught up with her with much effort (for he was lame), he tried to enter her, but she, being the model of virginal self-control, would not let him; so as he ejaculated, his semen fell on her leg. In revulsion Athene wiped it off with some wool, which she threw on the ground. And as she was fleeing and the semen fell to the earth, Erikhthonios came into being."[145]

Building on the tale, Hyginus says of the child *'the lower part of whose body was snake-formed. [that] They named him Erichthonius, because eris in Greek means 'strife', and khthon means 'earth'.'*[146]

---

[142] Walter Burkert, *Greek Religion*, p. 170.
[143] http://www.theoi.com/Olympios/Hephaistos.html
[144] Homer, (800BCE) *Odyssey* 8.
[145] Apollodorus, *The Library 3.187*.
[146] Hyginus, *Fabulae 166*.

Not only is Erichthonius reptilian or *drakon*[147] (dragon) but he also shares the first part of his name with Ares' child Eris. The disruption of normal parenting patterns is also a motif that will occur again in relation to Ares, Hephaestus, Athena and Aphrodite. Although this incident is sometimes referred to as the rape of Athena, there is very little suggestion that Hephaestus ever poses any danger – instead the tale highlights the lame God's lack of seductive power and prowess. Despite the cuckolding and occasional bout of laughter at his expense,[148] Hephaestus does seem to fare better than Ares in the great epics and poems and, at one point, Homer describes how Hephaestus unleashes his power in battle at the behest of Hera:

> "First he kindled a fire in the plain and burned the numerous corpses that lay there in abundance, slain by Akhilleus, and all the plain was parched and the shining water was straitened . . . So the entire flat land was dried up with Hephaistos burning the dead bodies. Then he turned his flame in its shining into the river. The elms burned, the willows and tamarisks, the clover burned and the rushes and the galingale, all those plants that grew in abundance by the lovely stream of the River. The eels were suffering and the fish in the whirl of the water who leaped out along the lovely waters in every direction in affliction under the hot blast of resourceful Hephaistos. The strength of the River was burning away; he gave voice and called out by name: `Hephaistos, not one of the gods could stand up against you. I for one could not fight the flame of a fire like this one. Leave your attack"[149]

This is interesting given the smith-god's subjugation to Athena (discussed below) as well as the generally accepted view of Hephaestus as a relatively minor deity in the Olympic pantheon (certainly in comparison with the other deities discussed here). Burkert feels the need to explain this sympathetic treatment of Hephaestus and says: 'The craftsman god becomes the model of the all-fashioning creator; perhaps the Iliad poet was also thinking of himself in the image.'[150] This quote is important in that it demonstrates the way in which a deity's fortune can rise and fall depending on who is charged with creating or maintaining their legacy at a particular point in history.

The motif of love, betrayal and jealousy illustrated in the *Iliad* is not limited to Hephaestus' marriage bed: it runs through the lives of

---

[147] Philostratus, *Life of Apollonius of Tyana* 7.24.
[148] See the *Iliad*.
[149] Homer (800BCE) *Iliad 21*.
[150] Walter Burkert, *Greek Religion*, p. 168.

his favoured people. There is an Hellenic legend that Aphrodite had the men of Lemnos abandon their wives for Thracian women because her worship was neglected. In revenge the Lemnian women killed their husbands and children, (a similar legend states that all Athenian descendants were slaughtered). From this comes the phrase *'Lemnian deed'* meaning a shameful act.[151] Aphrodite becomes a catalyst for disaster and discord between the representatives of her husband, lover and rival in this myth of jealousy and revenge that poisons and usurps family bonds and love. Interestingly, Aeschylus portrays the murderous Lemnian women as a *'woman's race'* similar to the Amazonian descendants of Ares, adding another intriguing, yet elusive, bond between the sons of Zeus and Hera.[152]

> *"... Strong, mighty Hephaistos, bearing splendid light, unwearied fire, with flaming torrents bright: strong-handed, deathless, and of art divine, pure element, a portion of the world is thine: all-taming artist, all-diffusive power, 'tis thine, supreme, all substance to devour: aether, sun, moon, and stars, light pure and clear, for these thy lucid parts [of fire] to men appear. To thee all dwellings, cities, tribes belong, diffused through mortal bodies, rich and strong. Hear, blessed power, to holy rites incline, and all propitious on the incense shine: suppress the rage of fire's unwearied frame, and still preserve our nature's vital flame."*[153]

As already mentioned, Hephaestus had a temple within the Athenian Agora, it was situated in the ancient metal workers' quarter and is now the best preserved of Greek temples. The temple was decorated with scenes of battle and heroism and contained statues of Athena and Hephaestus – note that the offspring of Hephaestus's failed seduction of Athena, Erikhthonios, became the first Athenian King. As with Ares there is little archaeological evidence of other temple worship, but there are a number of records of rites and festivals held in honour of Hephaestus. Some of these, such as torch races celebrating his gift of fire to mankind and the Khalkeia (Bronzes) festival, were originally celebrated by all peoples but later became private ceremonies observed by craftsmen (and particularly metal workers). Aelian gives a particularly evocative account of a Sicilian grove with sacred trees and an ever burning fire where hounds fawned on the kind man, ripped to pieces the man with hands stained with crime, and chased away the man who had lain

---

[151] Brewer, *Dictionary of Phrase and Fable*, 'Lemnian Deed'.
[152] Aeschylus, (458BC), *The Libation Bearers*.
[153] Taylor, *Orphic Hymn 66 to Hephaestus*.

on the bed of debauchery[154] - one doesn't have to look hard to guess who might have inspired this tradition.

> "Sing, clear-voiced Mousa, of Hephaistos famed for inventions (klytometis). With bright-eyed Athene he taught men glorious crafts throughout the world,--men who before used to dwell in caves in the mountains like wild beasts. But now that they have learned crafts through Hephaistos the famed worker (klytotekhnes), easily they live a peaceful life in their own houses the whole year round. Be gracious, Hephaistos, and grant me success and prosperity!"[155]

One way of exploring the power of Ares and Hephaestus is through fire. Ares can be seen as destructive wild-fire, spreading fear and chaos, destroying everything in its path; in contrast Hephaestus is the controlled and creative fire which can work metal, transform, purify (and at times be used in battle). I have mentioned the motif of bronze and I think it is important to consider that the smith works with metal and bends it to his will, while the soldier wears it and is protected by it. For me, Ares and Hephaestus seem to spark off each other, to bend around each other, to intermingle and entwine like glowing metal in the furnace. Like the Soldier, Ares is fierce and direct, but like the Smith, Hephaestus both manipulates the metal he works and bends his art to its nature in order to bring out its best qualities. The archaeological and historical evidence of cult worship support connections with Athena and Aphrodite for both Gods, hint at shared aspects, and suggest a filial bond forged of animosity and rivalry.

Olympian Order

In early accounts both Ares and Hephaestus are described as the sons of Zeus and Hera – making them the most likely heirs to the Olympian throne. Later, Hephaestus was popularly believed to be born of Hera alone; supposedly as her revenge on Zeus for birthing Athena by himself, but this explanation is flawed because Hephaestus acted as Zeus's *'midwife'* at Athena's birth and so had to be born first. Ovid later tells of a similar conception for Mars (the Roman equivalent to Ares) saying:

> "I nipped the clinging flower with my thumb,
> Touched Juno, and as I touched her breast she conceived.
> Pregnant now, she travelled to Thrace and the northern shores

---

[154] Aelian, (2nd-3rd century CE) *On Animals* 11. 3.
[155] White, *Homeric Hymn 20 to Hephaestus*.

> *Of Propontis: her wish was granted, and Mars was born."*[156]

It is also worth noting that these later tales result in Ares, Hephaestus, Athena and Aphrodite all being the progeny of lone parents - products of *'love gone wrong'*, illegitimate children conceived in anger, violence or fear. Who knows why the Greeks and Romans had such a fascination with creating single-parent offspring for their ruling deities – my suspicion would be that it suited the ruling classes to have no potential successors to their chief God. It is also worthwhile considering the threat Ares and Hephaestus pose as patrons of neighbouring regions (particularly the larger Thrace) as well as two civic groups essential to the state function (craftsmen and soldiers). Burkert hints at the possibility of powerful roots for Hephaestus stemming from a tradition of smith-kingship in the Late Hittite tradition[157] and it is interesting to note the figure of the magickal smith, lameness, vengeance and power in other traditions[158] (e.g. the Northern European Weland/Volund, and Biblical Tubal-Cain). However, by the time of the Greeks, Burkert claims, *"The Greek cities relegated craftsmanship to a secondary place in favour of the warrior arete"*[159] (note the root from 'Ares' - war).

Regardless of the status of those who enjoyed their patronage, Hephaestus and Ares fare no better than many of their siblings in attracting their parents' affection – and do significantly worse than some. While Hephaestus is flung from Heaven by either one, or both, of his parents, in the *Iliad* Zeus says to Ares:

> *"To me you are the most hateful of all the gods who hold Olympos. Forever quarrelling is dear to your heart, wars and battles ... were you born of some other god and proved so ruinous long since you would have been dropped beneath the gods of the bright sky."*[160]

For her part, their mother often seems completely devoid of maternal instinct - when she isn't throwing new-born Hephaestus to the Earth, she is siding with the other Olympians against Ares. I particularly like Homer's description of Hera's wrath at rampaging Ares during the Trojan War:

---

[156] Ovid, *Fasti: Book V* (trans. Kline.)
[157] Walter Burkert, *Greek Religion*, p. 167.
[158] Nemet-Nejat, *Daily Life in Ancient Mesopotamia*, p. 294.
[159] Walter Burkert, *Greek Religion*, p. 167.
[160] Homer (800BCE) *Iliad* 5.699.

Vs.

> *"There Hera stayed her horses, and spoke to Zeus the son of Kronos, lord of all. 'Father Zeus,' said she, 'Are you not angry with Ares for these high doings? See how great and goodly a host of the Achaeans he has destroyed to my great grief, and without either right or reason, while the Cyprian and Apollo are enjoying it all at their ease and setting this unrighteous madman on to do further mischief. I hope, Father Zeus, that you will not be angry if I hit Ares hard, and chase him out of the battle.' And Zeus answered, 'Set Athena on to him, for she punishes him more often than any one else does'."*[161]

For all his kindly nature we know from the tale of the adultery of Ares and Aphrodite that Hephaestus can take vengeance when needed. Unlike his brother who might bellow in anger and attack head-on (often wound up by others), Hephaestus uses his technical skills to entrap his enemies (presumably because he would lose in a direct attack). The Ares-Aphrodite net is in fact a reprise of an earlier trap set by Hephaestus for his mother Hera in revenge for her maternal rejection and his fall from Olympus. In this myth he sends a gift of a throne to Hera which, when sat upon, effectively traps her – it is only when his friend Dionysus gets him drunk that he eventually agrees to release Hera.[162] Despite these occasional misdemeanours, however, both Ares and Hephaestus largely work in support of their parents' interests. In one instance Aeschylus portrays Hephaestus's defence of his father against accusations of cruelty toward Prometheus (who stole Hephaestus's fire), saying *'the heart of Zeus is hard, and everyone is harsh whose power is new'*;[163] in some ways this seems like rather a back handed compliment as Hephaestus isn't denying that Zeus has a hard heart – it is more that he seems to recognise the reasons for this. While Ares seems to be controlled by the manipulations of his family, Hephaestus appears more as a willing pawn and at times a colluder. In the Iliad he counsels peace between his mother and Zeus:

> *"Hephaistos the renowned smith (klytotekhnes) rose up to speak among them, to bring comfort to his beloved mother, Hera of the white arms: 'This will be a disastrous matter and not endurable if you two are to quarrel thus for the sake of mortals and bring brawling among the gods. There will be no pleasure in the stately feast at all, since vile things will be uppermost. And I entreat my mother, though she herself understands it, to be ingratiating toward our*

---

[161] Homer (800BCE), *Iliad*, Book V.
[162] Pausanias, *Description of Greece*, 1.20.3
[163] Aeschylus, *Prometheus Bound* 34-35.

> *father Zeus, that no longer our father may scold her and break up the quiet of our feasting. For if the Olympian [Zeus] who handles the lightning should be minded to hurl us out of our places, he is far too strong for any'.*"[164]

He goes on to subject himself to divine laughter by taking on the role of cup-bearer which causes the assembled company amusement at his expense – but it also restores the peace. We can see here that Hephaestus has accepted Zeus's power and so seeks to maintain the status quo by soothing his father – this was a lesson learned after a previous attempt to take his mother's side in an argument resulted in his second fall from Olympus, this time at the hands of his father.[165]

It is important to bear in mind that Hera's coolness is not limited to her two sons, as Burkert says *"Never is Hera invoked as mother, and never is she represented as a mother with a child... Her womanhood is confined to her relationship with her husband."*[166] Hephaestus and Ares are not the sons of a *'mother-goddess'*; they are the sons of a Queen and King who are more committed to each other, and to power, than they are to their children. Although this piece isn't about them, to be fair to Zeus and Hera I should note that the King and Queen of Olympus don't have an easy job by any means and need to cultivate every advantage available.

As we have seen from the Homeric hymn to Ares, the war-god is described as the *'defender of Olympus'*. In *The Fall of Troy* Ares *'darted, swift and bright as thunderbolt terribly flashing from the mighty hand of Zeus'*[167] (contrast this with the similar description of Hercules earlier and note that perhaps Zeus moves his favour amongst his sons when he feels like it). As we know, Ares is sometimes said to be the embodiment of fire or war, and sometimes he was worshipped as a sword. I find the idea of him taking on the role of the thunderbolt of Zeus particularly compelling because Hephaestus is said to forge these (and also note that Zeus only gives his daughter Athena the right to wield his thunderbolts). In the image of the thunderbolt we find a perfect fusion of the smith who creates the weapon, the soldier who has the courage to strike with it, and the leader who has the power and wisdom to direct it – perhaps the fiery tensions in Olympus are required for this fusion to be achieved?

Hephaestus is made lame by one or both of his parents but Ares is *'harnessed in bronze'*[168] (consider also his entrapment in the

---

[164] Homer (800BCE), *Iliad, Book I*.
[165] Homer (800BCE), *Iliad, Book I*.
[166] Walter Burkert, *Greek Religion* p. 133.
[167] Quintus Smyrnaeus, *Fall of Troy* 7.400ff.
[168] White, *Homeric Hymn to Ares*.

Vs.

bronze barrel, the controlling of his son's horses with a bronze manger, and the net Hephaestus forges to catch his wife and her lover in the act.)[169] Although Athena is said to punish Ares most often, it is Hephaestus who is able to trap and channel his power and so bend it in service to Olympus (note again the idea of the Smith, the metal and the fire of the forge).

In the writings of Homer and the temples of the Athenian Agora we see the achievement of harmony and spiritual unity completed. The Iliad paints one scene where the intrigues and skirmishes of Olympus seem forgotten - Ares and Athena take to the battlefield clad in fine armour (presumably forged by their brother):

> *"And Ares led them, and Pallas Athene. These were gold, both, and golden raiment upon them, and they were beautiful and huge in their armour, being divinities, and conspicuous from afar..."*[170]

Lamed Hephaestus is the Smith who serves and, once tamed, Ares discharges the will of Olympus. This fusion in myth is mirrored in Athens at the height of its glory where Plato describes the city wardens (or police of Athens) as *'the officers of Ares.'*[171] In Athena's city the war-god shares his temple with Aphrodite and Athena, while lame Hephaestus is paired not with his wife but with the Goddess whom he helped to birth and who later refused his advances. Through a complex set of symbols, myths, and sleights of hand, the power-mongers of Olympus ensure that these two brothers place themselves and their powers at their disposal – any threat they might have presented is directed towards each other in the heat and clamour of the battle and the forge.

Counter-myth

The tale of how Zeus Olympios avoided the fate of his father and sealed the animosity of his sons.

Fair Providence hath decreed that the King of the Gods shall be overthrown by a triad of his lawful progeny. So it was that, led by Zeus, the sons of Rhea de-manned Father Kronos (as he had done to father Ouranos before him) and divided his kingdom in three; and the greatest portion went to Zeus, leader of the Gods. Praise be to Zeus Olympios [of Olympus]!

Once enthroned Zeus liked not the prophecy and quickly determined to change it. To this end he let it be known that by swallowing his first bride, Metis [wisdom] and her unborn child, he had tamed the future to his own will. But it was not so and Zeus

---

[169] Homer, *Iliad*, Book V.
[170] Homer, *Iliad* 18.516.
[171] Plato, *Laws* 670b.

Vs.

Kosmetas [of divine order] knew it. Praise be to Zeus Megistos [most great]! Praise be to Zeus Nomos [law]!

Now Zeus cast about for a new Queen who would be both beautiful and faithful, but with a love of power as strong as his own. Pure Hestia he discarded for her lack of ambition. Passionate Demeter too - for she loved her children better than her consorts. In Hera Hyperkheria [she whose hand is above] he found a Queen who knew the worth of power. The white-armed maiden matched his every desire and so he submitted to her yoke. Upon the peak they made their pact; Zeus Horkios [keeper of oaths] named Hera his Queen of Heaven and, as the Goddess took the throne, so he channelled her ambition to his own ends. Zeus Teleios [husband of Hera] we bow before Thee! Hera Gamelia [of marriage] we adore Thee!

To the sons of this blessed union the powers of heavenly fire were given. The sweet air of Heaven rang with their laughter and the clashing of arms. Delighters in competition these brothers two, each surpassing each in turn so their strength and valour grew. None could match the bronze-armed sons of Hera Basileia [queen], not the golden arrows of Leto's twins, nor the quick-silver feet of the trickster. Hera Krusothronos [golden-throned] smiled to see her sons outshine all Zeus's unlawful issue; how magnificent the Queen of Immortals looked, her chariot pulled by the horses of Ares, her feet shod with Hephaestus-crafted sandals of pure gold. Mother and sons sped across the skies as fiery comets - cities fell in trembling wonder before these divine brothers and rose up higher and more magnificent in their honour. Glory to Thee Ares Obrimos [mighty and strong]! Everlasting fame to Hephaestus Lampados [torch]!

All this Zeus saw with brooding looks and thunder in his heart. Fair Providence whispered in his ear once more while, inside his very skull, the clamouring of the child of Metis grew louder each day and his head seemed ready to split. The power of this entombed heir set even Zeus Laphystios [devourer] to tremble, and he knew that soon Providence would have her way and his crown would crack and his sons be united. Each day he sat upon the mountain peak, watching the world and bargaining with his clamouring child – two oaths he demanded in return for freedom, yet still the child refused. Hail to Thee Child of Metis [wisdom]! Hail to Thee warrior youth!

Strange to tell, it was the last daughter of fallen Ouranos who brought the answer Zeus Akraios [of the peak] sought: foam born Aphrodite, rising from the frothing ocean in naked splendour. As he watched the Cyprian set her foot upon the shore, Zeus Kronidês [son of Kronos] saw his chance and quickly set his chariot on its homeward journey. That night Zeus Meilichios [honey-eyed], whispered to his Queen of a secret plot, hatched by her own gentle Hephaestus, to kill Mighty Zeus and snatch Hera from the throne. Long into the night he spoke, offering cunningly derived proofs – it is not hard to convince a jealous sovereign that another covets the seat

Vs.

of power. Before daybreak and the coming of clear-sighted Eos [dawn], the Queen of Heaven flung her son down from Olympus and his body was broken upon the shores of Lemnos. Hail to Thee Hephaestus Kyllopodiôn [crooked foot]! Hail to Thee Hera Teleia [wife of Zeus]!

From the fair isle of Lemnos and the depths of the blue sea Hephaestus Polymêtis [resourceful, of many crafts] received nurture and teaching. Drawing power from the fires of Gaia [earth], he made himself anew and claimed the powers of the Smith for his own. While Aithaloeis Theos [the sooty god] prepared for vengeance, Zeus let it be known that his once-beloved son had abandoned Olympus. To Ares, Zeus Phratrios [of brotherhood] whispered of an elder son impatient with the younger, of plans for adventure and heroic deed hatched with a mind to shame fiery Ares and prove Hephaestus the greater. Ares Thouros [furious] raged at this reported betrayal, his warrior-pride unchecked by the gentle arts of his absent brother. Hera too was scorched by rage, quelling doubt and regret with righteous anger – and who would deny that the duty of the Queen is to defend the throne from those who threaten it? An easy task to weave a tale of unnatural birth and render Hephaestus Khalkeus [bronze-smith] no more the son of Zeus, merely a whisper was needed to send it speeding upon the backs of the winds. Hail to thee Zeus Semaleos [of weather signs]! Hail to Thee Zeus Euanemos [of fair wind]!

And now Zeus Philanthropos [kindly] brings Aphrodite Ourania [heavenly] to Olympus and, arduous as he finds himself for this Goddess of Love, she too must play her allotted part and bend to his design. Often he arranges for the Seductress and his younger son to meet, as if by chance, in some bower or grotto. How fateful it is then, that Aphrodite Hetaira [courtesan] should return the passion of ardent Ares Gynaikothoinas [feasted by women]. Providence at last colludes in Zeus's plot. So it is that the trap is laid and all too easy to spring: the Smith returns, exacting his revenge by trapping Hera in a throne, the very symbol of her power, and what more fitting reward for her release can Zeus Tropais [awarding the trophy] give his truant son than the hand of fair Aphrodite Areia [of Ares]? Hail to Three Aphrodite Nymphia [bridal]! Hail to the marriage of Love and Art!

How Ares Chalcocorustes [armed in bronze] rages as his brother's triumph rips his heart in two! Compassion and love are as ashes in his mouth as he speeds from Heaven. To Thrace he descends to expend his rage and grief in warfare and battle-frenzy. How easy it is for the tale to spread that he too was conceived through un-natural means; how little Ares cares if he is heir or no - for love is lost to him. Hail to Three Ares Aphneius [abundant]! Hail to Thee Ares Brotoloigos [murderous]!

And now the last act of our tale is come. The child who fought so long sees defeat and clamours no more, instead accepting the terms

Vs.

of Zeus Asbameus [protector of oaths]: to be born woman and remain forever Virgin. So Athen becomes Athena, most beloved of Zeus's children, neither son nor mother of an heir. By the axe-stroke of Hephaestus is the Goddess released from her father's skull: and never will the bronze brothers know that, as brother, she promised the overthrow of Olympus but, as sister, she would enslave our heroes to their father's purpose. Hail to Thee Athena Chalkiokikos [of the brazen house]! Hail to Thee Zeus Euergetes [benefactor]!

Through your mysteries conflict turns to peace.

Bibliography
Aelian, *On Animals* 1, Books 1-5, trans. Scholfield, A.F. Loeb Classical Library, 1958.
Aeschylus, *Prometheus Bound,* Translated by Herbert Weir Smith, 1926, http://www.perseus.tufts.edu/hopper/text?doc=Perseus%3atext%3a1999.01.0010
Aeschylus, *The Libation Bearers* Translated by I. Johnston May 2005, Malaspina University College, online at:
http://records.viu.ca/~Johnstoi/aeschylus/libationbearers.htm
Aeschylus, *Eumenides*, Translated by E.D.A Moreshead http://classics.mit.edu/Aeschylus/eumendides.html
Apollodorus, *The Library* Translated by Sir James George Frazer, 1921 http://www.theoi.com/Text/Apollodorus1.html
Aristophanes, *Birds*, 414 BCE,
http://classics.mit.edu/Aristophanes/birds.html
E.C., Brewer's *Dictionary of Phrase and Fable.* Cassell, 2003.
Burkert, W., *Greek Religion.* Basil Blackwell, 1985.
Cerneko, E.V. *The Scythians 700-300BC*, Osprey Publishing, 1983
Euripides, *The Cyclops,* Translated by E.P. Coleridge at http://classics.mit.edu/Euripides/cyclops.html
Herodotus (The History of), Book III, http://www.sacred-texts.com/cla/hh/hh3030.htm
Hesiod, *The Theogony of Hesiod,* Translated by Hugh G. Evelyn-White, 1914 http://www.sacred-texts.com/cla/hesiod/theogony.htm
Homer, *Iliad*, trans. Butler, Samuel. Dover Publications, 1999.
Homer, *Odyssey,* trans Butler, Samuel. Boomer Books, 2008.
Hyginus, *Fabulae* Translated by Mary Grant at http://www.theoi.com/Text/HyginusFabulae4.html#166
Kline, A.S., *Ovid: Fasti*, online at:
http://www.poetryintranslation.com/PITBR/Latin/Fastihome.htm
Nemet-Nejat, K.R., *Daily life in ancient Mesopotamia.* Greenwood Press, 1998.
Pausanias, *Description of Greece* 1: Books I and II, trans. Jones W.H.S. Harvard University Press, 1969.
Philostratus, *Life of Apollonius of Tyana*, Translated by Conybeare
Plato, *Laws*, trans. Jowett, B. Prometheus Books, 2000.
Quintus Smyrnaeus, *Fall of Troy*, Loeb Classical Library no. 19, trans. Way, A.S. Loeb, 1913.
Seneca, *Medea,* Translated by Frank Justus Miller at http://www.theoi.com/Text/SenecaMedea.html

Spawforth, T., *The Complete Greek Temples.* Thames & Hudson, 2006.
Taylor, T., trans., *Orphic Hymns.* London, 1792.
Virgil, *Aeneid* trans. Dryden, John. Penguin Classics, 1997.
White, E., trans., *Shield of Heracles.* 1914
http://ancienthistory.about.com/od/homer/a/HomerTOC.htm
White, E (Trans) (1914), *Homeric Hymns.* BiblioBazaar, 2007.

Websites:
Perseus Digital Library: http://www.perseus.tufts.edu/hopper/
Thrace: http://www.thracian.info
Theoi Greek Mythology: http://www.theoi.com

Vs.

RIDERS UPON SWIFT HORSES

the Divine Twins of Greek myth

by Karen F. Pierce

> "Bright eyed Muses, tell of the Tyndaridae, the Sons of Zeus, glorious children of neat-ankled Leda, Castor the tamer of horses, and blameless Polydeuces. When Leda had lain with the dark-clouded Son of Cronos, she bare them beneath the peak of the great hill Taygetus, - children who are deliverers of men on earth and of swift-going ships when stormy gales rage over the ruthless sea. Then the shipmen call upon the sons of great Zeus with vows of white lambs, going to the forepart of the prow; but the strong wind and the waves of the sea lay the ship under water, until suddenly these two are seen darting through the air on tawny wings. Forthwith they allay the blasts of the cruel winds and still the waves upon the surface of the white sea: fair signs are they and deliverance from toil. And when the shipmen see them they are glad and have rest from their pain and labour.
> Hail Tyndaridae, riders upon swift horses! Now I will remember you and another song also."
> ~ Homeric Hymn to the Dioscuri (XXXIII)[172]

Introduction

Divine twins are found in the myths of many cultures, and it has been noted that patterns and similarities abound throughout these stories. Mythologically many divine twins are believed to derive from an Indo-European prototype, as represented by the Asvins in the *Rig Veda*, a collection of hymns dating from around 2000-1700 BCE, the archaic period in Indian culture. One of the most famous set of twins are Castor and Polydeuces (Castor and Pollux),[173] collectively known as the Dioscuri (sons of Zeus) or as the Tyndaridae, an epithet that

---

[172] Translation by Allen et al (1936).
[173] Throughout this paper the Latinised forms of Greek names will be used, being those probably more familiar to a general audience. Hence, Castor and Polydeuces rather than Kastor and Polydeukes, and Dioscuri rather than Dioskouroi, etc. Pollox is the Roman version of Polydeuces.

appears to relate to their step-father Tyndareus, although some believe his character was invented to explain their collective name. They are Greek heroes, who take part in heroic (although not particularly outstanding) adventures; but who assume a greater mythical mantle at the point of death, and beyond. When Castor is mortally wounded, Polydeuces, unable to face the idea of life without him, appeals to Zeus to grant immortality to his brother (for in the majority of stories about the twins one is immortal and one mortal); and subsequently they share this immortality between themselves, spending one day in the heavens, and the next beneath the ground.

It is immediately apparent that there is a distinctive duality about Castor and Polydeuces; the twins are dead, and not dead; mortal and immortal; forever separated in their immortality (in some variants), and yet together as deities (in others). In life and in death they are not obviously polar opposites, not drawn as good and evil, but complementary and loyal. The stories attached to them do not end at the point of death/deification and there are sightings of them reported within Classical texts, usually coming to the aid of whoever they appear to. Their heroism goes beyond death, and they are worshipped as deities both at home (Sparta), further afield in Greece, and beyond to Rome, and even to the *'Celtic world'*.

To try to understand these particular divine twins a little better, we will first take a look at their mythical life and death in Part 1, exploring important motifs and highlighting those that represent their archetype. Part 2 will move on to their cult, which survived for many centuries, and will discuss the signs and symbols that are an essential part of their mythical *'genetic make-up'*. At the same time comparisons to other divine twins will be made, namely the Asvins and the Baltic Divine Twins, as we explore the similarities most apparent between them. By doing so we may also throw some light on the concept of divine twins in general.

Part 1: Mythical life and death

- Birth

Myths are living and breathing entities, especially in their oral form; a different slant for a different audience, a re-interpretation for a new moment, but a core truth beneath the veneer, which is why we have variations in our mythical stories. Once written down they tend to become more static, fixed to the page, and there is a tendency to believe that some versions are 'truer' than others. Instead we should try and listen to what each variant has to tell us, as each story has its own validity. However, we should also take into consideration for whom the tale was intended, a gender specific gathering or a rich patron perhaps, as most poets will have some kind of bias.

Within Greek myth the Dioscuri are no exceptions to the rule of multiple versions, from the moment of their birth to Castor's last breath we are left juggling with slightly differing, though overlapping, versions of their *'truth'*. The differences may be slight at times, but all give us some insight into the duality of their being.

Castor and Polydeuces were born to Leda, but there is some confusion over their father: was he Zeus or Tyndareus, did they have a dual paternity? At times they are both mortal, at others both divine, and perhaps the most widespread belief makes one mortal and one divine, bringing an interesting duality to their life and death.

In our earliest poetic sources, the Homeric epics, we learn relatively little about Castor and Polydeuces, the actions of these poems taking place after their death and apotheosis. In book three of the *Iliad* Helen is looking for them on the battlefield to no avail (they are already dead), but here we first learn of the attributes traditionally associated with the twins. Castor is described as *'tamer of horses'* and Polydeuces as *'good at the fist'* i.e. boxing. The same epithets are also used in the *Odyssey*, and are repeated in subsequent literature. In book eleven of the *Odyssey* the twins are said to have been fathered by Tyndareus, although they were shown special favour by Zeus so that they could share alternate immortality. It may appear strange that their divine birth is not acknowledged within the Homeric epics, especially when their sister Helen is named as a daughter of Zeus on seven occasions. Homer is obviously aware of their semi-divinity, but instead chooses to emphasise their mortal aspects. To him they are Tyndaridae rather than Dioscuri. If they are not sons of Zeus, their shared immortality might take on a different slant. It could be perceived that they earned it by their actions rather than their birth.

Unusually for heroes they have two Homeric Hymns composed about them.[174] A number of these hymns, such as the *Hymn to Demeter*, are of substantial length, but both the hymns to the Dioscuri are comparatively brief. They are similar in content, though no. 33 is longer than no. 17. They are undated but thought to have been written at least prior to Theocritus *Idyll* 22, which is believed to have imitated the description of the storm; it is thought they may even have been composed before the 6th century BCE.[175]

These Hymns record the earliest literary evidence for the appellation *'Dioscuri'* which by the 5th century BCE had become their established title,[176] although it only appears in the title of the Hymns (To the Dioscuri). Despite this title within them they are still collectively called the Tyndaridae, although they are described as

---

[174] The Homeric Hymns are a collection of poems, or preludes, of unknown author written over a number of centuries.
[175] Theocritus lived in the first half of the 3rd century BCE. Allen et al (1936, 436) mention an inscription found at Cephallenia which is believed to indicate that the Hymn was well known before the sixth century BCE (*IG*. IX.1.649).
[176] Dios kouroi = sons/youths of Zeus. The earliest epigraphic evidence is on an inscription from Thera, dated possibly as early as the 7th century BCE (*IG* XII.3.359).

sons of Zeus and Leda.[177] Thus whilst in Homer they are both mortal (sons of Tyndareus), in the *Homeric Hymns* they are both divine (sons of Zeus). It is within Pindar's *Nemean Ode* 10 that we have the dual paternity laid out in detail for us, at the point of Castor's death, when Zeus reveals to Polydeuces that Leda slept with him and Tyndareus in the same night.[178] Leda's relations with Zeus are (later) viewed in the guise of rape as many divine/mortal couplings are, and an element of bestiality is added (as with many other divine/mortal rapes). She is said to be raped or seduced by Zeus in the form of a swan. More often this story is attached to the siring and birth of Helen, but the rape/birth stories are sometimes mingled. Thus Leda is raped by Zeus as a swan and bears an egg (or two) and from this egg hatches not only Castor and Polydeuces, but also Helen (and possibly Clytemnestra as well). As noted the whole Zeus/Swan/Egg myths are more fully detailed in relation to Helen, and there are even other variants in which the goddess Nemesis is the one who is actually raped by Zeus in the form of either a swan or goose after she has gone through many metamorphoses of creatures (including a fish) in an attempt to escape, with all the overtones and similarities of other metamorphic traditions including the rape of Thetis. Nemesis lays the egg, which is subsequently given to Leda to hatch; nothing is ever simple in Greek myth![179]

Although the swan/egg motif is not overemphasised for the Dioscuri, and as such is probably a conflating of two myths (theirs and Helen's), it is still a minor recurrent theme, even within art. There are vase paintings which depict Leda and the egg; sometimes the Dioscuri are shown standing around as adult males, which demonstrates that the egg is about Helen rather than them, whilst other depictions show the three of them within, or emerging from the egg.[180]

---

[177] As mentioned above scholars believe that their foster father Tyndareus was invented to explain their original collective name – Tyndaridae – but do not know what this name originally meant. See for e.g. Burkert (1985, 212).

[178] This particular Ode was composed in the 5th century BCE in honour of Theaeus, son of Ulias, for a wrestling victory at Argos. The inclusion of the Dioscuri story is particularly relevant since a distant relative of the winner had apparently once entertained two strangers in his house, who subsequently showed themselves to be the Dioscuri, and henceforth they were regarded as the family's patrons.

[179] There is a myth about another pair of twins, Eurytos and Cteatus, sons of Actor and Molione (and commonly referred to as the Molionids) who were born from a silver egg. See Ibycus fr. 285 *PMG* ; Plutarch *De. Frat. Am.* 478C. Additionally within Orphic cosmology there was a Cosmic Egg from which a divine being named Phanes emerges; this figure is regarded as the first born god and fills the world with radiance.

[180] See for instance a marble sarcophagus, Aix-en Provence, Granet Museum; *LIMC* IV s.v. *Helene* 11; 2nd century CE; a Stucco relief , National Museum of Rome 113217; *LIMC* IV s.v. *Helene* 12 / *LIMC* III s.v. *Dioskouroi/Castores* 146; Vespasian epoch; and a mosaic, Treves, Imperial residence; *LIMC* III s.v. *Dioskouroi/Castores* 145; 4th century CE.

Vs.

In book three of Pausanias' *Guide to Greece*, he mentions Leda's egg which he claims is now contained within a sanctuary of Hilaera and Phoebe (the Leucippides), and is hanging from the roof tied with ribbons (3.16.1). If there had been an actual egg that Helen or the Dioscuri had emerged from, surely it would only have survived as cracked egg shell, since by necessity their birth would have broken the egg (though perhaps the ribbons are holding the fragments together). However, it is interesting that a symbolic or representational egg was deemed important enough as a sacred object to be included in the sanctuary. It also indicates that there was a close link between the Leucippides and Leda, which would presumably have been through the Dioscuri. We have a Spartan relief carving of the Dioscuri[181] which depicts an egg above the two figures. On first look the egg is surrounded by what could be described as ribbons, which would tie in nicely with Pausanias' description, however on closer inspection they are actually snakes, which are a common Dioscuric symbol (see below).

Whether born from an egg or not, intriguing birth stories of the twins lend greater mystique to their myth, but also possibly have older origins and relate back to earlier divine twin prototypes. Whether both originally divine or not, the story of Castor being mortal and Polydeuces immortal captures the imagination of the poets (and to a certain extent is reflected in their sisters, where we have a mortal Clytemnestra alongside the immortal Helen).

- **Exploits**

As adults the heroic exploits of the twins fall into three categories; their exploits on the Argo with Jason, rescuing their sister Helen from Theseus, and their relations and confrontations with another set of twin brothers, Idas and Lynceus, which ultimately leads to their death and immortalisation.

Relatively little is made of their activities on the Argo, although Polydeuces does demonstrate his boxing skills when he fights and defeats Amycus, the arrogant King and bully of the Bebryces. Polydeuces does sometimes have the epithet *'good at the fist'* and this story ably demonstrates why.[182] Without meaning to belittle the Argo stories, which do after all exemplify the idealised masculinity and heroic status of the twins, I believe that the myths attached to the brothers' rescue of Helen, and interactions with Idas and Lynceus are more important to the archetypal divine twin concept. Although, their presence on the Argo does demonstrate their experience as sea voyagers, and hence adds to their status as saviours of those at sea.

---

[181] Spartan relief carving on blue marble, Sparta Museum 575; 525-500 BCE.
[182] See Apollonius Rhodius *Argonautica* 1.147-51, 2.1-97 and Theocritus *Idylls* 22.

Vs.

- **Rescuing Helen**

Before Helen's more famous abduction by Paris to Troy, she was also abducted by the Greek hero Theseus when she was much younger (some sources say she was as young as 7 or 10), her beauty already being apparent. He desired her and wished to marry her, abducted her and took her to Aphidna where she was placed with his mother Aethra for safe keeping, while he went off to attempt to fulfil an even more foolish mission with his friend Perithous, to abduct Persephone from Hades. While he was absent the Dioscuri ably rescued Helen and captured Aethra in return.[183]

Isocrates' *Helen* written c.370 BCE was written as an encomium to Helen, but within it he digresses to praise the Athenian hero Theseus; as such this text give us an illustration of Athenian power versus Spartan might, with the Athenian hero making a mockery of all that is of Spartan importance – their royal family, their heroes, their *'trophy'* woman. In this version little is made of the Spartan heroes' actual triumph and rescue of Helen. Isocrates' muffling of the Dioscuri's exploits emasculates, disempowers and renders them as nothing against the power of Theseus, and hence we see how an author's bias can twist a myth to their own agenda.

In Plutarch's version (*Theseus* 31.2) he describes Helen as being abducted from the dancing floor of the temple of Artemis Orthia; snatched from a physically liminal place – outside the city boundaries. Neither purely wild, nor purely civilised, but from the edge of society.[184] Artemis herself represents liminality and the transition from virginal maidenhood to marriage. These details are significant to a story (see below) told by Pausanias (4.16.9-10) which involves the abduction of Spartan girls after the prevention of an initial attack by the appearance of the Dioscuri and Helen.

During their mission to rescue Helen the Dioscuri ransack the villages of Attica until they find her. We have stories here about the rivalries between Sparta and Athens (especially demonstrated in Isocrates' telling), which bring the myth down to a local level; however we are also seeing a more universal myth being

---

[183] The main sources for this story are Isocrates, Plutarch, Diodorus Siculus, and Apollodorus. The difference in tone in these versions does illustrate to a significant extent what difference a poet's bias and agenda can make to a myth.

[184] Cole (1998) states that 'Sanctuaries of Artemis were often located some distance from inhabited settlements, at the extremities of a city's territory. Sacred space on a border defined the limits of a city's territory and protected the transitional area that divided one community from another.' (27) She goes on to suggest that 'There was a recognisable correspondence between the vulnerability of a city's women and the vulnerability of a city's borders...Violation of the safety of females at these sites was a sign of ritual failure and indicated that the security of the polis was threatened by a war with its neighbours.' As Cole herself notes, the story of Helen's abduction by Theseus from the sanctuary of Artemis Orthia can be seen as a good example of a mythological tale illustrating the perception of women and boundaries as interconnected. We are learning not only about Helen's mythology, but about enmities between Attica and Sparta.

demonstrated: the abduction of a sun-maiden, and her rescue by the twin-riders, an older indo-European myth, seen also in the Vedic myths and elsewhere (see below). This myth is tied to Helen as much as it is to the Dioscuri – perhaps even more so, as we see it repeated later in her story, when she is abducted by Paris. In some sense Castor and Polydeuces are conspicuously absent at this point in Helen's myth and thus fail in their role as her saviours by not rescuing her from Paris. The logical explanation for this which the poets from Homer onwards have given, is that Castor and Polydeuces have already died. In their place we have Menelaus and Agamemnon coming to the rescue, two brothers (though not twins) who are ultimately successful. The two sets of brothers appear to have comparative story patterns within myth, as we see that the fate of the brothers in the afterlife reflects to a certain extent that of the Dioscuri. Just as Castor is mortal and Polydeuces immortal, Agamemnon dies and Menelaus is granted eternal life with Helen in the Elysian Fields.[185] The repetition of this mythic pattern of abduction and then rescue by two brothers is important and demonstrates the older roots it derives from.

- **Relations with twins**

There are other stories attached to the Dioscuri that demonstrate their links to the archetypal divine twins, and these involve their relations with two other sets of twins, one set male, and one set female. It is perhaps here more than anywhere that we see a polarity in action that isn't apparent between Castor and Polydeuces themselves.

The rivalry between them and the male twins, Idas and Lynceus (sons of Aphareus) inevitably leads to the death of these mortal twins and the death/deification of the Dioscuri. Idas and Lynceus are superficially portrayed as the *'bad'* twins to Castor and Polydeuces' *'good'* twinness, but their actions are not any more evil or worse than anything Castor and Polydeuces actually do. They are also avatars of Greek masculinity, but ultimately do not have Zeus on their side. There are two variations on their fatal quarrel, one involving women and one involving cattle.

Idas and Lynceus were engaged to the daughters of Leucippus, their cousins Phoebe and Hilaera.[186] However, the Dioscuri wished to marry the girls themselves and carried them off, some versions say they kidnapped them on their actual wedding day. Hence we have Castor and Polydeuces acting in the wrong initially. In a world where the abduction of woman was, if not common-place, then certainly not unknown, Castor and Polydeuces have already rescued their sister

---

[185] See Homer *Odyssey* 4.561-569.
[186] According to some sources all six twins were cousins as Tyndareus, Aphareus and Leucippus were brothers.

from one such abduction, but are guilty themselves in this case. Abduction marriage is a concept that is mentioned throughout ancient sources, and comes to be reflected even in marriage ritual.

Idas and Lynceus, unsurprisingly, pursue Castor and Polydeuces and the fatal fight ensues. Other versions add to the story and relate how the fight actually came about due to a quarrel over cattle. The four of them took part in a raid and stole some cattle from Arcadia (all four equally as guilty in the initial wrongdoing). When they were trying to divide up the spoils Idas duped/tricked the Dioscuri and took all the cattle for himself and his brother. To take revenge the Dioscuri lay in wait for them, but Castor was spotted and killed; Polydeuces then slew Lynceus and Zeus brought down Idas. Polydeuces refused to accept his individual rights to immortality while his brother lay dead, so Zeus granted that they spend half their time among the Gods and the other half among the dead (or half in the heavens, and half under the ground). It isn't clear whether this meant they were always apart, or whether they shared their days together (different sources indicate both ways); although the general impression is that they were separated, when we come to look at their appearances it seems they are always seen together, and indeed this is one identifying factor.

Castor and Polydeuces are no better or worse that Idas and Lynceus in many respects, their only unique factor is their connection to Zeus, plus the fierce loyalty and love that Polydeuces has for his brother is shown to be extremely admirable.

To return to the female twins, there are interesting connections to horses (much as the main epithet of the Dioscuri is *'riders upon swift horses'*). Phoebe and Hilaera are the daughters of Leucippus, whose name means *'white horse'*. Pausanias (3.16.1) relates that in Sparta there was a sanctuary of Phoebe and Hilaera, where young maidens officiated as priestesses and were called *'the colts of the Leucippides'* after them. As we will discuss below Castor and Polydeuces are very much associated with horses and are even called the *'White colts of Zeus'* by Euripides. To have their brides essentially named as *'white mares'* is very significant. It is also interesting that in Sparta at least the Leucippides had their own cult. Although it is evident that the Dioscuri were deified shortly after carrying off their brides they did however apparently have time to consummate the marriages and sire a child each. Phoebe bore Mnesileus/Mnasinous (to Polydeuces) and Hilaera bore Anogon/Anaxis to Castor.[187] No more is known about them, or what happened to the Leucippides after the Dioscuri were deified.

---

[187] Apollodorus *Library* 3.11.2; Pausanias 2.22.6, 3.18.13; *Schol. Lycophron* 511. The names are slightly different in these sources. See Gantz (1993, 324-25).

Vs.

Part 2: Cult and symbolism
- Cult

Cult activity towards the Dioscuri was not restricted to their hometown of Sparta. The mythical stories about them were widespread (through time and space), and they were venerated throughout Greece and abroad; perhaps most notably at Rome where a temple was built in their honour in the forum. They even apparently reached the *'Celtic world'* according to Diodorus Siculus[188] who mentions that the Celts who *'dwell among the ocean'* venerate them, and have the tradition that the Dioscuri appear to them at sea. An altar was also found at Paris depicting them alongside various deities including Cernunnos, Jupiter and Vulcan.

Primarily of course we find evidence of their veneration throughout Greece. The 2nd century CE travel writer Pausanias is a wonderful source for stories of local cult activity, even though not much detail may be realised, the mention of a shrine or a temple helps to demonstrate how widespread some beliefs were, and the importance of some heroes or deities to a wide range of people. The Dioscuri (and Helen too), do have a *'home locality'*, a geographic area where they are *'local'*; i.e. Sparta and the state of Laconia. Myth places them at this location, and cult activity reinforces the connection; but myths and cults do travel, and the popularity of the Dioscuri is revealed to us thanks to a great extent to Pausanias.

Within Sparta itself Pausanias mentions several places sacred to the Dioscuri, including Castor's tomb, above which a sanctuary to the Dioscuri had been built at a later date (3.13.1); another sanctuary to them and the Charities (Graces) (3.14.6); at the racecourse the Dioscuri stand as Starting Gods (presumably statues) (3.14.7), and near a small trading square there is an altar to them as the Dioscuri of Counsel (3.13.6). There is even a house that had apparently been built by them (when they were mortal), and Pausanias (3.16.3) relates the story telling how they came to the new owner, a Spartan called Phormion, disguised as foreigners, and asked if they could stay in the room they had loved most when they were alive. Phormion told them they were welcome to stay in any room but that one which now belonged to his virgin daughter. The next morning his daughter had vanished and two statues of the Dioscuri were found in the room, along with a table with sylphium on it.[189] Abduction of a young maiden is not outside the remit of their mythical archetype, as we will see below, and it is curious to see if this story in some way reflects a deeper level to their myth, or if it is just an oddity.

Sparta was also known for having a duel kingship that appears to be tied up with the veneration of the Dioscuri. Herodotus (5.75)

---
[188] Diodorus Siculus *Library of History* 4.56.4.
[189] A magical, powerful medicinal plant that has not been identified in modern times.

relates a change in policy which meant that only one king would go out with the army, and one would stay in the capital. He notes that the same would follow for the Tyndaridae (one with the army, one at home). It is inferred that this may have referred to idols or images of Castor and Polydeuces; and thus the kingship and power was intrinsically linked to deity.

Throughout the rest of Greece there are various sanctuaries and temples. Some places have carved images of the Dioscuri, for instance in Argos within a temple there were figures of the Dioscuri, the Leucippides and their sons Anaxis and Mnasinous;[190] all were carved in ebony (2.22.6).[191] Elsewhere there are small bronze statues of the Dioscuri by the sea, on the island of Pephnos (3.26.3) and possibly also on a promontory as Brasiai (3.24.5). Both are locations in Laconia, and help to demonstrate the belief in the Dioscuri as *'sea gods'*.

- **Appearances**

The veneration of the Dioscuri as deities is promulgated/enhanced by the appearances they made to people within *'historical'* time, not only within Greece, but perhaps more surprisingly in Italy/Rome. These appearances make the divine twins more real, closer to man than some Gods; perhaps having once been mortal they are more easily able to walk amongst mortals again, and lend their aid to certain causes.

One story told by Pausanias (4.16.9-10) informs us how the Dioscuri, in conjunction with their sister Helen, prevented an attack on Sparta one night. Aristomenes of Messenia had attacked a nearby city earlier, but when attempting a night time march on Sparta was turned back by these deities. Interestingly, not just the Dioscuri, but Helen as well.

However, although they saved Sparta, Aristomenes was still at large in Laconia, and the next day he and his men captured the virgin maidens who danced at the temple of Artemis (at Karyai); kidnapping the girls from important families he took them to a Messenian village, and left some of his men to guard them. Perhaps unsurprisingly, after becoming drunk they attempted to rape the girls. Aristomenes tried to stop the sexual attacks, but his men paid no attention to him; thus he killed the most drunken perpetrators. The girls were subsequently ransomed back to their families. Why

---

[190] The Dioscuri are also portrayed with their sons in Athens, within the sanctuary dedicated to them; they are standing whilst their sons are shown seated on horses. Within this sanctuary there are also paintings showing their voyage on the Argo, and their marriage to the Leucippides.

[191] Close to this shrine is a sanctuary to Eileithuia (Goddess of childbirth) which was dedicated by Helen after she fell pregnant by Theseus and gave birth in Argos to Iphigeneia. She gave her child to her sister Clytemnestra to bring up (Pausanias 2.22.7). This is an interesting variant on Helen's myth (and Iphigeneia's).

are these stories linked? Was it just coincidence that after the Dioscuri and Helen saved Sparta, the very next day another atrocity was committed?

The story has almost more bearing on Helen that her brothers; she too was abducted from a temple of Artemis, she too was raped (in some versions), before being rescued by her brothers. Here we seem to have their myth being re-enacted. It is possible that the story of the appearance of Helen and the Dioscuri was added in order to make the abduction and rape of noble daughters more palatable, and even to help strengthen their cult activity at this time. The implication also being, that to enable the protection of the city, unpleasant personal sacrifices sometimes have to be made. Like Helen these girls were returned home after their ordeal, and they may well have turned to their local deities for support in a time of need.

Another appearance, this time somewhat anonymously, demonstrates that they come to the aid of those who have faith in them. The Thessalian prince Scopus refused to pay the poet Simonides his fee after the poem he composed honoured the Dioscuri more than Scopus. During the banquet at Scopus' palace Simonides was summoned outside by two youths; once he had left the building the roof collapsed and killed everyone within (*Poetae Melia Graeci* 510).

The state of Messenia laboured under a curse ascribed to the Dioscuri for a great while. Pausanias believed that it came about due to the actions of two Messenian youths – Panormos and Gonippus, who dressed up in white tunics and red cloaks, and rode into the Laconian camp carrying spears on magnificent horses at a time when the Laconians were celebrating a feast to the Dioscuri. Thinking that the Dioscuri had come among them they bowed down and prayed to them, Panormos and Gonippus proceeded to ride amongst them, piercing them with spears, and killed a great many. By impersonating the Dioscuri at a feast in their honour they brought the wrath of the gods down upon their own state.

So the Dioscuri act as saviours to those in need, and help those who have faith in them, loyalty being one of their traits; but they are also quick to bring vengeance upon those who go against them. Before moving on to the Roman cult it should just be mentioned that one way of venerating the Dioscuri was by the act of *'theoxenia'*. A feast was spread out on a table, along with two amphora, with a couch for two; in vase painting the Dioscuri are shown riding to the feast, or flying over the feast on their horses. Parker (2009) notes that although such *'table-offerings'* were common in Greek cult, they were normally held within a shrine rather than in the home, and believes that *"the domestic setting in the case of the Dioscuri creates an added intimacy"*.

Vs.

- **Castores**

As mentioned above the cult of the Dioscuri spread far and wide (notwithstanding the archetypal divine twins in the Baltic) and they were adopted by the Romans primarily under the name of the Castores. It perhaps seems strange that their collective name should stem from the twin who was originally mortal, although with their joint deification they stood on equal footing as saviours, heroes and gods. Ward (1968) makes an interesting point that also highlights a duality within the twins that we had not previously considered; that Castor was the war-like twin and Polydeuces the more passive/domestic twin.

There was a universal belief in pre-modern societies that the birth of twins indicated that dual paternity was involved.[192] Invariably this led to the belief that the mother of twins was an adulteress; or that she had been visited by a spirit, demon or god. This had varying results ranging from the killing of one or both of the twins, and their mother, to the preferential treatment accorded those blessed by god, with the twins regarded as semi-divine. Along with this belief of dual paternity is the idea that therefore there are tangible differences in the twins; good and bad, dark and light, clever and foolish, mortal and immortal, etc. Up to this point we have not really identified any particular differences in the Dioscuri apart from them being mortal and immortal, and that Polydeuces is *'good with fists'* and Castor is the *'tamer of horses'*. Ward (1968, 21-22) discusses a study by Stig Wikander that demonstrates an early distinction between the Asvins that is not so apparent in the Vedic Hymns.[193] One twin is the warrior and represents the second function from Georges Dumezil's trifunctional hypothesis of sovereignty, military and productivity in proto-Indo-European society,[194] whilst the other is concerned with domestic duties and animal husbandry representing the third function. Ward carries this contrasting behaviour to the Dioscuri, although the distinction is not quite as clear cut. In *Homeric Hymn 33* Castor is the *'tamer of horses'* whilst Polydeuces is *'blameless'* or *'virtuous'*.[195] Elsewhere Castor is honoured as the founder of the horse race, whilst Polydeuces founds the hound race. Horses are animals of warfare and dogs are domesticated and associated with home and farm. In Indo-Iranian

---

[192] As indeed we see with Castor and Polydeuces and elsewhere within Greek myth with Heracles and Iphicles.

[193] Wikander looks at the twin sons of the Asvins in the Mahabharata and in Indo-Iranian mythology. (Wikander, S. (1957) 'Nakula et Sahadeva.' *Orientalia Suecana* 6: 66-96.)

[194] Dumezil's theory has been much criticised since it was first published in 1929, although conversely it has also been embraced by notable scholars too. It does at least provide a basic framework for addressing Indo-European mythology and society.

[195] See also Alcman fr. 2 where Castor is the tamer of swift steeds and a skilled horseman, whilst Polydeuces is 'glorious'.

myth one twin was a *'tamer of horses'* and the other twin *'virtuous and patient'* which does demonstrate a striking similarity in this case. We do, however, have Polydeuces described as *'good with the fist'* which is more war-like than being *'virtuous'*; though it could be argued that boxing was a more *'domestic'* or *'localised'* activity rather than riding into battle.

This brings us back to the Roman Castores, and why Castor was seen as the more prominent twin. If, as Ward suggests, the twins did have a war/domestic duality then the adoption by the Romans of Castor over Polydeuces would make more sense. He highlights the account in Dio Cassius (LVII.14.9) of the younger Drusus being prone to anger, beating a distinguished citizen, and earning himself the nickname *'Castor'*.

The cult of the Dioscuri in Rome as the Castores led to a temple being built in the Forum,[196] the remains of which are still visible today; they were also said to have appeared to various Romans in times of need, much as they did to the Greeks. In the battle of Lake Regillus between the dictator Aulus Posumius and Octavius Mamilius of Tusculum they were seen fighting on horseback (it was due to this intervention that Postumius subsequently dedicated the temple to them).[197]

- **Signs, Symbols and Attributes**

The Dioscuri are associated with a number of sacred symbols, though as Parker (2009) notes they mostly just *'stress the idea of twinness'*. In art and literature we see them portrayed with the *dokana* (two upright parallel beams of wood with two cross beams), two amphora, a pair of snakes, two shields, two stars and they are often seen wearing *piloi* - distinctive shaped hats (the shape is likened to half an eggshell). They also have strong connections to horses and to the sea. There is little to say about the amphora or the shields, although the shields might indicate their prowess as warriors,[198] however the other symbols do reveal some aspects of the twins.

- **Dokana**

Plutarch (*De Fraterno Amore* 478a-b) describes the *dokana* and says that the indivisible form of this symbol is highly appropriate to

---

[196] See Strabo *Geography* 5.3.5, Ovid *Fasti* 1.705 and Cicero *De Natura Deorum* 3.5.
[197] They also appeared to the governor Publius Vatinius to inform him that King Perses had been taken prisoner and that the Romans were victorious. Although not acting as saviours in this instance, but rather as messengers of victory. (Cicero *De Natura Deorum* 2.2 and 3.5).
[198] A maxim among Spartan warriors was that they either came back from battle with their shield, or on it (i.e. dead). The implication being that a coward running from battle would drop his shield.

the brotherly love of this pair. A 2nd century BCE marble votive relief depicting the Dioscuri includes several of their archetypal symbols including two amphora, a snake and two *dokana*.[199] Having two *dokana* seems to belie the original idea of the symbol, and perhaps indicates a lack of understanding on the part of the artist, or over-enthusiasm perhaps. Whereas an earlier marble stele from the 6th-5th century BCE depicts the *dokana* with an additional two inner beams between the two lintels, with a pair of snakes on the main uprights.[200] It has been suggested that the *dokana,* as well as being an obvious symbol of united twinness, could perhaps also represent a gateway, and may have connotations of initiation, or have been used in a *'rite of passage'*. Its physical shape as well as pertaining to a gateway is also reminiscent of alphabetical symbols like the runes.

- **Snakes**

One aspect that snakes are supposed to represent is healing, and as such we have the symbolic Rod of Asclepius (not to be confused with the Caduceus)[201]. Although we don't have much evidence of the Dioscuri as healers there is one story that tells how Phormio (a Chrotonian strategist) was wounded in the foot during a battle against the Locrians. The Dioscuri appeared and healed him. There is also an inscription from the shrine of Asclepius at Epidaurus that calls to the Dioscuri alongside Asclepius, the Charities (Graces), Mousai (Muses) and Moirai (Fates). In comparison there are many hymns that tell of the Asvins' powers as magical healers and physicians. It is possible that the healing nature of the divine twins has become diluted over time and that the twins have become generic saviours rather than healers, as there is also no evidence of the Baltic Sons of God having any such powers. Ward, (1968, 18) however, suggests that this is down to the source material; that we have an abundance of prayers and incantations praising the healing powers of the Asvins, but that no such material for the Greek or Baltic twins has survived. Without the evidence of the prayers we have been left with practically no indication that they

---

[199] Marble votive relief, Verona, Museo Maffeiano 555; *LIMC* III s.v. *Dioskouroi* 122; 2nd century BCE.
[200] Marble stele, Sparta, Museum of Archeology 588; *LIMC* III s.v. *Dioskouroi* 224; 6th-5th century BCE.
[201] The rod of Asclepius is a staff with a single snake entwined around it, and is associated with medicine, healing, astronomy and, of course, the Greek god Asclepius. In contrast the Caduceus is a herald's staff entwined by two snakes, akin to a double helix, the staff is topped off with wings. Associated firstly with Iris, then later Hermes, it can symbolise commerce, deception, theft and death. The two symbols have become confused in modern times, especially in North America where the Caduceus was adopted by the Medical Department of the United States Army in 1902, and also by the American Medical Association for awhile (although they abandoned it in 1912 and subsequently adopted the rod of Asclepius).

are healers, apart from their snake symbol, which could also represent death and transformation as exemplified by their apotheosis.

- Stars

The two stars associated with the Dioscuri are highly indicative of their celestial nature, also seen in the Asvins and the Baltic twins. They are perhaps most famously associated (in modern and classical times) with the constellation Gemini; the Hellenistic writer Hyginus (*Astronomica* 2.22) states that it was as a reward for their services to friendship that Jupiter (Zeus) put them in the sky as stars.[202] The idea of turning them into stars in these instances stems from the shared half life/death granted to the brothers at Polydeuces request; one day in the heavens, the next underground. It seems to be the later Latin sources that match them up with the Gemini constellation, although they are associated with stars elsewhere.

Depictions on coins and gems of the Roman world from the 3rd to 1st century BCE show them with stars above their heads, and sometimes also with a crescent moon above them too in the later periods (with the crescent moon on its back, like a lucky horseshoe shape).

As well as being identified with the Gemini constellation they are also associated with the Morning and Evening star (Venus) – stars that are separated by day. The immortal Polydeuces is matched to the Morning star which rises up into the heavens, whilst Castor, the mortal twin, is seen as the Evening star which slips below the horizon at the end of the day into the ground. The Baltic twins are also linked to the Morning and Evening star, for instance one daina/song (368-33803) names the Steeds of the Moon (Morning and Evening star) as the suitors of the Sun Maiden.

The association with stars wasn't just in the Roman period, for the Spartans too had linked the Dioscuri with them. In the temple to Castor and Polydeuces at Delphi golden stars had been set up in their honour to commemorate the victory of Lysander over the Athenians because the Dioscuri had been seen with the Spartan fleet at that battle. These golden stars subsequently disappeared just before the Spartans were defeated at Leuctra. The loss of the stars was seen as a warning to the Spartans of an impending defeat. However, as Cicero notes, their disappearance probably had more to do with the actions of thieves than the actions of gods.[203]

Similar to and connected with their symbolisation as stars is their relation to the phenomenon of St Elmo's Fire, an electrical discharge causing a glow, commonly appearing around the mast and rigging of ships. Sailors believed this was the Dioscuri appearing to

---

[202] See also Ovid *Fasti* 5.697, and *Metamorphoses* 8.370.
[203] Cicero *De Divinatione* I.34.75 and II.32.68. See also Plutarch *Lysander* 12.1.

them, and was a good sign, similarly they were believed to appear as stars in times of need too.[204]

Their attributes as saviours and their symbols as stars have become overlapping. They are seen as stars because of their deification, but also they appear in this format when they are coming to the rescue of those at sea (they appear in person too). Gods, saviours, stars - their presence in the heavens is continually referenced, as is the celestial nature of our other divine twins. One of the Latvian dainas describes them thus:

Two lights are burning at sea
In two silver lanterns
They are lit by God's Sons
While waiting for the Sun Maiden
(365-33776)

Whilst the Asvins are called *'Shining'* and *'Silvery'* (TA 1.10.2) and *'Lords of Light'* (RV 8.22.6; 10.93.6), and they drive a chariot with either *'Dawn'* or the Sun Maiden in it (as do the Baltic Twins). Scholars cannot agree exactly what celestial body the Asvins represent as they are seen as the first rays of light at dawn, as the sun and moon, the constellation Gemini, lightning etc. This is unlike the Dioscuri who are more firmly represented as stars (and St Elmo's Fire). We should also not forget that they are all offspring of a sky god.[205]

The celestial nature of all these twins is tied up with their relationship to the Sun Maiden. They are her charioteers taking her across the sky, her suitors, her brothers, her rescuers and her abductors. In the *Rig Veda* the sister of the Asvins is Surya (a feminine form of the Sun), she is also called Daughter of the Sun. In the Baltic traditions, both the Latvian and Lithuanian twins have a sister who is also called *'Daughter of the Sun'*. The Dioscuri have Helen who is not directly a sun maiden (in Greek myth), but whose attributes and place in their myth do link her to this Indo-European prototype to a certain extent.[206] The Indo-European tradition has the twins as both brothers and suitors of the Sun Maiden. Greek myth has, however, separated these strands out, a polyandrous and

---

[204] See for instance Alcaeus fr. 34, Plutarch *Lysander* 12.1, Diodorus Siculus *Library of History* bk. 6, Seneca *Hercules Furers* 552, Statius *Silvae* 3.2.1 and Pliny *Natural History* 2.37 (101). See also Diodorus Siculus *Library of History* 4.43.1 for a story concerning the stars appearing over the heads of the Dioscuri during a rescue at sea, although this occurred before the Dioscuri's deification and it was actually the Kabeiroi, deities of Samothrace who saved the sailors.

[205] The Asvins are the Sons of Dyaus (the sky) RV 4.43.3 and Sons of God – Divo Napata; the Dioscuri are Sons of Zeus/Sons of God; and the Baltic myths have the Latvian Dieva Deli, and the Lithuanian Dievo Suneliai (both Sons of God).

[206] See Clader (1976, especially 49-62) and Skutch (1987). The figure of Helen may indeed be derived from a Sun Maiden.

incestuous theme perhaps being unpalatable. So whilst Helen is their sister and they rescue her from Theseus, they also have the Leucippides as their brides. Sister and brides are separated, and the twins get a woman each. However, the Dioscuri do also play some part in the supervising of the courtship of Helen.[207] The names of the Leucippides are however celestial in nature, although they are connected to the moon rather than (or as well as) the sun. Phoebe meaning *'Pure, Bright'* or *'Shining'* and Hilaera *'Softly shining'*; both names are also used as epithets for the moon goddess Selene.

- **Horses**

As has been seen from the earliest poetical evidence the Dioscuri are closely associated with sailors and the sea, and with horses. Castor and Polydeuces are the *'riders upon swift horses'* who are paired with two white colts, the Leucippides, whilst Castor on his own is a *'tamer of horses'*. We find altars dedicated to them at racecourses in Sparta and Olympia, and they are also the *'starters'* at the course in Sparta. They are frequently depicted with horses in art; either riding them, or in chariots drawn by them (and occasionally stood next to them). Pindar called them *'White horses'* (*Pythian Ode* I.66 (126) and Euripides called them *'White colts of Zeus'* in his lost play the *Antiope*. These connections to horses are part of the tradition of divine twins, thus the Asvins of the *Rig Veda*, whose name means *'Owner of horses'* and in the Baltic tradition there are many instances where the horses of the divine twins are described. The divine twins' horse-drawn chariot is frequently seen to fly through the sky, although less so with the Dioscuri (though see Euripides *Helen* 1663).[208]

---

[207] See for example Hesiod's *Catalogue of Women* where the courting is done through the Dioscuri and Tyndareus.

[208] There is also the interesting occurrence of a horse sacrifice made by Tyndareus at the time of the Contest of the Suitors for Helen's hand. All the Greek leaders, the best men in Greece came to compete for Helen. A potentially volatile situation with only one man being able to win the 'prize', Tyndareus (or Odysseus) came up with the idea of getting the suitors to swear an oath, effectively binding them from creating harm, and offering protection the one who would win. (Hence when Paris stole/raped/ abducted/seduced Helen from Menelaus the Greek leaders bound by their oath came to his support and formed the army that went to sack Troy). Pausanias states (3.20.9) that Tyndareus sacrificed a horse and made the suitors stand on the pieces of the horse to make their pledge. When all had sworn the oath the horse was buried. Pausanias is the only one who describes the sacrifice, but in Hesiod's *Catalogue of Women* the Dioscuri do play a large part in the Contest of the suitors (courting being done between them and Tyndareus). It can be no coincidence that the animal chosen for sacrifice is the animal most associated with them, and most sacred to them. There are no other exact examples of this kind of oath.

- **Sea**
The connections of the Dioscuri to the sea seem slightly odd and don't bear much relation to their life. Although they did join the Argonauts on their voyage of adventures, the only story that really features them is one in which the boxing skills of Polydeuces are highlighted. However, from the *Homeric Hymns* onwards they are seen as saviours of sailors, and this tradition continues down so strongly through the centuries that Pope Gelasius I in 5th century CE attests to a cult of Castores that the people do not want to abandon; it has also been suggested that the Church replaced the divine twins with a pairing of their own in the form of Peter and Paul who became the patron saints of travellers. It is not so much that the Dioscuri have a strong sea-faring connection, but more that they act as saviours to various people, and in conjunction with their celestial nature they have been adopted to a certain extent by sailors.

Conclusion

The divine twins of mythology, as here exemplified by Castor and Polydeuces are an enduring phenomenon. They appear in various guises in many cultures; and it is difficult to ascribe a single reason why this might be so. The *'mystery'* of (human) multiple births may have helped the mythical counterparts; having living proof of deity living amongst society. Alternatively their celestial origins may touch a basic need within our collective psyche to have the movements of Sun and Moon anthropomorphised for us. Whatever the reason, the 'riders upon swift horses' have watched over many travellers, and remain with us even today as the constellation Gemini.

Bibliography
Allen, T. W., Halliday, W. R. & Sikes, E. E. (1936) *The Homeric Hymns.* Oxford: Clarendon Press.
Auge, C. (1986) *'Dioskouroi (in Peripheria Orientali).'* In, *Lexicon Iconographicum Mythologiae Classicae* (vol. III) Zurich & Munich: Artemis Verlag.
Burkert, W. (1985) *Greek Religion.* Oxford: Basil Blackwell.
Cole, S. G. (1998) *'Domesticating Artemis.'* In, Blundell, S. & Williamson, M. (eds.) *The Sacred and the Feminine in Ancient Greece.* London: Routledge. 27-43
Gantz, T. (1993) *Early Greek Myth: a Guide to Literary and Artistic Sources.* Baltimore: The Johns Hopkins University Press.
Grottanelli, Cristiano (1986) *'Yoked horses, twins, and the powerful lady: India, Greece, Ireland and elsewhere.'* In *Journal of Indo-European Studies* 14: 125-52.
Gury, F. (1986) *'Dioskouroi/Castores.'* In, *Lexicon Iconographicum Mythologiae Classicae* (vol. III) Zurich & Munich: Artemis Verlag.
Hermary, A. (1986) *'Dioskouroi.'* In, *Lexicon Iconographicum Mythologiae Classicae* (vol. III) Zurich & Munich: Artemis Verlag.

Vs.

O'Brien, S. (1982) *'Dioscuri elements in Celtic and Germanic mythology.'* In *Journal of Indo-European Studies* 10: 117-36.
Parker, R. C. T. (2009) *'Dioscuri.'* In, Hornblower, S. & Spawforth. A. (eds.) *The Oxford Classical Dictionary.* Oxford: Oxford University Press.
Pierce, K. F. (2000) *'Helen of Troy: Heroine or Goddess?'* In *White Dragon* 26 (Imbolc): 4-9.
De Puma, R. D. (1986) *'Dioskouroi/Tinas Cliniar.'* In, *Lexicon Iconographicum Mythologiae Classicae* (vol. III) Zurich & Munich: Artemis Verlag.
Shapiro, M. (1982) *'Neglected evidence of Dioscurism (divine twinning) in the old Slavic pantheon.'* In *Journal of Indo-European Studies* 10: 137-65.
Skutsch, O. (1987) *'Helen, her name and nature.'* In *Journal of Hellenic Studies* 107: 188-93.
Ward, D. (1968) *The Divine Twins: an Indo-European myth in Germanic tradtion.* Berkeley: University of California Press.

Vs.

THE SCORPION & THE BRIDAL BED

A Paradoxical Tale of two Star Crossed Lovers: Innini & Dumuzi

by Vikki Bramshaw

> **Note:** *Although their stories and characters often differ, it is virtually impossible to study the Goddesses* Inanna *and* Ishtar *as separate entities. Therefore when referring to them interchangeably I will be using the name* Innini - *an older origin of both names*[209] – *and when I am referring to one or the other individually I will name them as either* Inanna *or* Ishtar, *respectively. However the character and portrayal of Innini's consort and son – who was known as both* Dumuzi *and* Tammuz – *remains comparatively constant throughout the legends. So for ease, I have used the name* Dumuzi *for the majority of references to the God, only citing* Tammuz *when I am referring specifically to his Akkadian nature.*

> *"Tammuz, the lover of your earliest youth ... yet you struck him and turned him into a wolf ... so his own shepherds now chase him, and his own dogs snap at his shins. Thou smotest him and didst cause him to dwell in the Netherworld ... me likewise, thou lovest - and would make me as he is."*[210]

The legends of the Sumerian *Inanna & Dumuzi* (or Akkadian *Ishtar & Tammuz*) are drawn from a vast amount of both contrasting and complimentary Sumerian and Akkadian literature, some of which dates back to at least 3,000BCE. In its simplest form, the original myths of Innini and Dumuzi are the accounts of two star-crossed-lovers; a tale of passion and love - yet also of betrayal, disaster and death. Inanna, the beautiful goddess of creation, falls head over heels in love with the handsome shepherd Dumuzi. The young couple become sweethearts and marry, consummating their

---

209 *The Name of the Goddess Innin*, I.J Gelb – Journey of Near Eastern Studies Vol.19 / *Tammuz and Ishtar*, S.Langdon.
210 Text: *Epic of Gilgamesh*, Tablet VI.

union upon a bed of date-fruits and precious lapis lazuli whilst the whole world celebrates the abundance of harvest. Yet in subsequent myths, Inanna spitefully sets the eye of death upon her lover and causes him to descend into the netherworldly realms of the dead – thus condemning all of mankind to drought and famine.

> *"High and low, there is weeping ... the wailing is for the plants; they grow not. The wailing is for the barley; the ears grow not ... the wailing is for the great river; it brings the flood no more."*[211]

Innini herself is an enigma. As Queen of Heaven and Earth she reflects the unification of both the upperworld and underworld, and as Mistress of both the Morning and Evening Star she embraces both light and dark and male and female aspects. She is a goddess of fertility and abundance, yet also of destruction and bloodshed – indeed, one of her symbols is the double-headed axe, symbolising the authority to both grant and destroy life. She was considered a formidable war deity particularly in Babylonia and Assyria, and so strong was Ishtar's association with war that the battlefield itself was referred to as her *'playground'*. However this protective side of her nature also meant that Innini was sometimes considered a tutelary Goddess: *"O' come, enter our house, and with this thee may enter thy kindly shadow."*[212] If infuriated, she was more than willing to cast storms and pestilence: *"with the charging storm you charge, with the howling storm*[213] *you howl ... with all evil winds you rage!"*[214] yet as a harvest deity, she was honoured as the provider of fruits and vegetation: *"I step onto the earth, and grass and herbs sprout up."*[215]

The Babylonians certainly recognised the two sides of Innini's character, and she was often depicted on vases and wall plaques with maces and other weapons in one hand and date clusters in the other, clearly demonstrating the two extremes of this enigmatic Goddess. (See Fig. 11)[216] An inscription to Innini found at the temple of Nippur also reflects the dual personality of Innini, in a paragraph that acts as both a blessing on the temple and its architect but also a curse upon those who might cause damage:

> *"May the Great Mistress of Nippur, the supreme lady ... look upon this work with joy, and may a word favourable to me be put on her lips. May she set as my fate life of long days, a goodly number of descendents, physical and*

---

[211] *Sumerian & Babylonian Psalms*, S Langdon .
[212] *Proceedings of the Society of Biblical Archaeology* 1901, 120, 18f.
[213] The term 'Howling Storms' was sometimes also used to refer to disease.
[214] *The Exaltation of Inanna*, WW Hallo & JJA van Dijk.
[215] *Sumerisch-Babylonische Hymnen nach Thontafeln griechischer Zeit*, GA Reisner.
[216] Such as the Seal of Adda, 2,300 – 2,200 BCE.

spiritual well-being ... But - he who will destroy in mischief the inscription containing my name, or will change its place, may the Great Mistress of Nippur frown on him in anger, and annihilate his name and his seed in all the lands!"[217]

Figure 11 - Innini with weapons (war) & date clusters (fertility). The Greenstone seal of Adda, 2,300 – 2,200BCE.

---

217 *Esarhaddon's Inscription from Nippur*, A Goetze.

Vs.

Inanna and Ishtar were already equated with each other as early as 3,000 BCE. The origin of the Akkadian name *Ishtar* can be found in the Semitic *Attar* (the evening star), and the Sumerian *Inanna* can be traced to at least twenty other Goddess names and epithets - in particular *Gestin'anna* the heavenly Goddess of the vine, *Nin-anna* the lady of the heavens, and *Innin* - who is the best attested, and probably the oldest.[218] *Innin*, or *Innini*, was both mistress of the heavens and a goddess of agriculture, which included products sourced from the rivers such as reeds.

Although Inanna and Ishtar are indeed cut from the same cloth, it is clear that the two goddesses evolved well beyond simple epithets and became important independent deities in their own right - particularly with the cross pollination of Semitic culture. Certainly, there are distinct differences between Ishtar and Inanna which are clearly reflected in their mythology. For instance, *Inanna* was instrumental in Dumuzi's murder, whilst in most tales, *Ishtar* has nothing to do with Tammuz' death; and *Inanna*, the *'Faithful Queen'* expressed an aversion to prostitution[219] whilst *Ishtar*, *'Courtesan of the Gods'*, is remembered for her sacred courtesans.

One of the most interesting differences between Inanna and Ishtar is their relationship with the God Dumuzi, or the Akkadian Tammuz. The terms *'husband'* and *'son'* were often used interchangeably for the God (the root word for Dumuzi, *'Damu'* meaning both *'consort'* and *'son'*) however the emphasis was, on the whole, that of *husband and wife* in the earlier Sumerian legends of *Dumuzi & Inanna* and that of *parent and child* in the later Akkadian legends of *Ishtar & Tammuz*. It has been suggested that this distinction occurred due to cultural differences - the original Sumerian faith was focused on the divine relationship between *husband and wife*, whilst the religious structure of the later invading/co-existing Semites was primarily focused on the relationship between *son and mother*.[220] However in truth, like so many other dying and rising Gods, Dumuzi/Tammuz fulfils both roles of son *and* lover – and even brother.

The defining character of Innini and Dumuzi largely depended upon the basic economies of the local cult centre.[221] In the mountains where the economy was largely based on animal husbandry, Dumuzi originated as the Divine Shepherd and Innini as Patroness of Flocks, *'she that passes before the cattle, who loves the*

---

218 *The Name of the Goddess Innin*, I.J Gelb – Journey of Near Eastern Studies Vol.19 / *Tammuz and Ishtar*, S.Langdon.
219 Such as within the text *Mother of Transgression.*
220 *Tammuz and Ishtar*, S.Langdon .
221 It is interesting that in the text *Dumuzi's Wedding*, Inanna is described as having four 'attendants' - a shepherd, a farmer, a fowler, and a fisherman; all four of whom appear to represent regional aspects of Dumuzi.

shepherd ... she is the shepherdess of all lands'[222] - the *'wild cow'* and Goddess of Mountains. Both Inanna and Ishtar are depicted wearing horned headdresses - a symbol of divinity which is usually considered as associated with planetary correspondences, but is also a likely reminder of Innini's ancient connection with sheep, goat and cattle herding.

> "Shepherd of Heaven, son of Ea thou art. Husband of Ishtar the bride - leading goat of the land. Clothed in the girdle band bearing the shepherd's staff. Creating the seed of cattle, lord of stalls."[223]

Historically, herds of animals have been connected with kingship and wealth (and still are in certain parts of the world, such as South Africa) and as the custodians of their kingdom the title of *'Shepherd'* was also shared by the Kings of Sumer. Dumuzi was also referred to as the compassionate protector, and the health of the land was seen as synonymous with the health of the King who was deified and sometimes addressed as the *'wild bull'*.[224]

> 'Great Mistress of Nippur ... the exalted one, the distinguished one, glorious among gods; Innini, the supreme lady who is caring for the King.'[225]

In the plantations where date palms were grown, Innini was known as *Gestin'anna 'Spirit of the Harvest Storehouse'*[226] and Dumuzi was *Amaushumgalana* - the harvested date-fruit itself.[227] Dumuzi was also associated with the spring harvest of beer and barley. Known as *'The Green One'*, images of barley stalks and ploughs symbolised Dumuzi's fertility and abundance, which was celebrated with acts of fertility magic as the mortal personification of Dumuzi - the King as *'Gardener'* - would take part in ritual lovemaking just before the harvest.

Ritual lovemaking – Hieros Gamos, or The Sacred Marriage – was one of the three most important cult dramas of Mesopotamia[228] and was practised as a highly organised and respected element of temple

---

222 Text: *Iddin-Dagan Text*.
223 Text: *Iddin-Dagan Text*.
224 A metaphor for 'shepherd', and a title of Dumuzi.
225 Inscription of dedication to Innini, temple of Nippur. Sourced from *Esarhaddon's Inscription from Nippur*, A Goetze.
226 Or Nin-anna, 'Lady of the Date Clusters' – generally accepted, but disputed by P Collins in *'The Sumerian Goddess Inanna'*.
227 A separate deity equated with Dumuzi after 2,000BCE - P Collins in *'The Sumerian Goddess Inanna'*
228 The remaining two being the Ritual Lament of Dumuzi's death, and Travel Rites of the Underworld.

worship. Several cylinder seal images show ritual lovemaking taking place within the temple and even upon the temple altar[229] as the King took part in Hieros Gamos with the *Nu-Gig*, or the *Ishtaritu* – the trance-mediums, or *'sacred prostitutes'*[230] who embodied Innini during the rite. According to many researchers [231] the Sacred Marriage aimed to bind the powers of fertility (Dumuzi) to the Spirit of the Storehouse (Innini) and it is possible that lovemaking was used as a vehicle of creation through ecstatic experience. The text *The Courtship of Dumuzi & Inanna* describes how the divine couple performed the Sacred Marriage upon a pile of date-fruits - perhaps significant of the connection between their union and the prosperity of the land. As the two united, so the powers of fertility and harvest were wed.

> *"May there be floodwater in the Tigris and Euphrates,*
> *May the plants grow high on their banks*
> *and fill the meadows,*
> *May the Lady of Vegetation*
> *pile the grain in heaps and mounds.*
> *O my Queen of Heaven and Earth,*
> *Queen of all the universe,*
> *May he enjoy long days in the sweetness of your loins."*[232]

In contrast to her role as *Faithful Queen*, Innini as *Hierodule of Heaven* (Sacred Prostitute) was characterised as having an insatiable appetite for men; in fact in one text she is described as the one whom even 120 lovers could not exhaust! She was the personification of feminine desire; a Goddess who embraced sexuality and rejoiced in its unifying power. This aspect of the Goddess Innini is still largely misunderstood; this may be due to the demonisation of earlier deities by the later Semitic religions, as well as biased interpretations by early historians who may have been led by prejudices set by the religious (and moral) *'status-quo'*. The Greek historian Herodotus stated that every Mesopotamian woman was obliged to go to the temples of Ishtar and have intercourse with a stranger who cast a coin in her lap;[233] but it is now generally accepted that his story was rather imaginative[234] and, contrary to popular opinion, the *Nu-Gig* were not women of low moral standards. The title of *Hierodule* originally meant *'sacred work'* or *'servant of the holy'* and according

---

[229] Such as scenes from the Middle Assyrian Temple of Istar at Assur.
[230] Due to modern application, the term 'prostitute' may not be appropriate given the religious significance of the Hieros Gamos.
[231] Such as T. Jacobsen in *The Treasures of Darkness*
[232] Text: *The Courtship of Dumuzi & Inanna*.
[233] *The Histories*, Herodotus - Book 1, Chapter 199 .
[234] *Gods, Demons & Symbols of Ancient Mesopotamia*, J. Black & A. Green .

to Mesopotamian law, the priestesses of the Sacred Marriage followed strict ethical guidelines.[235]

It is likely that the *Nu-Gig* were highly respected for their trade, and even held a certain amount of authority in relation to the lovemaking rite itself. Certainly, Inanna does not give herself freely to Dumuzi - and demands lavish gifts and the promise of a privileged life in return for her agreement to the union and her hand in marriage. The text *The Blessing of the Bridegroom* (which is also believed to be an actual account of Sumerian ritual) even describes Inanna ready to *'view'* the bridegroom - a position of authority in which she decides if Dumuzi (and therefore his mortal representative, the King) is *'satisfactory'* for the proposed union. Many of Innini's priestesses were even married women with children, and in her mother aspect Innini was also patroness of the childbirth aspect of fertility, holding the title of Begetting Mother, *"In the home where the mother gives birth, a protecting shadow am I"*[236] whilst in other texts, Innini is referred to as a virgin goddess – she who is *'consecrated'* or *'set aside'*– which is perhaps a suggestion of the importance of purity within ritual lovemaking.

> *"Not only is it sweet to sleep hand in hand with him, sweetest of sweet is too the loveliness of joining heart to heart with him."*[237]

Upon the shores of the Tigris and Euphrates rivers, Innini was *Nina*: *'Lady of the Waters'*. Dumuzi followed suit and became associated with inundation, travel and fishing; Dumuzi was *ab-zu*, *'Lord of the Deep'* (the waters of the netherworld) and *Nin Girsu*, *'Lord of the Flood'*: *"He that from the flood is risen, I would embrace ... return O Lord, create the rising waters ... and the granaries shall be heaped."*[238] The Sumerians were so dependent upon the freshwater rivers that their cities could literally rise and fall as a result of a change in the watercourses. They relied heavily upon the river to irrigate their crops, yet were also at the mercy of the widespread flooding which was so common in ancient Mesopotamia. This was somewhat of a predicament for those who worshipped the River God Dumuzi, who were caught within an intriguing paradox – lamenting Dumuzi's absence during the dry summer months, yet also fearing the might of his returning floods which brought devastation and death.

Dumuzi's transformation into a water deity also resulted in an interesting variation in the nature of the *Descent* myth, as the

---

[235] *Sacred Prostitution in Israel and the Ancient Near East*, S M Hooks.
[236] *Sumerian & Babylonian Psalms*, S Langdon - 13,29.
[237] Text: *Dumuzi's Wedding*.
[238] *Babylonian Liturgies*, S. Langdon - 99-103.

Vs.

location of Dumuzi's divine sacrifice shifted from a descent into the earth to a descent into the water: *"The raging flood brought him low, him that has taken away to the lowerworld."*[239] The hymns of Dumuzi as River God describe how the *Gallu* - demons of the underworld - seize Dumuzi and drag him beneath the waves to his death, as Innini mourns in unbearable anguish at the loss of her consort. The Gallu of the underworld also appear in another death myth, outlined in the text *The Dream of Dumuzi,*[240] which is relevant to Dumuzi as Shepherd God. In this tale, Dumuzi is shepherding when he is attacked and murdered by the Gallu, and Innini is distraught at the death of her consort/son:

> *"Howling in sorrow for her husband, the heavenly queen for her husband wails ... for her husband who sleeps, the child who sleeps; for her husband who is dead, for the child who is dead."*[241]

The myth of the river descent was re-enacted by the Mesopotamians, who placed a symbol of the dying God upon a sinking boat and cast it into the river as part of their ritual lament: a religious event that was carried out at the peak of the dry season when the land was notorious for food shortages. Obscure references in old texts also refer to the drowning of the Goddess Innini herself, who is cast out into the river on a sinking boat in a similar way: *"in a sunken boat thou art."*[242] This may be a connection to other myths in which Innini follows Dumuzi into the underworld, to try to bring him back to life following his divine sacrifice.

Divine sacrifice was an important part of early worship and religion as a whole, and the Sumerians were particularly interested in the paradoxical themes of death and resurrection; motifs which were clear in the element of water which, like Innini, so easily granted both life and death. However, by far the most popular legend of the death of Dumuzi can be found within the text *The Descent of Inanna*. In this particular myth however, it is Inanna *herself* who sets the eye of death upon her husband Dumuzi, and causes his descent to the underworld. It is also within this myth that we see some of the most striking parallels in terms of conflict and union within their relationship.

Having courted, married and consummated their union, Inanna receives notice that her brother in law - the husband of her dark Underworld sister, Queen Ereshkigal - has died. Inanna decides to attend his funeral, but it soon becomes clear that rather than

---

[239] *Sumerian & Babylonian Psalms*, S. Langdon - 312, 10.
[240] Text: *The Dream of Dumuzi.*
[241] *Tammuz*, V. Scheil.
[242] *Tammuz & Ishtar*, S. Langdon .

offering her condolences, Inanna intends to take the opportunity to usurp her sister of her position as Queen of the Underworld instead. But Ereshkigal soon becomes wise to this and murders Inanna, keeping her corpse hung horribly upon a meat-hook for three days whilst Dumuzi continues to govern Sumer. Immediately, we can see that a reversal of roles has occurred; Inanna the Queen of Heaven has descended into the underworld, whilst her mortal lover Dumuzi has risen to the status of King and is ruling Sumer in her absence. Eventually, Inanna's attendant raises the alarm, and with the help of the God Enki Inanna is brought back to life and released - but only with the agreement that she must send another soul back to the underworld in return. Making the decision of who to send in her place was at first an extremely difficult decision - until she arrives home to find that Dumuzi - her one true love - is so busy with the affairs of the state that he appears to have not even noticed that she was missing. Enraged, she immediately sets the eye of death upon him and he is seized by the Galla, who drag him into the underworld and to his death. So now the roles have reversed yet again - as Inanna ascends back to the upperworld and to her throne, whilst Dumuzi descends to the underworld and his death.

> *"She looked at him, it was a look of death; spoke to them, it was a word of wrath; cried out to them. It was the cry of 'guilty! Take this one along!' and Holy Inanna gave the shepherd Dumuzi into their hands."*[243]

Later in the tale it becomes clear that whilst Dumuzi was murdered at Inanna's hand she still feels a strong sense of love for him, and she begins to lament for her dead husband:

> *"My lady weeps bitterly for her young husband. Inanna weeps bitterly for her young husband. Woe for her husband! Woe for her young love! Woe for her house! Woe for her city."*[244]

Dumuzi is also sorely missed by the people, whose crops cease to grow and whose animals will no longer breed because of Inanna's grief and Dumuzi's absence. In direct contrast to the earlier hymns such as *The Courtship of Dumuzi & Inanna*, the material in *The Descent*, *The Dream of Dumuzi* and *The Return* appears distinctly different; Innini and Dumuzi's legend has turned from a fairytale love story into a nightmare of demons, anger, murder and mourning, as drought and famine quickly grip the land:

---

243 Text: *The Descent* (From the Great Above to the Great Below).
244 Text: *The Return*.

Vs.

"The churn was silent. No milk was poured.
The cup was shattered. Dumuzi was no more.
The sheepfold was given to the winds."[245]

Later in the *Descent* tale, an arrangement is made with Ereshkigal in which Dumuzi shall remain in the underworld for half the year whilst his sister, Gestin'anna (herself an aspect of Inanna) takes the other half. When Gestin'anna is called to the netherworld, Dumuzi is set free - and inundation and fertility returns to the land. The roles of Innini & Dumuzi have reversed once again, and the cycle of life may continue.

And so in this twist of fate and to ensure the seasons, Innini – Goddess of life, and the source and store and harvest – also seems doomed to destroy all that she loves. What makes the legends of Innini & Dumuzi so interesting in terms of this particular anthology is the role that their myths have to play in the paradoxes and inevitabilities of life; abundance and poverty, peace and war, virginity and sexuality, drought and flood - and even life and death itself, which is guaranteed by Innini and Dumuzi's journey between the upperworld and the underworld. The revival of one deity coincides with the death of another, and the act of Hieros Gamos occurs at that one sacred moment in time when the God and Goddess meet in a place of equilibrium - half way between heaven and earth.

As a final note, a cylinder seal from the Early Dynastic Period shows a large scorpion - one of Innini's symbols - hiding beneath the mattress of Innini & Dumuzi's bridal bed.[246] In ancient Babylonian religion, the scorpion represented both protection and death; an intriguing antithesis and a fitting symbol perhaps, foretelling the eventual doom of our star-crossed lovers, Innini and Dumuzi.

Bibliography
Baring, A. & Cashford, J. *The Myth of the Goddess: Evolution of an Image.* Penguin, 1993.
Black, J & Green, A: *Gods, Demons & Symbols of Ancient Mesopotamia.* University of Texas Press, 1992.
Collins, P: *The Sumerian Goddess Inanna*, Institute of Archaeology, UCL [Publisher and Date]
Farrar, J & S: *The Witches Goddess: The Feminine Principle of Divinity.* Phoenix Publishing, 1987.
Gelb, I J: *The Name of the Goddess Innin* (Journal of Near Eastern Studies Vol.19).
Goetze, A: *Esarhaddon's Inscription from Nippur* [Publisher and Date]
Hallo, W & Van Dijk, J J A: *The Exaltation of Inanna.* Yale University Press, 1968.
Herodotus, *The Histories*, Book 1, Chapter 199. Penguin Classics, 1996.
Hooks, S M: *Sacred Prostitution in Israel and the Ancient near East* [Publisher and Date]

---

245 Text: *The Dream of Dumuzi.*
246 Cylinder seal Early Dynastic Period 2800BCE..

Vs.

Jacobsen, T: *The Treasures of Darkness: A History of Mesopotamian Religion*. Yale University Press, 1978.
Langdon, S: *Sumerian & Babylonian Psalms*. Cornell University Library, 2009.
Langdon, S: *Tammuz & Ishtar: A monograph upon Babylonian Religion and Theology*. Cornell University Library, 2009.
Lyon, D G: *Consecrated Women of the Hammurabi Code* (Studies in the History of Religions). McMillan Co. 1912.
McCall, H: *Mesopotamian Myths*. British Museum Press, 1990.
Proceedings of the Society of Biblical Archaeology 1901, 120, 18f.
Reisner, G A: *Sumerisch-Babylonische Hymnen nach Thontafeln griechischer Zeit*. W. Spemann, 1896
Scheil, V: *Tammuz*. In *Revue d'Assyrologie* Vol 8.161-169
Wolkstein, D & Kramer, S.N.: *Inanna: Queen of Heaven and Earth*. Harper Perennial, 1983.

Vs.

INANNA AND ERESHKIGAL

A Necessary Encounter

by Sophie Nusslé

> "*From the Great Above
> she opened her ear to the Great Below
> From the Great Above,
> the goddess opened her ear to the Great Below
> From the Great Above
> Inanna opened her ear to the Great Below.*"[247]

Iraq, late March-April 2003

It's dark. I am lying outside our temporary shelter under the vast vault of the Southern Iraqi sky, gazing at the gaudy stars that cluster against the black silk of night, jewels on a Gulf State princess. I have been here since the evening star, Venus, rose clear and bold, as she has for millions of years, as she did when the Ancients of this land, Sumerians and Babylonians, first named her. Inanna. Ishtar. I whisper her name. Now, despite the competing brilliance and pattern of hundreds of constellations, she commands my attention, removing my mind from the days behind me, the days ahead, the false security of the desert night. In the silence and darkness, I see flashes of light and hear distant gunfire. The Americans and British armies are charging through the country, the Americans racing their Abraham tanks ahead towards the oilfields and Baghdad, while the British seize the South. What I am seeing and hearing is the battle for Basra.

I have been in Iraq three days, and tomorrow I shall lead my team into our first prisoners-of-war camp, to register the detainees and check that the 3rd Geneva Convention is applied.[248] Inanna, Ishtar,[249] Queen of Heaven and Earth, goddess of love and sex - she

---

[247] Wolkstein, Diane and Kramer, Samuel, *Inanna: Queen of Heaven and Earth*, p. 52.
[248] The Third Geneva Convention is part of the Law of Armed Conflict, and covers the treatment, condition and registration of Prisoners of War. The International Committee of the Red Cross (ICRC), of which I was a delegate, is mandated to control how it is being applied by the armies in conflict.
[249] Throughout this article I use Inanna and Ishtar interchangeably: the one is the Sumerian name of the goddess, the other her Akkadian name, used by the Babylonians. The story of her descent to the Underworld to see her sister Ereshkigal,

who carries the blessings of life and civilisation, whose vitality ensures that the bull mounts the cow, that man and woman make love, that grain grows abundant and the date palm is weighed down with fruit - has taken on yet another of her myriad roles, in her own homeland: the destroyer, the tempestuous mistress of storms and of war. She has brought the two at once, blasting sandstorms, tanks and troops up the length of the two rivers.

Is she once again descending into the Underworld, leading her ancestral people into the deathly realm of her sister, Ereshkigal? Am I going there myself, during this journey into Iraq at war, drawn irresistibly down by some inner compulsion, as Inanna was? Did the Americans and British, when they drove their tanks across the border, cross the threshold into the realm of Ereshkigal, unleashing war, terror, death on a large scale, freeing the demons that had been frozen in Saddam's unhappy country? If so, they don't know it yet. Like Nergal, god of war, blasting his way into Ereshkigal's dominion to seduce its mistress in a lusty Babylonian tale, they only think of conquering the lady and making her beg for more, fuelled by rock-and-roll and testosterone, Fox News and the scent of early success and minimal casualties. The embedded journalists have all caught war fever, and speak only of approaching victory and rebirth for Iraq. They don't realise that rebirth always comes at a price.

First encounter

Long before I came to Iraq and became interested in Ancient Mesopotamia, I met Inanna in the story of her descent to the underworld and her meeting with her sister Ereshkigal. I first read the myth in *Descent of the Goddess,* written by a Jungian analyst, Silvia Brinton Perera. Its premise is that Inanna's descent traces the natural descent of women into their own shadow-self, often through depression, and the ultimate rebirth of the self by integrating the shadow and light side of the personality. At the time I read it, I was going through a painful depression: Brinton Perera's analysis gave my personal story a meaning I hadn't found elsewhere, guilt-ridden as I was by wasted time and lost opportunities. I found the original story in an anthology of myths and hymns of Inanna published by Samuel Kramer, an American Sumerologist and Diane Wolkstein, a mythographer and storyteller. I clung to Inanna's story of descent and return, and the opposite tale of Ereshkigal receiving her, removing Inanna's signs of power, then killing her. In my imagination, I saw myself as Inanna visiting Ereshkigal, and I replayed the story many times in my mind. As I pulled myself out of the dust heap of depression, the reason for my being there was less important than the acknowledgement that this was a common part

---

and what befell her there, was told in several known versions in Sumerian and Akkadian.

of the cycle of life and that travelling through the underworld of depression could be empowering. I didn't question the tale or its use in Jungian psychology: it became my story.

The Descent of Inanna

> *"My lady abandoned heaven and earth*
> *to descend to the underworld*
> *Inanna abandoned heaven and earth*
> *to descend to the underworld*
> *She abandoned her office of holy priestess*
> *to descent to the underworld."*[250]

Although I first encountered these words as a drowning woman might see her life spiralling round her as she sinks, it wasn't long before my poet's eyes took an interest in them. The repetition of the line and the rhythmic scansion trick the logical mind into rest and awaken the mythical, imaginative mind. Very soon, we are following Inanna on her great journey. We don't know what will happen, we only know we must go too.

Before she left, Inanna adorned herself with the sacred *me*, an untranslatable word, which conveys variously *'attributes of power and civilisation'*, *'laws of nature and civilisation'*, *'protective emblems of a deity and city'*. The *me* take the form of tangible precious objects - a short lapis-lazuli necklace, two long rows of beads, a robe, a diadem, a breastplate, eye-shadow and the measuring rod and line that all the gods carried. There is a back-story to how Inanna acquired the *me*, which is worth retelling as it illuminates her character and her relationship with the god of wisdom, who plays a crucial role in the *Descent* story. Enki, god of wisdom and sweet waters, originally held the *me*. One day Inanna, at the height of her confident youth and beauty, decided to visit Enki in his sacred place in the city of Eridu. Enki, in avuncular fashion, received her and laid out a feast for her. They drank and exchanged stories late into the night. Softened by good cheer and beer, Enki gave the *me* to Inanna, one by one, toasting her as he did so.

To each gift, Inanna replied: *"I take them!"* and toasted her uncle in return.

Once she bore the seven *me*, she enumerated all that they contained - that is, everything, good and bad, that was part of life in a Sumerian city. Having received the art of making decisions, Inanna rose swiftly with her treasures, left Enki and boarded her boat to bring the *me* back to her city of Uruk. The next morning, hungover and grumpy, Enki realised what he had handed away and sent envoys to fight Inanna, raise the water-level to capsize Inanna's boat

---
[250] Wolkstein and Kramer, *Inanna, Queen of Heaven and Earth,* p. 53.

and reclaim the *me*. Inanna in turn deployed her minister Ninshibur to fight off the envoys, and steered the boat coolly through the flood. Eventually, Inanna and Ninshibur reach Uruk, offloaded the *me* - only to find out there were many more than Enki had passed on: Inanna's courage and decisiveness had raised more power. Enki declared that she won them fairly and proclaimed an alliance between their two cities.

These, therefore, were the *me* that Inanna wore as she prepared for her great journey to the underworld. Because she won them from the god of wisdom and with her own courage and intrepidity, they contained both wisdom and audacity, age and youth. Once she had armed herself with the *me*, Inanna turned again to her assistant, Ninshibur. She explained to her she was going to visit Ereshkigal and instructed her where to find help if she didn't return after three days. Inanna then abandoned all her cities and temples, her Heaven and Earth, and travelled to the Great Below.

Why did she go?

This has remained a mystery, which various psychologists, mythographers, feminist scholars, Pagan practitioners and Mesopotamia specialists have tried to explain. Neither the Sumerian version of the myth, nor the later Babylonian version, are explicit about her reasons. Thorkild Jacobsen, following the opinion of the elder gods Enlil and Nanna, sees it as the whim of a reckless girl;[251] Johanna Stuckey as the remnants of a matriarchal religion where Inanna and Ereshkigal, sisters in the myth, were formerly a single goddess that oversaw heavens, earth and underworld - Inanna's descent is explained as an attempt to reclaim that feminine unity of power that had been severed by male gods.[252] Psychotherapists, on the other hand, explain Inanna's reasons in modern psychological terms, as the desire of the personality to encounter and integrate its shadow. All seem to reveal more about the preoccupations of the commentators than the key to what drew Inanna to Ereshkigal. But the beginning of the story itself suggests a possible answer:

"From the Great Above she opened her ear to the Great Below"

Kramer and Wolkstein write that the Sumerian word for *'ear'* is the same as the word for *'wisdom'*. The line above, therefore, can equally be translated as: *'From the Great Above, she set her wisdom towards the Great Below'*. Ear, listening and wisdom are united in a single word. Are we to infer that the path to wisdom necessarily passes through the underworld? That any deity or human who wishes to attain wisdom must experience such a descent and confront her adversary, the ruler of the underworld? We can't be certain from the language alone, but another clue lies in the first

---

[251] Jacobsen, Thorkild. *The Treasures of Darkness, A History of Mesopotamian Religion.*
[252] Stuckey, Johanna. *Inanna's Descent to the Underworld*, in Matrifocus 2005, vol 4-5.

story I related, the visit of Inanna to Enki, who gave her the sacred *me*. Among the list of *me* we find: *Descent to the Underworld; Ascent from the Underworld.* In other words, the god of wisdom gives Inanna the force that urges her to abandon her life and go to meet Ereshkigal. As we will see below, he also wields the force that will bring her back to life.

The occasion Inanna chose for her journey was the funeral of Ereshkigal's first husband, Gugulanna, the Bull of Heaven. Though it is not mentioned in the text, we know from the famous *Gilgamesh* epic that Ishtar sent the Bull of Heaven against Gilgamesh when the hero turned down her love, and that Gilgamesh and Enkidu, Gilgamesh's friend, kill Gugulanna. Unless these two myths are unrelated, it's reasonable to assume that Inanna would know Ereshkigal would not welcome her. Yet still she went.

As Inanna approached the outer gate, Ereshkigal's gatekeeper, Neti, asked what led her *"on the road from which no traveller returns"*. Inanna explained that she came to attend Gugulanna's funeral. Neti had her wait while he informed his mistress of this surprise visitor. He described Inanna as *'tall as heaven, wide as the earth, strong as the foundations of the city wall.'* She had come with the *me*, he said, she had come prepared. Ereshkigal reacted fiercely. *"She slapped her thigh and bit her lip."* She gave her orders: stop Inanna at each of the seven gates of the Underworld, and remove one item from her at a time: *"Let the holy priestess of heaven enter bowed low."*

And so Inanna descended, and at every gate she was asked to surrender a piece of her power. When she objected, she was told not to question the ways of the underworld. She arrived before Ereshkigal naked and powerless.

The encounter between the two sisters was brief:
> *"Ereshkigal rose from her throne*
> *Inanna started towards the throne.*
> *The Annuna, the judges of the underworld surrounded her.*
> *They passed judgement against her.*
> *Then Ereshkigal fastened on Inanna the eye of death.*
> *She spoke against her the word of wrath.*
> *She uttered against her the word of guilt.*
> *She struck her.*
> *Inanna was turned into a corpse,*
> *A piece of rotting meat,*
> *And was hung from a hook on the wall."*[253]

In contrast with the dialogues that enliven the rest of the myth, this passage tolls inexorably. The sisters didn't exchange a word. The judges pronounced their verdict and Ereshkigal executed Inanna with the sword of her look and word. The bright queen of Heaven and

---
[253] Wolkstein and Kramer, *Inanna: Queen of Heaven and Earth*, p. 60.

Vs.

Earth, the life-force of the land, the goddess of love and war died an ignominious death and was casually hung on a meat hook to rot.

The Babylonian version of the myth gives us a glimpse of the effect of this death in the upper world:

> "After Lady Ishtar had descended to the nether world,
> The bull springs not upon the cow, the ass impregnates not the jenny,
> In the street the man impregnates not the maiden.
> The man lies in his own chamber, the maiden lies on her side."[254]

It also expands on Ereshkigal's reasons for disposing of Ishtar:

> "Lo, should I drink water with the Anunnaki?
> Should I eat clay for bread, drink muddied water for beer?
> Should I bemoan the men who left their wives behind?
> Should I bemoan the maidens who were wretched from the laps of their lovers?
> Or should I bemoan the tender little one who was sent off before his time?"

Iraq, April to August 2003

We are driving along a dusty road in the Southern Iraqi desert in a convoy of three cars, clearly marked as humanitarian cars - though who cares about the protective emblem these days? In Baghdad one of our colleagues, driving a similar vehicle to deliver surgical equipment to a hospital, was gunned down by an Abraham tank just three days ago. Not long after the fall of Saddam, the nascent Iraqi resistance was to shoot one of our electronics engineers at close range as he stood outside his car near Babel, the ancient Babylon. Humanitarians have become targets. The border between Ishtar's and Ereshkigal's dominions has all but disappeared in the ubiquitous dust. When we crossed the border from Kuwait, we entered a liminal zone between the outer and underworld, and I never know exactly when I am in one or the other. War in Iraq is treacherous, uncertain - a green grove might hide mines, a smiling face might distract from the hand that sets off the bomb, while a fierce-looking scarred warrior might offer you a basket of ripe apricots.

It's 6am, and we are on our way to a prison camp. By 1pm it will be too hot to continue working under the implacable sun, so we leave early. Along the road, we see the long debris of the First Gulf War, twelve years earlier - rusted remains of tanks and armoured cars belonging to the Iraqi army that was retreating - or rather fleeing - from Kuwait. The Coalition bombed them intensively from the air during their rout. 40,000 died, for the most part young conscripts.

---

[254] *The Descent of Ishtar*, Ancient Near Eastern Texts, trans. E.A. Speiser.

Vs.

Then Saddam sent his helicopter gunships and warplanes to bomb his Shiite people, who were rising up against him throughout the South. It's estimated that 100,000 civilians died in that campaign, in full view of the Coalition forces that stood by on the opposite bank of the river, refusing to intervene or enforce a no-fly zone they had only just proclaimed.

"*I saw it happenin*", a sergeant in the Marines told me once, "*back in '91. I was ashamed of what we were doin', letting all those folks down, letting them get butchered by Saddam. That's why I'm glad we're back again. We got a job to finish we should've done twelve years ago. We owe it to them.*"

I have no doubt he believed that sincerely, but his notion of history was sketchy. The twelve years he mentions were a mere blink in the timeframe of this country, and at the same time, one of the hardest and most painful periods this land has known. In Iraq, history is everywhere. Recent history, modern history, ancient history. It whispers through the date palms by the two rivers, it rises from the dust of the desert, it peeps out of the faces of children, it shows in the pockmarked buildings of every city, it comes out in torrents from the Iraqis when they speak of the invasion: "*Who do they think they are, these Americans? We have a history of 8000 years, we are the cradle of civilisation, we have given birth to heroes like Gilgamesh and Salaheddin - and they come here with their tanks, their wild music, their ignorance, their obsession with oil and their terrible manners... They don't know us, they don't understand us, they don't know our past, our culture, our losses. They don't understand what we have been through. We are glad to be rid of Saddam, but we don't want the Americans here.*"

Sometimes, I answer that they might be doing what Ishtar did, travelling to the underworld; and they nod, but add that they're not sure whether they will return to America wiser and more respectful than they came. I don't remind them of the mass rape of their historical artefacts from the National Museum by their own fellow-citizens during the three days of mayhem and looting that followed the fall of Saddam on the 9th April. Most Iraqis are too tired and too poor to care. The looting was just the culmination of years of Saddam's hyperbolic dictatorial rule, and of the cruel sanctions imposed after the First Gulf War. In true United Nations style, after the army it authorised did nothing to prevent the massacres in the South, the world imposed a blockade on Saddam that hurt his people and barely touched him. His only answer was to turn the screw a little tighter and lay waste the marshes and date palm groves of the South. Basra's own poet Shakir Al-Sayyab said it best, about another time of loss and rebirth:

"*And in the village, Ishtar is dying of thirst,*
There are no flowers on her forehead
And in her hands there is a basket, its fruits are stones

Vs.

Which she casts at every woman. And in the palm trees
On the city's shore, there is a wailing."[255]

On every road, checkpoints have been set up, manned by young soldiers who stand in the sun all day in their heavy anti-bullet gear and helmets, stopping every vehicle. The backlog of cars is long. Heat and the fear of bombs are making us all edgy. At that time, most suicide bombers operate at checkpoints. We surrender our papers and authorisations at every roadblock. Sometimes, the message to let the Red Cross through hasn't come down the chain of command, so we are detained pending verification. At one gate, a young black woman in full combat gear approaches our landcruiser. Fear stretches her skin and suffuses her velvet eyes as she holds her gun up to the window, the trigger finger quivering. It wouldn't take much for an accident to happen. I speak to her, show her my papers and the gun lowers a fraction, enough to reassure. *"Just doin' my job, ma'am. We gotta check everyone. Some bad folks get dressed up and paint their cars with a red cross and then blow themselves up and kill people."* She's right. On the internal news yesterday, there was a report of a car bearing a red crescent emblem spewing out armed men who opened fire. I experience again the shifting threshold between Ishtar and Ereshkigal. In this land, I am as suspicious in the eyes of strangers as they are in mine, as likely to bring death as relief.

We arrive at the camp, which has become our own underworld. Thousands of Iraqis were detained as the coalition troops advanced towards the North. The occupation force has been arresting many more since the fall of Saddam. Some are clearly soldiers, prisoners of war. Some are just as clearly gangsters, generally held separate from the others - for in the dying days of his regime, Saddam let them all out of prison, intending to make the country ungovernable. Some are foreigners, young men who flocked to Iraq to fight for the Arab cause. The rest are civilians, a mix of common law and security detainees. When Saddam fell, the Iraqi prison service was disbanded: the whole of the detention work now falls on the coalition's military police, British and American. For reasons best known to themselves, the coalition has built its main prison camp in a desert devastated by sandstorms and old wars. Everyone inside it - prisoners, guards, humanitarians - eats dust and bakes in the sun. The military sleeping quarters, at the entrance of the camp, is barely better than the prisoners': same overheated tents, same scorching heat, same dirt that penetrates everywhere. I wonder if the Ancients got their idea of hell from this dour area. *Where dust is their fare and clay their food.*

---

[255] From *City of Sindbad*, by Badr Shākir al-Sayyāb (Basrah, 1926-1964). This poem was published in 1960 and excoriates the failures of the 1958 revolution of Gen. Qasim.

Vs.

The Ascent of Inanna from the Underworld

Inanna had made preparations with her assistant Ninshibur in case she did not return after three days. That deadline past, Ninshibur followed her mistress's instructions to the letter. She dressed herself in mourning rags and ashes, and went to beg the god Enlil for help. Enlil reminded her that the laws of the underworld were inflexible and he could do nothing for the foolhardy Inanna. Inanna's father, Nanna, gave her the same answer as Enlil. Finally, Ninshibur went to Enki, Inanna's uncle, god of wisdom and sweet waters. In Sumerian, *'sweet waters'* - is also the word for semen: Enki is the great inseminator.

Enki didn't hesitate. Inanna was a daughter after his own heart, and, like his water, her vitality was necessary for life on earth. He fashioned two creatures from the dirt under his fingernails, neither male nor female. Shamanic shape-shifters and threshold-crossers, they slipped past the gates of the underworld as flies. When they reached Ereshkigal, they found her moaning as though in labour. As she cried, they cried with her, showing her a compassion she couldn't find in the sterile creatures of the underworld.

We are not told why Ereshkigal is experiencing labour pains, but it is inferred in the text that her pain follows on from Inanna's death. It is impossible, the tale seems to suggest, to take someone's life, to torture them (as happens in the Babylonian version), without feeling pain, without one's own life-force revolting against the choking out of life. Ereshkigal was alive with the pain of birth - as well she might, as she was about to give birth to Inanna's revival. The kindness of Enki's creatures won her over and she promised them whatever they wanted, offering them the water-gift or the grain-gift. We learn that the lady of death owns two vigorous signs of life - water, grain, both of which hide below ground before emerging. But Enki's creatures were after the bigger prize - she that embodies the principle of life itself, Inanna. They asked for her corpse and despite Ereshkigal's reluctance, she gave it to them. They revived Inanna and alive, she set out for home, stopping at every gate to retrieve her powers.

As she left, the judges of the underworld once again surrounded her:

> *"No one ascends from the underworld unmarked*
> *If Inanna wishes to return from the underworld,*
> *She must provide someone in her place."*[256]

To ensure this sacrifice was carried out, Ereshkigal dispatched her demons with Inanna. After refusing to give up her faithful Ninshibur or her two sons, who were all deep in mourning for her, Inanna came upon her husband Dumuzi, who sat on his throne, dressed in splendid clothes, indifferent to his wife's disappearance.

---

[256] Wolkstein and Kramer, *Inanna: Queen of Heaven and Earth*, p. 68.

Enraged, she decided against him. Her words are a repetition of her own execution in the underworld:
> "Inanna fastened on Dumuzi the eye of death
> She spoke against him the word of wrath.
> She uttered against him the cry of guilt."[257]

Inanna had changed during her time in the underworld: through humiliation and death, she had absorbed some of Ereshkigal, just as Ereshkigal had assimilated some of Inanna in facing and killing her. Now, Inanna becomes the one condemning another to death. The two, Inanna, Ereshkigal, became one continuum in life and death.

In a subsequent story, Dumuzi's sister Geshtinanna, goddess of the vine, pleads for his life, and Inanna agrees that she should spend half the year in the underworld, while Dumuzi will spend the other half. This arrangement portrays neatly both the Sumerian night sky, where constellations representing Dumuzi and Geshtinanna appeared and disappeared at different times of the year, and the agricultural year, which was divided between the grape and the grain (Dumuzi, as well as being the shepherd, was a grain god). Thus Inanna's wisdom, acquired during her hard journey, is complete and she and Ereshkigal have become a united force of balance: they regulate heavens, earth and underworld in harmony, half the year given to one life force, half the year to the other, while the god or goddess who has finished their task *'dies'* and remains in the underworld for six months.

After Iraq

I spent less than six months in Iraq. I was due to return after a break, but the bomb at the UN headquarters in August, and a subsequent bomb outside the International Red Cross headquarters in Baghdad, caused all departures to Iraq to be frozen. Our headquarters were moved to Amman in neighbouring Jordan, and all humanitarian operations towards Iraqi prisoners and civilians set off from there in small ultra-mobile teams. Only delegates who spoke Arabic joined them, which excluded me, to my mingled sadness and relief. I holidayed up in the Swiss Alps, went walking every day, picked blueberries, played with my nephew and niece. I didn't send a loved one to Iraq in my place, but hundreds of humanitarians remained risking their lives and freedom to bring help and comfort to ordinary Iraqis. The insurrection against the Americans grew and was severely repressed, then gradually morphed into a civil war, as ever-more violent militants and terror organisations opposed each other in a dirty territorial and ideological war. Both insurrection and civil war killed thousands of soldiers and civilians. What was already dangerous work for humanitarians became at times almost suicidal,

---
[257] *Ibid.*, p. 71.

yet still, Iraqi and foreign humanitarians kept going, bringing to their work their life-force and their desire to see the country grow out of its misery and its fratricidal conflict.

The underworld that was Iraq in 2003 has never left me. Just as years before, in the midst of private pain, I had found solace with Inanna as she journeyed below and was reborn, this time I consciously experienced Ereshkigal's realm - the tangible underworld of Iraq at war, the emotional underworld in which most of its people were living, and my own grief for so much lost life, for a ravaged countryside, for a battered people - Ishtar's proud people, lamenting the death of Dumuzi, as became the yearly tradition in Babylon. Yet it was only after I had left the physical reality of Iraq that I was able to grieve for it, and to feel and express my anger at what I had witnessed, my guilt at being alive and safe. I mourned for a long time. Like waters mingling together, my grief intermixed with other, earlier and later grief, both personal and linked to my work. In 2006, impelled by memories of Iraq and by a more recent heartbreak, I took part in a shamanic experience that retraced over several days, in a series of four long journeys, the descent of Inanna to the underworld, her encounter with Ereshkigal and the experience of death, rebirth and return. Through this work at the centre of my own underworld, through my own meeting with the mysterious Ereshkigal, who underneath her stern exterior lives and resonates as intensely as Inanna, through my own shamanic death and rebirth in her domain, I was able to make sense of much of what I had experienced in my life. More importantly, I learnt to balance the forces of light and dark, to assimilate them in my life as part of a single cycle: rather than lurching from one to the other, uncontrollably and at a great cost to myself.

Switzerland, August 2003

I am lying outdoors under a pristine Alpine night sky. Meteor showers are falling around me, stardust exploding in death and life. I draw to myself the encrusted robe of night, wrap it close around me, pluck down the crown of heaven, slip the necklace of stars over my head and a ring of Saturn around my wrist, draw darkness onto my eyelids, protect myself with a shining breastplate of light. I'm sleeping out here tonight, enclosed between the interwoven darkness of the sky, the earth and the mountainous underworld. I am home.

Bibliography
Jacobsen, Thorkild. *The Treasures of Darkness, A History of Mesopotamian Religion.*
Stuckey, Johanna. *Inanna's Descent to the Underworld*, in Matrifocus 2005, vol 4-5.
Wolkstein, Diane and Kramer, Samuel. *Inanna: Queen of Heaven and Earth. Her Stories and Hymns from Sumer.* Harper and Row, 1983.

Vs.

ARE FREYJA AND FRIGGA THE SAME GODDESS?

by Katie Gerrard

The contemporary heathen pantheon[258] lists Freyja and Frigga as separate goddesses, with separate characteristics and different roles within mythology and within heathen practise. Whilst it is very clear within the heathen viewpoint that Freyja and Frigga are to be considered as distinct entities, many texts and dictionaries[259] will combine the two goddesses within listings and continue to consider them together. Where does this discrepancy come from? Has one group really got it so very wrong?

Our information on the two goddesses comes from various places. Much of the information we have on Norse beliefs and culture comes from the collection of ancient Scandinavian heroic tales often referred to as *'the sagas'*. The most widely read primary source on Norse mythology is Snorri Sturluson's *Edda* (also known as the *Prose* or *Younger Edda*.)[260] Snorri Sturluson was a Christian, writing about 1200 CE so it is unclear how much he may have been influenced by Christian ideas and mythology. Scholars of the Norse goddesses also use a collection of stories called the *Poetic Edda* (found within the *Codex Regis* manuscript) which was written around the same time as Snorri's *Edda* but looks to have been compiled from older traditional sources. This is often referred to as the *Elder Edda*.

Information on Frigga and Freyja is also found in many different secondary sources. Within the romanticism found in turn of the century art and music, for instance, a number of works of art were created on the theme of the Norse myths; Arthur Rackham in particular painted many images of Frigga and Freyja. Information can also be found in modern academic and folkloric studies, where an invaluable scholarly approach is taken in dissecting the information found within the primary evidence in order to build up a picture of the goddesses. Modern pagan and heathen authors have also combined the *Eddas* and *Sagas* with their own personal experiences and the goddesses in order to put the two goddesses

---

[258] See Diana L Paxson, Essential Asatru, 2006.
[259] Sorita D'Este and David Rankine, *Isles of the Many Gods*, 2007.
[260] *Edda*, Snorri Sturluson.

within a context where they can be used within a practical modern religious framework.

On first impressions, the personal experiences of a contemporary heathen may not seem as concrete and solid as the evidence put together by an academic, especially if they are not backed up by any research. However, personal experiences are being increasingly trusted by those undertaking personal work and seeking personal understanding of different deities. These experiences come from meditations, from trance work, from channelling (invoking the deity into a person), and from attempts to get in touch with and directly experience the energy of that particular deity. These personal experiences have a name within contemporary paganism, UPG (Unsubstantiated Personal Gnosis)[261] and are often referred to within magazine and web-based articles. Where it is clear that information on a deity comes from UPG, many contemporary pagans are happy to use this information when piecing together their own practises.

Where our information comes from originally helps us to understand why the viewpoints on whether Freyja and Frigga are the same goddess are so different. It has been suggested that at some point Frigga and Freyja might have been the same goddess,[262] but that they were separate by the end of the Viking era. It has also been suggested that the Germanic tribes held the two to be one and the same deity, but that the Scandinavian tribes considered the two to be separate.[263]

Freyja and Frigga were goddesses that the *Eddas* tell us came from two different tribes – the Aesir and the Vanir.[264] The Aesir lived in Asgard and were the main subject of the *Eddas*. The two tribes were at war with each other for many years, a war which ended with the exchange of two hostages. Njord, the father of Freyja, was the Vanir hostage that went to live with the Aesir. He took his children with him, the twins Freyr and Freyja, which shows us that Freyja is a Vanir goddess. Frigga on the other hand is very much of the Aesir, the wife of Odin (who is the leader of the Aesir) she is the Queen of Asgard. Academics have suggested that the Vanir and Aesir wars represented two rival sets of beliefs from two rival tribes and that the Aesir were the gods of the conquerors who, instead of ignoring the Vanir gods of those they had taken over (and thus forcing the worship of them underground and undisclosed), assimilated the most popular into their own pantheon.[265]

---

[261] Lafayllve, Patricia M. *Freyja, Lady, Vanadis*, 2006.
[262] Diana L Paxson, *Essential Asatru*, 2006.
[263] Lynda C Welch, *Goddess of the North*, 2001.
[264] Heather O'Donague, *From Asgard to Valhalla*, 2008.
[265] HR Ellis Davidson, *Gods and Myths of Northern Europe*, 1969.

Vs.

If this is the case, then was the worship of Freyja and Frigga similar to that of Odin and Wodan in that the deities were similar, but given different names by different tribes? To answer this question would be difficult, unless we looked again at the evidence that joins and separates the god Odin to his namesakes Wodan and Wotan. One thing very clearly marks out Frigga and Freyja as different to Odin/ Wodan/ Wotan. This is that Frigga and Freyja appear in the same texts and even the same stories alongside each other and very clearly as different characters.[266]

Freyja's name translates as *'Lady'* and she lives in Sessrumnir (the hall of the many seated). She has a chariot drawn by two cats (whose names translate as honey and amber) and a sow called Hildisvine.[267] She has two daughters whose names are both types of treasure. Freyja is called the most *'glorious'* of the Aesir, she rides into battle every day as leader of the Valkyries and has the first choice of the slain to come and live in her hall. Freyja is associated with seidr and witchcraft and taught seidr to the Aesir.[268]

Within the Norse literature Freyja is involved in several myths. One of these sees her as a guide to her mortal lover, the hero Ottar, who she helps on his quest and eventually helps to shape shift into a boar.[269] Another of these shows her sleeping with four dwarves in payment for them making her the beautiful golden necklace Brisingamen; and then losing that necklace and agreeing to start a war between two human tribes to gain it back. Another story tells of the Aesir asking Freyja to pretend to marry a giant (basically making her *'bait'* for catching the giant), she refuses this with much anger, and instead Thor dresses as Freyja.[270] In *Lokasenna*[271] Loki accuses Freyja of sleeping with many different people, including her brother Freyr. Njord steps in here and suggests that a woman of Freyja's standing is perfectly entitled to sleep with whoever she likes. *Ynglingasaga* tells us that Freyja is a priestess and *Egil's Saga* tells us that a young woman committing suicide was expecting upon death to join Freyja, suggesting that unmarried women of noble death joined Freyja in her hall.

Another myth tells of Freyja's husband Odr going missing and Freyja mourning for and searching for him.[272] In this story she weeps tears of red gold (amber?) and searches in many different places using a series of different names including Mardel, Mardoll, Skialf, Syr, Gefn, and Horn. Based on this story, Freyja has sometimes been associated with the Greek goddess Demeter and

---

[266] *Edda*, Snorri Sturluson, Everyman.
[267] Diana L Paxson, *Essential Asatru*, 2006.
[268] Sheena McGrath, *Aysiniur*, 1997.
[269] *Edda*, Snorri Sturluson, Everyman.
[270] Hilda Ellis Davidson, *Thor's Hammer*, appeared first *The Folklore Journal* 76, 1965.
[271] *The Poetic Edda*, Penguin.
[272] Sheena McGrath, *Aysiniur*, 1997.

Vs.

therefore become symbolic of the earth[273] or of the earth mother: a similarity that draws strong parallels with Frigga, who, like Demeter, is a grieving mother. This, as well as the references made to Freyja's sow, has caused some to consider that Freyja is a fertility goddess.[274] The link with fertility draws further conclusions that Frigga and Freyja are the same goddess, due to Frigga's links with childbirth and fate.

Is Freyja a fertility goddess? Certainly, the story of her searching for Odr draws parallels with the story of Demeter's wandering the earth during her mourning for Persephone. Yet there is no mention of nature within this story and the only link we can find to the seasons are the tears of red gold which some have suggested as being associated with the falling leaves of autumn. This is an interesting theory, but we need to remember that Scandinavian seasons are very different to those that are found in the UK and North America.

The parallels in the story of Demeter and Persephone are interesting however, and are not the only parallels with Greek writing that are found within the Norse literature of this time.[275] It is not at all unlikely that the authors could have heard or read Latin versions of the Greek myths as trade between European countries was widespread at this time and Christianisation was in progress. Perhaps instead, we can look at the other motif in Demeter's story, specifically that of the initiation of Demophon into the Eleusinian rites. This fits in with Freyja's character far closer than the fertility symbolism, especially when you consider the initiatory undertones in the Ottar myth.

The other symbol of Freyja given to represent fertility is the sow.[276] But is the sow really an emblem of fertility? This is possibly another misunderstanding based on the assumptions that we make about the sow and what it represents within the Norse culture. The sow is called *'Hildiswine'*, *'war pig'*. Does this sound like a fertility symbol or a symbol of battle? Fertility of the fields and of animals was considered a male attribute[277] and associated with Freyja's brother Freyr. Childbirth was the jurisdiction of Frigga, although there are mentions that associate Freyja with childbirth, although that these were misrepresentative of the times has been argued.[278]

Frigga is the wife of Odin and takes her place as the Queen of Asgard. She is the daughter of Fiorgynn which makes her a child of

---

[273] Lynda C Welch, *Goddess of the North*, 2001.
[274] HR Ellis Davidson, *Gods and Myths of Northern Europe*, 1969.
[275] Consider also how *Voluspa* in the *Poetic Edda* parallels the Greek oracles.
[276] HR Ellis Davidson, *Gods and Myths of Northern Europe*, 1969.
[277] Sheena McGrath, *Aysiniur*, 1997.
[278] Lee Hollander, commentary on *The Prose Edda*, 1962.

the earth giants.[279] Her name means *'beloved'*[280] and she has a cart drawn by rams.[281] Her hall is Fensalir which means *'hall in the marshes'*[282] and her symbol is the keys of the house[283] which she is pictured with dangling from her belt. This is an important symbol as it marks her out as an authority within the home, the keeper of the keys and the maker of decisions. Frigga spins the wool that is woven into the web of wyrd (the web that holds the fates of mankind) and because of this she holds the key to prophesy and knows the fates of mankind. *Lokasenna*[284] tells us that Loki was considered crazy to upset Frigga as she alone knew what his fate would be. This suggests a deep level of respect bordering on fear for Frigga and her knowledge. Frigga has a collection of handmaidens who are named as Fulla, Saga, Eir, Gefjun, Siofn, Lofn, Syn, Hlin, Var, Vor, Snotra, and Gna.

Within the myths, Frigga plays an important part in the leading up to Ragnarok – the end of the world as we know it. Frigga's son Baldur (the beautiful) is having dreams in which he dies and goes to Helheim (the underworld, the place of the dead). Frigga and Odin set about finding out what these dreams mean and when they find out that Baldur will die Frigga sets about trying to change the course of fate.[285] Instead of changing his fate, Frigga's actions help to bring it about and she is left grieving and waiting for Ragnarok.

In another myth, Frigga's cunning becomes evident. During a war between the human tribes the Winnilers and the Vandals, Frigga's favourite (the Winnilers) were not Odin's favourites and therefore Odin was about to declare victory on the Vandals. Frigga disorientated Odin by turning the bed round the wrong way and asking the Winniler ladies to cover their faces with their long hair. On awakening, Odin saw the Winniler ladies and asked 'Who are these Longbeards?' thus naming them, which ensured that he claimed them as his own which meant he had to give them victory.[286] (I believe Odin's naming of the Longbeards to echo the Norse practise that a father claimed a child as his on naming it.)[287]

In another story, Frigga has a servant melt down a statue of Odin (the payment of this was sleeping with him), and the gold made into a necklace. When Odin finds out about this he leaves Frigga and Asgard and journeys throughout the worlds.[288] This has stark

---

[279] Diana L Paxson, *Essential Asatru*, 2006.
[280] Sheena McGrath, *Aysiniur*, 1997.
[281] Diana L Paxson, *Essential Asatru*, 2006.
[282] Diana L Paxson, *Essential Asatru*, 2006.
[283] Sheena McGrath, *Aysiniur*, 1997.
[284] *The Poetic Edda*, Penguin.
[285] Kevin Crossley Holland, *The Penguin Book of Norse Myths*, 1996.
[286] Sheena McGrath, *Aysiniur,* 1997.
[287] Jenny Jochens, *Women in Old Norse Society*, 1995.
[288] *Saxo Grammaticus.*

parallels with two significant stories of Freyja – the mourning for the loss of Odr and the story of Brisingamen. These stories, as well as the name of Freyja's husband, became the backbone of Stephan Grundy's article *Freyja and Frigg* which gathered evidence together suggesting that Freyja and Frigga had been the same goddess originally.[289]

Another key motif in Grundy's article is the parentage of Frigga and Freyja. Freyja's father is Njord, who is associated with the earth goddess Nerthus (a link which comes from the name Njardr, as in Njordr/ Njardr) and some authors have suggested that the two may be the same deity.[290] Frigga is the daughter of Fiorgyn, who is often coupled with Fiorgvin (sometimes said to be her brother or her mate.)[291] This makes for similarities in Frigga and Freyja's parentage. Certainly the Fiorgyn/ Njord link is an interesting one, however, Nerthus was more of a Germanic deity than Scandinavian and within the Scandinavian tales, Njord takes a wife in Skadi, the frost giant. Brian Branston has suggested that the name Fiorgynn might have originated in Eastern Europe.[292] He also links the name with Jorth (or earth) and suggests that Fiorgynn was an earth goddess.

One reason that is often given for Frigga and Freyja being the same deity, is that it is unclear which of the two goddesses the English day of the week *'Friday'* is named after. Is it Frigga or is it Freyja? Both seem to fit. If we look at English place names we can see that both Frigga and Freyja have places named after them[293] (as do Odin and Thor, also named in the days of the week). Friday has been associated with love (for example, Friday's child is loving and giving), and therefore the suggestion has been made that whichever goddess Friday is named after is the goddess of love and equated with the Roman Venus.[294] Which goddess is associated with love – Freyja or Frigga? Britt Mari Nasstrom suggests that Freyja is coupled with Venus and that Snorri Sturluson has cast Frigga instead into more of a Juno role.[295] On first consideration, Freyja seems to fit more into this role considering that beauty and sexuality are her virtues. But is love considered to be part of beauty and sexuality? Does sexuality equal love? Frigga rules marital and maternal love as the wife of Odin and mother of Baldur. Which love did the Norse praise most highly?

---

[289] Stephan Grundy, *Freyja and Frigg*, first appeared in *The Concept of the Goddess*, edited by Sandra Billington and Miranda Green, 1998.
[290] Lynda C Welch, *Goddess of the North*, 2001.
[291] Lynda C Welch, *Goddess of the North*, 2001.
[292] Brian Branston, *The Lost Gods of England*, 1957.
[293] Sheena McGrath, *Aysiniur*, 1997.
[294] Brian Branston, *The Lost Gods of England*, 1957.
[295] Britt Mari Nasstrom, Freyja, *The Great Goddess of the North*, 1995.

Vs.

The etymology of Frigga and Freyja's husbands (Odr and Odin) also cannot be ignored. It looks almost certain that the two names have come from the same root source suggesting that Odr and Odin are the same whether or not Frigga and Freyja are.[296] Both Odr and Odin went missing.[297]

While considering which of the two goddesses is associated with love, it is also worth looking at which is associated with beauty. Certainly, the first thought would be that Freyja rules this area. However, if we look at the Eddas again we can see that the deity most associated with beauty is Baldur – the son of Frigga.[298] Jenny Jochens, writing on the lives of Norse women, points out that within Norse literature, descriptions of beauty tend towards male beauty rather than female.[299] Men's appearances are often described in far more detail and with more admiration than women's beauty, and the women who are championed (particularly within the heroic and family sagas) are those who are cunning and quick thinking.[300] Was beauty (like the fertility of the fields and of animals) also more often thought of to be a male virtue by the Norse?

Both Frigga and Freyja are associated with what we consider now as supernatural virtues. Both are owners of falcon feather cloaks that allowed them to shapeshift.[301] Freyja has been associated with seidr – the witchcraft of the Norse and can be associated with initiation (based on the story of Ottar). Frigga is never described as being involved with seidr, however, she is described as knowing the fates of mankind and of spinning the wool that the web of wyrd is made into. This gives her the gift of prophecy which is a virtue often associated with witchcraft through the ages. Interestingly, in modern heathenism seidr is now associated with prophesy.[302] There is also confusion regarding the goddess Gefjun. Gefjun is mostly associated with Freyja and often said to be another of Freyja's names.[303] Yet in *Lokasenna*, Gefjun is also associated with knowing the future and therefore the gift of prophesy.[304]

Looking at heathen practise today, it is very clear that Frigga and Freyja are considered as having very separate energies and they are invoked as separate entities, although there are similarities between the two goddesses. However there are no more or fewer similarities and differences between them than there are with the other

---

[296] Britt Mari Nasstrom, Freyja, *The Great Goddess of the North*, 1995.
[297] Britt Mari Nasstrom, Freyja, *The Great Goddess of the North*, 1995.
[298] *Edda*, Snorri Sturluson.
[299] Jenny Jochens, *Women in Old Norse Society*, 1995.
[300] Jenny Jochens, *Women in Old Norse Society*, 1995.
[301] Kevin Crossley Holland, *The Penguin Book of Norse Myths*, 1996.
[302] See Jenny Blain, *Nine Worlds of Seid-Magic* for more information on seidr and witchcraft.
[303] Sheena McGrath, *Aysiniur*, 1997.
[304] *The Prose Edda*.

goddesses in the Norse pantheon, or for that matter, between the goddesses of other European pantheons.

Perhaps we can look at Freyja and Frigga as being two different kinds of women, the mistress and the wife, or as different stages of a woman's life. Frigga's role is as wife and queen. She holds the keys to the house and is associated with the wifely roles of childbirth and the fixing of problems. Odin comes to Frigga for advice and we remember her cunning and problem solving aspects. Freyja's love of gold and beauty and her sexual confidence and her freedom are the virtues that we remember. Both goddesses are held up as ideals of women, almost as fantasy figures.

In concluding, we need to look towards the title question again. Are Frigga and Freyja the same goddess? More importantly, we need to look at the discrepancies between the heathen trail of thought and the academic. What separates the goddesses and what brings them together?

Firstly, we need to consider the UPG and the religious practises of heathens today. Certainly, there can be no question here that the goddesses are separate entities. However, modern paganism sometimes also puts goddesses that were once linked under different headings. For example the Roman and Greek Diana and Artemis originally came from the same source but the Romanisation of Diana gave her a different energy and feel to the goddess Artemis and more modern Italian descriptions of Diana[305] are different again. Deities change and adapt to the people that are worshipping them.

What does the evidence suggest when looking at antiquity? As we have shown, there is evidence that can be seen to suggest that at some point they were the same deity, for example the parentage, the similar mythological stories, and the confusion with the days of the week. But is each of these enough to say with certainty that they, at some point, were the same deity? Certainly, there is just as much evidence to suggest that they were not considered to be the same deity, the clearest of these being that they appear together in the same myths. The writing style of the Norse literature does follow the classical style in that a character is described using different names or versions of their names, but this is clearly not the case with Frigga and Freyja as the characters interact with each other. *The Prose Edda*, which is considered to be one of the oldest sources, for example (in the story *Lokasenna*)[306] shows them very clearly as separate characters. Moving on from the *Prose Edda*, however, we see that occasionally Snorri seemed to attribute the same things to both goddesses[307] (for example the falcon cloak) so the confusion between the two started even at this stage. It is worth remembering,

---

[305] Charles Leland, *Aradia: Gospel of the Witches*, 1899.
[306] *The Prose Edda*.
[307] Britt Mari Nasstrom, *Freyja, Great Goddess of the North*, 1995.

however, that Snorri Sturluson was already secondary evidence (as in, he was writing about beliefs that were dying out and were not his) when it was written.

If Freyja and Frigga are not the same goddess, how can we explain the evidence that suggests that they are? This is evidence upon which academics have built theories for many years. Perhaps, instead of suggesting that Frigga and Freyja have come from the same source, it is more accurate to suggest that Frigga and Freyja are deities from the same pantheon who are often confused with each other. The two goddesses are often mentioned in the later Norse literature alongside the Virgin Mary especially for childbirth charms. In fact one of these charms describes Mary opening the womb with her keys, but the keys are a symbol of Frigga.[308]

Frigga and Freyja are goddesses from the same pantheon that have, in antiquity and even in the modern day, been confused with each other. Evidence exists that suggests that they may have come from the same source, but the amount of evidence that exists, especially when combined with the evidence that suggests that (especially within Norse society) they existed and functioned as separate deities, is not enough to fully conclude that they were at one point the same goddess. Within modern pagan thinking it is clear that Frigga and Freyja are not the same goddess; whether or not they originally existed as one single goddess is not clear enough to decipher one way or another. My suspicions lie in the reasoning that they were two separate goddesses whom authors in antiquity confused occasionally.

Bibliography
Blain, Jenny. *Nine Worlds of Seid-Magic*. Routledge, 2001.
Branston, Brian. *The Lost Gods of England*. Thames & Hudson, 1957
Crossley-Holland, Kevin. *The Penguin Book of Norse Myths: Gods of the Vikings*. Penguin, 1996.
D'Este, Sorita & Rankine, David. *The Isles of the Many Gods*. Avalonia, 2007.
Ellis Davidson, H.R. *Gods and Myths of Northern Europe*. Penguin Books Ltd., 1969.
Fisher, Peter (trans.) *Saxo Grammaticus: The History of the Danes*, Books I-IX: I. English Text; II. Commentary: Bks.1-9. D.S. Brewer, 2008.
Grundy, Stephan. *Freyja and Frigg*, first appeared in *The Concept of the Goddess*, edited by Sandra Billington and Miranda Green. Routledge, 1996.
Hollander, Lee. *The Poetic Edda*. Translated with an introduction and explanatory notes. University of Texas Press, 1962.
Jochens, Jenny. *Women in Old Norse Society*. Cornell University Press, 1995.
Lafayllve, Patricia M. *Freyja, Lady, Vanadis*. Outskirts Press, 2006.
Larrington, Carolyne (trans.). *Poetic Edda*. Oxford Paperbacks, 2008.
Leland, Charles. *Aradia: Gospel of the Witches*, 1899.

---

[308] Lynda C Welch, *Goddess of the North*, 2001.

Vs.

McGrath, Sheena. *Asyiniur: Women's Mysteries in the Northern Tradition.* Capall Bann Publishing, 1997.
Nasstrom, Britt Mari. *Freyja, The Great Goddess of the North.* Almqvist & Wiksell Internat, 1995.
O'Donague, Heather. *From Asgard to Valhalla.* I.B.Tauris, 2008.
Paxson, Diana L. *Essential Asatru: Walking the Path of Norse Paganism.* Citadel Press Inc., U.S., 2006.
Sturluson, Snorri. *Prose Edda.* Trans. Byock, Jesse L. Penguin Classics, 2005.
Welch, Lynda C. *Goddess of the North.* Red Wheel/Weiser, 2001.

HIDDEN CHILDREN OF THE GREAT M/OTHER

The resolution of binary oppositions into complementary polarities in Wicca

by Melissa Harrington

Wicca is a pantheistic, egalitarian, ecological, diverse, post modern, feminist Nature Religion, which fits better into the contemporary spiritual zeitgeist than the struggling patriarchal monotheisms that seem to have had their day. Thus Wicca has risen like a phoenix from the flames of secularism to take its place in the dawn of a new religious consciousness.

When Gerald Gardner published *Witchcraft Today* in 1954 it would have been hard to predict that Wicca would become a global faith in less than a century, but not impossible. For Wicca has an appeal beyond its 21st century psychosocial norms, which goes to the heart of all religions: that of resolving the split between the body and soul, the human and the divine.

Binary Oppositions

The first chapter of *Genesis* describes Elohim dividing the light from the darkness and calling the light day and the darkness night. That division of light and dark has manifested in the philosophies and doctrines of many religions, and forms the basis of dualism.

It is the easiest division that one could make, and yet it forms the basis of most prejudice and negative stereotyping, where Other - as in not-I - becomes Other - as in different, hard to understand, wrong, then bad. And yet its basis may be biological.

The cognitive development of the human being is a fascinating and complex process that has spawned millions of studies and theories, but a lot of them seem to hinge on the issue of differentiation. It seems we are born to make our own identity in relation to others, to construct ourselves in relation to 'the Other'.

It seems we are born to differentiate to make sense of the world. Saussaruen linguists argue that binary oppositions are integral to the production of meaning, and is the logic underlying all language, and thus we split the world into binary opposites. This is confirmed by contemporary psychologists who talk of schema theory. A schema is a template we build of the world so we do not have to learn everything anew each day. We can fit new information onto what we already know, and find a match of best fit, so things make sense. Analytic psychologists, such as Melanie Klein, have built a large body of work on *'splitting'*: how we spilt things into *'bad'* and *'good'*, sometimes including parts of ourselves, and how we can project these categories onto others. This has been adopted successfully by clinicians working with patients with mental illness.

The Sociological Other

Pierre Bordieu was a sociologist who worked in the grand narrative traditions that are typified by the work of Marx and Freud; he examines the symbolic sets of differences between male and female. In his discussion of the generative formula of antagonistic forces he created a diagram that he calls a synoptic diagram of pertinent oppositions.

Social scientists have explored difference in terms of its construction via binary opposition, and shown how this usually means that one term is privileged more than the other, that one becomes the norm and one *'the Other'*. They show that this can be used negatively for exclusion and marginalisation of people who are construed as *'Other'* or outsiders. Jacques Derrida discussed the deprivileging of one of a binary opposition. French feminist writers have taken Derrida's thesis and elaborated upon it in terms of gender, pointing out that power oppositions lead to social divisions that are inevitably gendered.

Luce Irigaray is a French feminist philosopher who has iconic status in feminist academia. Her writings offer a critique of patriarchy that encompasses philosophy, linguistics, and psychoanalysis and representation theory. Her work over decades moves from describing how the differences in male and female speech patterns show the invisibility of women in society, to suggesting ways to recognise sexual difference between the genders, and attempt to make this work in society, rather than aim for an equality that is impossible. She discusses the Other thus:

> *"Who is the other, the Other ...? How can the other be defined? Levinas speaks of 'the Other' ..., of 'respect for the Other..., of the 'face of the Other'.... But how to define this Other which seems so self evident to him, and which I see as a postulate, the projection or the remnant of a system, a hermeneutic locus of crystallization or meaning, etc... Who is the other, if the other of sexual difference is not recognized or known? Does it not mean in that case a sort of mask or lure? Or an effect of the consumption of an other ...? But how is transcendence defined?...*

Vs.

> *...What Levinas does not see is that locus of paternity, to which he accords the privilege of ethical alterity, has already assumed the place of the genealogy of the feminine, and has already covered over the relationships between mothers and daughters, in which formerly transmission of the divine word located...*
>
> *...The other sex, then, would represent the possible locus of the definition of the fault, the imperfection, of the unheard, of the unfulfilled, etc. But this fault cannot be named except by my other or its substitute. More precisely, there are at least two interpretations of the fault: that which corresponds to the failed fulfilment..., of my sex, the failure to become the ideal of my genre, and that which is defined in relation to the ideal of the other genre. These faults are not the same. For centuries, one has been cruelly masked by the other. This puts society permanently in the position of being ethically at fault, a position which often has the backing of religion."*[309]

Helen Cixous agrees that the gendering of difference is due to long term cultural determination. She wrote:

> *...Where is she?*
> *Activity/passivity*
> *Sun/Moon*
> *Culture/Nature*
> *Day/Night,*
> *Father/Mother,*
> *Head/heart,*
> *Intelligent/sensitive,*
> *Man*
> *Woman*[310]

The Witch as Other

Looking at these discussions of binary oppositions, splitting and deprivileging of 'The Other', it is clear that Witchcraft is Other with a capital O. The Witch has always been the Other on the edge of the village, on the edge of society; blamed for wasting cattle and blighting crops. She is the old woman, the worn husk that can no longer give birth, beyond her time, souring the milk by the very fact of her barren existence. No heed is paid to her wisdom, or her present capabilities for light work in contributions to the clan. Old ladies may babysit, but not if you have read the perennial fairy tale *Hansel and*

---

[309] Irigaray, quoted in *The Irigary Reader*, pp. 181-2.
[310] Cixous, Helen, "Sorties", English translation in *New French Feminism: an Anthology*, p. 90.

Vs.

Gretel. The young woman must be pure, she must be meek, good, obedient, beautiful, pre-marriage, all the qualities of Cinderella, or Snow White. The Witch however is different: she is the seducer. Nimue, Circe, Heide, Lilith, Morgana, Babalon; the vagina dentata, the fanny with fangs, the worst of all men's fears.

Erica Jong, whose feminist fiction sold millions, wrote the beautiful illustrated book *Witches*, in which she weaves together the myth and the magic of the Witch, how she is feared for the dark feminine power she wields, and how she has been repressed. Witches represent our shadow-side where lurk our darkest fears as well as our untapped powers and great unconscious reservoirs of power. This untapped potential, the hidden, the feared, the untouched reserves of natural bright power is more easily envisaged as Goddess power, a less pejorative term but infinitely woven with the powers of the Witch; for the old Goddesses became the demons and hags of the last few thousand years, now returned to their celestial thrones by the new Paganism. It is no wonder that Hekate, the great Goddess of antiquity should be a rightful Goddess for the contemporary Witch.

Witchcraft is the domain of women and of nature, ruled by the Moon and the Great Mother. Logic is left outside the circle where people of all paths leave their outer identities on the threshold, with their clothes. Craft is often practiced naked, or sky clad, so fashions and signals of rank can be left at the door, and the power can flow from the unfettered dance of the naked body, as the incense billows in golden candle light, and the temple shivers into another world when incantations in ancient tongues summon elder Gods.

The Gods of Witchcraft are the Old Ones who have long been banished but have never left out sleeping minds. They call to us from the dappled sunlight in the forest, and the living grass that sweeps like seas across the meadows. They whisper in the winds, and their faces flicker in the fires as midwinter softly wraps the land in a snowy mantle.

They are Gods who have lasted millennia, and shown themselves in the faces of so many different cultures: Thunder Gods, Forest Gods, Gentle Gods, and Gods that call their name as the deer rut under the deepening autumn sunset; They are Goddesses of love, of every hue from every era, such as Freyja and Aphrodite. They are Goddesses of war who ride through our mythic landscapes from Sekhmet in Egypt to Morrigan of the Celtic west, instilling admiration and devotion into the heart of many a young woman who seeks their strength and fortitude.

They are the Gods who were banished when their younger brothers came to rule with patriarchy, reason and culture; demonized they lurked in the shadows, until when our need was greatest they rose from the depths of our dreaming, like phoenixes of light with healing on their wings.

Vs.

The resolution of opposites in the circle.

Wicca actively resolves the power balance of binary opposites. It can be seen as a ritual enactment of the principals of yin and yang. The circle is a place in which paradoxes are resolved. It is a place where east meets west, and north meets south, fire meets water and the wheel turns. It is an alchemical vessel for transmutation of flesh and spirit into one, of human and divine into one. The Witch stands as alchemist at the centre of the circle, where heat and cold, wet and dry, merge to form the fifth element of spirit, where all is one and one is all.

Magic is the Witch's stock in trade. It has its own logic, but a logic that works when the conscious mind is shielded by the ecstasy of the Witches Sabbat, and power is raised that can not be held permanently in any vessel, but flows through like lightning; revivifying, healing, and enlightening those who held it for the split second it manifested, then melted into nothing.

And at Wicca's heart is the Goddess and the Witch, not split into opposing pairs, like Virgin vs. Mother, Maiden vs. Whore, but complementary. All female Witches carry the Goddess, as women they strive to embrace the dark and fertile ground that comes with the word '*Witch*'. They embrace the two together and reconcile the split within of Goddess and Witch, of Virgin and Whore, of Mother and Daughter, of woman and wife.[311]

In Wicca the Gods are invoked into human vessels. The divine is perceived to be within each of us, immanent in all nature, and to be available to be drawn upon at any time. This is expressed so beautifully in the *Charge of the Goddess* as rewritten in the mid-1950s by Doreen Valiente, that this text has become central to many forms of Modern Pagan Witchcraft.

> "...I who am the beauty of the green earth, and the white Moon among the stars, and the mystery of the waters, and the desire of the heart of man, call unto thy soul. Arise, and come unto me. For I am the soul of nature, who gives life to the universe. From me all things proceed, and unto me all things must return; and before my face, beloved of Gods and of men, let thine innermost divine self be enfolded in the rapture of the infinite."

We can see a soft juxtaposition of complementary polarity in the 'eight virtues of Wicca' in this paragraph:

> "Let my worship be within the heart that rejoiceth; for behold, all acts of love and pleasure are my rituals. And therefore let there be beauty and strength, power and compassion, honour and humility, mirth and reverence within you."

---

[311] See Rowntree, *Embracing the witch and goddess, feminist ritual-makers in New Zealand.*

And it is re-iterated that there is no split between human and divine, simply a matter of mystery that can be unveiled.

> *"And thou who thinkest to seek for me, know thy seeking and yearning shall avail thee not unless thou knowest the mystery; that if that which thou sleekest thee findest not within thee, thou wilt never find it without thee. For behold, I have been with thee from the beginning; and I am that which is attained at the end of desire."*[312]

If we examine the whole ritual corpus of Wicca we can see that it celebrates diversity, but weaves a seasonal dance that allows the God and Goddess to wield differing sorts of power as the year turns. And yet as they do this dance of life and death they worship each other, and seek completion in each other's arms.

In terms of its placement in our cultural imagination Witchcraft claims all that is natural; natural magic, natural healing, earth magic. It claims Gods such as Pan that are half animal, half man, half beast, in arithmetic that gloriously does not add up. It aims for the return to the innocence of Eden. Wicca hearkens to an ancient bucolic past. We no longer believe the Murrayite hypothesis of the Old Religion, an ancient hidden Witch cult in Western Europe, but the image and emphasis of ritual draws heavily on a dream of a place and time that may never have existed, but is recreated in our mythic dreams, and ambitions for a better world tomorrow.

Coming home

My doctoral research was on conversion to Wicca. It is generally accepted that one does not convert to Wicca, but rather one comes home. In my research I found plenty of evidence to support this strong feeling, but other interesting trends arose as well.

I found that many respondents had consciously turned away from the religion of their birth, then entered a period of quest before they came home to Wicca. Some had found the home-coming feeling strongest when they encountered their first friends who thought like them, others felt it at initiation. All had held their own form of Pagan belief for years before they found a faith community that believed the same things, which is one of the crucial parts of that homecoming.

Almost all were Christians who had disavowed their birth religions before joining Wicca. This disavowment was necessary, as they would not accept that this wonderful part of their life meant that they were evil and would burn in hell. Due to Christian doctrine they had to turn their back on their family's God of wrath and damnation in order to worship the Goddess as the Great Mother of all. The few respondents whom I found who had been born Hindu

---
[312] Valiente, *The Charge of the Goddess*, p. 54.

and Buddhist had not had to take such drastic steps, and incorporated aspects of both religions in their personal faith.

Men described coming to Wicca for a variety of reasons, but one of the main aspects of Wicca that appealed to them was that the Divine is seen as both male and female, with an emphasis on the Goddess. The Goddess called to these men, she had always been there in myriad forms, in myths, in art, in literature, in films: but always as an icon, an image, a dream mirage, until they found Wicca, where She made religion come alive for them.

Psychologists have shown that there is a case for the theory that we create the image of our Gods in the image of our parents. From the day we are born we see the world divided into male and female gender, and yet for the person born into patriarchal monotheism God is male, and there is a huge unspoken gap of the divine feminine.

Of course the Goddess is there in the Abrahamic faiths, but she is well hidden, and has been further hidden by androcentric translations of ancient texts. In Christianity she is explicit as the Virgin Mary, and is worshipped much as a Goddess (one of the reasons fewer Catholics feel the need to become Witches), but she is a strangely neutered Goddess; the Virgin Mother is a phrase that is a paradox in itself. In Wicca the Goddess is glorified in all her feminine faces, from the young virgin Brighde who brings in the first flush of Spring, through the Great Mother to Hecate, the dark Queen of the Underworld. Ancient Goddesses from pantheistic cultures are invoked, and a variety of mythic life cycles are celebrated as the year wheel turns. Respondents in my study spoke of the relief and joy that they felt when they could at last worship the Divine in a more wholesome form, and the positive effect that this had on them.

Men also described how they came to Wicca to worship the Goddess, but therein found the God. They mirrored the Wiccan myth of a God who came to lay his sword and crown at the feet of the Goddess, but therein found his true power. In coming to Wicca they found a religion they had not thought existed, one that honours the feminine face of the divine, but also honours the God, not as the dominant force over and above femininity but as a complementary partner.

Thus Wicca embraces the paradoxes and dichotomies of male and female and turns them to its adherent's advantage. It acknowledges and celebrates polarities rather than privileging one opposition over another. Wiccans describe the God and Goddess as complementary polarities, similar to the concept of the yin yang yu found in Taoism. Although the same male/female, dry/wet distinctions are made as in western oppositions, these are seen as necessary to each other, and each holding the seed of the other within itself.

Here we can see a relationship to the Jungian concept of the male Animus inside all women and the female Anima inside all men.

Part of the sacred technology of invocation in Wicca may lie in this complementary polarity, where the Priestess reaches deep inside herself, and far outside into the spiritual realm, to invoke the God into the Priest, and vice versa.[313]

Ritual

The Wiccan year wheel celebrates the Gods in all their aspects, and the deity in both its dark and light forms. Birth, growth, marriage, death and rebirth are all celebrated as the wheel turns. Thus deity is seen as both the giver and taker of life, the force which promises and fulfils rebirth. As the rites are enacted the Witch dances the dance of light and dark with their Goddess. In this dance it becomes possible to understand why the taker of life is also the giver of life, why the Great Witch Goddess Hecate should stand at the crossroads, and how she might be the midwife of new life as she cuts the cord that binds us to this earth.

Initiations take much symbolic form from the process of life and death, and the meeting of anima and animus. At each circle the Witches celebrate the union of complementary forces, and the rite is grounded when cakes and wine are consecrated, bringing down the energy of the rite into the ritual food and drink to share. This is done with the Priest kneeling before the Priestess, carrying the cup, while she carries the ritual knife, or the athame. They join cup of wine and ritual knife with the words *"as the athame is to the male, so the cup is to the female, and conjoined they bring forth blessedness"*, the Priest lifts the cup and the Priestess lowers the athame.

Some Witches draw on the writings of Dion Fortune and explain polarity in terms of the male being passive on the inner plane while active on the outer plane, while the female is passive on the outer plane and active on the inner plane, and that the cakes and wine symbolise this. Some say that this is just a hangover from sexual stereotyping that still places the woman at the centre of home and the man in the market place, but for whatever reason, it does, as a ritual symbolic act, enact the balanced polarity of the yin yang symbol. A reading of Taoist philosophy may indicate much as to the nature of Wiccan polarity concepts.

Esoteric notions of complementary polarities

Given Wicca's long roots in the ceremonial magical traditions it is not surprising that the union of opposites has long featured in Western esoteric thought. The Kabbalah maps the universe and the human conscience, and is a model of motion, whereby Sephiroth function like magnetic poles, each negative to the one above and positive to the one below, while the force of the universe flows

---

[313] See Vivianne Crowley, *Wicca: The Old Religion in the New Age*.

through its channels. In ritual and meditation it is not recommended to go straight up the middle pillar, straight into the eye of God, but to travel its paths in succession, integrating the energies of the complementary poles through which one passes.

Alchemy has a long and vivid tradition of mediating hot/cold, wet/dry etc., and it is in solving and coagulating, in melting down the prima materia to make the stone of the wise, that the gold is formed from dross.

Carl G. Jung's *Mysterium Coniunctionis*, is based upon the study of opposites, reviewing Medieval, Renaissance, and post-Renaissance alchemy from a psychological perspective as spiritual and mental transformation of the alchemist via the conjunction of Solar/Lunar, Male/Female, Spirit/Matter.

Various sacred texts that explore opposition and polarity are used by ceremonial magicians today. I particularly liked working with the *Thunder Perfect Mind* with O.T.O friends, in rites where this text from the second or third century CE was used as a modern Goddess invocation:

> "...I am the union and the dissolution.
> I am the abiding and the loosing.
> I am the descent, and they come up to me.
> I am the judgment and the acquittal.
> I, I am sinless, and the root of sin is from me.
> I am desire in appearance, and self control of the heart exists within me
> and interior self-control exists within me.
> I am the hearing which is attainable to everyone
> and the ungraspable utterance."[314]

Conclusion

Witches embrace the paradox of the shadowside; they embrace the deprivileged Other of feminine divinity, feminine sexuality and feminine power. In doing so they open up a new world of possibilities where existing power structures may not be the only ones, and a patriarchal religion may not be the only answer in a multi-faith world. In doing so they open up new possibilities of divinity, God, of Godhead, and of being human. In doing so they explore and claim territories that have long been *'occult'* i.e. hidden and considered heresy for centuries.

It is not surprising that this radical religious change is happening at a time when fundamentalist monotheistic Christianity is losing its grip on contemporary western society, where secular atheistic humanism concerns itself with equality and diversity, nor

---

[314] Mcquire, *Diotima – Materials for The Study of Women and Gender in the Ancient World*, 4.

Vs.

when feminism has informed some of the ethos of this fascinating new religiosity.

It is time that the Goddess sat once more beside her consort the God, and antagonistic dualisms were laid aside. Wiccans do so with joy and relief as they dance their spiral dance under the full moon, then walk away complete and completed. Many Wiccans claim to have had extraordinary results in healing rites, and spiritual states of consciousness. It is impossible to prove these claims scientifically, but if in the very least Wicca provides its followers with joy, peace and inspiration then its magic is well founded.

This is a book that will mainly be read by Pagan practitioners, and it is for that market that I have addressed this chapter, however, I think it is appropriate here to have the last word from Luce Irigary on meeting and embracing the Other:

> *"He risks who risks life itself...And who goes not into the abyss can only repeat and restate paths already opened up that erase the traces of gods who have fled. Alone, always alone, the poet runs the risk of venturing out side the world and of folding back its ripeness to touch the bottom of the bottomless. Saying yes to what calls him beyond the horizon. In this abandonment, one breath, at most, is left to him. First and last energy that is forgotten when is not short of it. Present everywhere, but invisible, granting life to all and to everything, on pain of death. ...Expiring in the other so as to be reborn more inspired...Leaving the already-consecrated temple to find traces of the ferial bond with the wholly other...whose breath subtly impregnates the air, like a vibration perceived by those lost in love. Their sense awakens, they boldly go forward and, sometimes, a song comes to their lips. ..In this opacity, this night of the world, they discover traces of gods who have fled, at the very moment when they have given up their salvation. Their radiance comes of their consenting that nothing shall ensure their keeping...Yet the breath of he who sings, mingling his inspiration with the divine breath, remains out of reach. Cannot be situated. Faceless. He who perceives it sets it off. Obeys the attraction. Goes to encounter nothing – only the more than all that is."*[315]

---

[315] Irigaray, quoted in *The Irigaray Reader,* pp. 213-218.

Bibliography

Bordieu, Pierre, *The Logic of Practice*. Cambridge: Polity Press, 1995.
Cixous, Helene *'Sorties'* in *La Jeune Nee*. Paris. Union General d'Editions, 10/12, 1975. English translation in Marks E and de Courtivron, I (eds) *New French Feminism: an Anthology*. Amherst M A. University of Massachussetts Press, 1980.
Crowley, Vivianne, *Wicca: The Old Religion in the New Age*. London: Aquarian Press, 1989.
Frese, Pamela R. and Coggeshall, John M., *Transcending Boundaries. Multidisciplinary approaches to the study of Gender*. New York: Bergin and Garvey, 1991.
Fortune, Dion, *The Mystical Qabalah*. The Aquarian Press, 1987.
Gardner, G. B., *Witchcraft Today*. London: Rider, 1954.
Gardner, G. B., *The Meaning of Witchcraft*. New York: Magickal Childe, 1959.
Harrington Melissa, *A study of conversion processes in Wicca, with specific reference to male converts*. Department of Theology and Religious Studies, Kings College, London, 2006.
Hetherington, Mavis E. and Parke, Ross D., *Child Psychology, a contemporary viewpoint*. McGraw Hill International editions, 1986.
Irigary – see Whitford.
Jong, Erica, *Witches*. New York: Harry N Abrahams Inc., 1981.
Jung, Carl G. M., *Mysterium Coniunctionis: an enquiry into the separation and synthesis of psychic opposites in alchemy*. London: Routledge and Kegan Paul Ltd., 1963.
Klein, Melanie, *The Psycho-analysis of children*. London: Hogarth Press, 1937.
McGuire, Ann *'Thunder Perfect Mind'*, pp. 39-54 in *Searching the Scriptures, Volume 2: A Feminist Commentary*. Ed. Elisabeth Schuessler Fiorenza. New York. Crossroad, 1994.
McGuire, Ann, *'The Thunder: Perfect Mind'*, in internet document *Diotima – Materials for The Study of Women and Gender in the Ancient World*, 2000. http://www.stoa.org/diotima/anthology/thunder.
Murray M. A., *The Witch-Cult in Western Europe*. Oxford: Oxford University Press, 1921.
Rowntree, Katherine, *Embracing the witch and goddess, feminist ritualmakers in New Zealand*. London: Routledge, 2004.
Young J. E., Klosko J. and Weishaar M. E., *Schema Therapy, a Practitioner's Guide*. London: The Guildford Press, 2003.
Valiente, Doreen, *The Rebirth of Witchcraft*. Washington: Phoenix Publishing Inc., 1989.
Valiente, Doreen, *The Charge of the Goddess*. Brighton: Hexagon Hoopix, 2000. (The text for The Charge of the Goddess is widely available on the internet).
Whitford Margaret, *The Irigaray Reader*. Oxford: Blackwell, 1991/1996.
Woodward, Kathryn, *Identity and Difference*. Milton Keynes: Open University, 1997.

Vs.

POLARITY MAGICK

by Diane M. Champigny

The early classic texts of Janet and Stewart Farrar were cornerstones of my becoming. They comment on their views regarding the distinction between *'gender magic'*, which utilizes men and women as opposites in rites, and *'sex magic'*.

> " . . . We would say categorically: sex magic as such should only be worked by a couple for whom intercourse is a normal part of their relationship – in other words husband and wife or established lovers in complete privacy."

They go on to say:

> " . . . If they approached it cold bloodedly as a 'necessary magical operation' that would be a gross abuse of their sexuality and their supposed respect for each other; if they rushed into it with a sudden and ill considered warmth, it could have effects on unexpected levels for which they are quite unprepared; worst of all it could effect them unequally, leaving one emotionally overwhelmed and the other with a burden of guilt. Sex magic without love is black magic."[316]

An important element of working within a Wiccan context is polarity. In *The Life and Times of a Modern Witch*, the Farrars note, "*Wiccan philosophy sees polarity as the great creative drive of the Cosmos, from macrocosm to microcosm; the tension between complementary opposites from which all manifestation proceeds, and without which manifestation is unthinkable.*"[317]

'Polarity' is the concept of complementary opposites which, when brought together, create manifestation. There are different ways of working with polarity, and techniques to work with polarity within one's self, as we have both masculine and feminine aspects within our individual beings. Regardless of personal human sexual preference, male/female polarity is the form that Nature chose to use for procreation.

---

[316] Farrar, Janet and Stewart. *The Witches Way*, p. 171.
[317] Farrar, Janet and Stewart. *The Life and Times of a Modern Witch*, p. 42.

Vs.

The practice we'll be focusing on here is that of the energetic interplay between Priestess and Priest, and it is this method of operation that is used in Alexandrian Witchcraft.

We can define the Law of Polarity as the concept that any pattern of data can be split into two *'opposing'* characteristics, each containing the fundamental nature of the other within itself. The *'opposite'* of a pattern contains information about that pattern, by providing information on what the pattern is not. Thus, control over a pattern's opposite facilitates control over the pattern itself.

Polarity should not be confused with dualism; an error that Westerners have been making for thousands of years and which has quite possibly led to more misunderstanding than any other theological concept in history. Dualism assumes that opposites are at odds with one another; polarity assumes that they embrace. Everything contains its opposite as is reflected in the Daoist *yin-yang-yu* symbol. Duality is the foundation of Reality.

Being related to sex magick, polarity magick is sex magick that is never consummated, like the north and south poles of two magnets which are not permitted to touch. Energy is drawn from the workers of polarity magick throughout the course of the working and not just in one burst of energy as is the case in coitus.

Dion Fortune states in the *Sea Priestess*:

> *"In this sacrament the woman must take her ancient place as priestess of the rite, calling down lightning from heaven; the initiator, not the initiated. She had to become the priestess of the Goddess, and I, the kneeling worshipper, had to receive the sacrament at her hands. When the body of a woman is made an altar for the worship of the Goddess who is all beauty and magnetic life, then the Goddess enters the Temple."*[318]

Polarity magick, or gender magick to use a more antiquated term, does not necessarily involve the act of sexual intercourse. There are many other ways with which to transcend the mundane and touch the infinite. Dion Fortune illustrates this aptly in her fictional books *The Sea Priestess* and *Moon Magic*. A careful study of these novels would serve the aspirant well and provide a lifetime of information with which to work. Some of my Elders (and myself) re-read them on a yearly basis (or every other year) to glean new insights. Every time we read them we are on a different leg of our spiritual Journey, so new vistas open up with each reading.

My personal experience working within a magickal partnership has been focused on duotheistic gender polarity. In my opinion, it is necessary to have a polar interchange, or both sides of the battery present, for a successful lifting of the veil. In the hands of well-

---
[318] Fortune, Dion. *The Sea Priestess*, pp. 160-1.

trained, experienced, consecrated Initiates, it could be an act as simple as the laying of the Priest's hand onto the lap of the Priestess. Going beyond Drawing Down the Moon within a ritual context, there is an oracular technique that is practiced between the Priestess and Priest. It consists of the Priestess being in a seated position, donning a veil or shroud (black is traditional, but colours may be used to channel a particular deity or force, such as red for Hekate, silver for Selene, blue for Isis, etc.) The Priest kneels at the Priestesses feet and either chants an appropriate rune, couplet, or *'takes the Priestess down'* by way of visualization. When the channel has been worked and well worn between the two, it could merely be the laying on of hands that sends the Priestess into the trance state. This technique can be used during ritual *amongst experienced practitioners,* or worked privately.

With regards to the issue of magickal polarity I tend to think of the principles of Chokmah and Binah, the masculine and feminine aspects on the Tree of Life – the two specific opposing principles of the universe. Think of these two principles as intuitive versus rational, holistic versus linear, analogue versus digital, or synchronistic versus cause-and-effect. Always remember that opposites attract and that like attracts like.[319]

Another way of looking at polarity is as a magnetic interchange, having a mutual sympathy and rapport with one's working partner – an energetic gestalt through which energy can flow and return. This vortex is built up with practice and is reinforced upon the planes. Over time, the level reached on the inner planes increases and higher forces may be contacted and communed with.

Ritual energizes the imagination and therefore stimulates emotion causing latent energies to come to the fore. It is the interplay of these energies that the working couple is attempting to tap into and work with. I can't stress the importance of alignment, rapport and sympathy enough. This type of work tends to open telepathic links between the parties. For example, knowing when the other person is going to call or arrive unexpectedly, getting a feeling for your partner's emotional state without knowing previous details, or receiving flashes of occurrences happening in the other person's life. It can also lead to having them tell you something you already were aware of that they didn't have to tell you, having them appear in dreams, doing ritual work on the astral and being able to compare notes and having them make sense, match up and be provable, etc. What you are attempting to form is an energetic circuit, through which both energies meet, flow and merge. This eventually creates the link or vortex that I refer to, which in turn leads to being able to *'speed dial'* the other person with little effort. Words are extremely tenuous when discussing this topic, and metaphor is sometimes the

---

[319] Diane M. Champigny, "*Lifting the Veil,*" p. 189, in *Priestesses Pythonesses Sibyls.*

only way to convey the concepts. It is the Lifting of the Veil, the Opening of the Door.

Usually, people are not ready for this Work before their 30's or 40's when their lives are already established with family and children. This poses a problem for most folks, as their spouses are not usually the ones with whom they work magickally. I have worked with my magickal partner for many years. He was originally my teacher and Initiator and we've come full circle so to speak. We are Brother and Sister in the Art. Our relationship has never been sexual, but that has not hindered or stopped our progress in any way. Again, polarity magick is not necessarily sex magick. Our rapport is such that it is like having each other on speed dial because the connection has been built and maintained over time. We employ some of the initial techniques such as breath work, power passage and energy exchange, but are able to simply use a form of entrainment that *'gets us there'* without too much preparation. Entrainment is a technique of grounding and centring yourself, then meeting face to face with the person standing in ritual posture, looking deeply into each other's eyes (or if that is too much at first, focusing on the *'third eye'* or pineal gland and jumping off from there.) You can also use entrainment with each other's energy centres or chakras. It is important not to break the connection during this Work and to breathe in synch with the person. An established magickal couple will know when things are *'cooked'* and then move forward with the Work. A key point to keep in mind is that polarity magick is experiential, part of the Western Mystery Tradition, and cannot be fully (or even partially) grasped by armchair study.

Sources/Further Reading:
Ashcroft-Nowicki, Dolores. *First Steps in Ritual*. Aquarian Press, 1982.
Ashcroft-Nowicki, Dolores. *The Tree of Ecstasy*. Aquarian Press, 1991.
Champigny, Diane M. *"Lifting the Veil"* in *Priestesses Pythonesses Sibyls*, ed. Sorita d'Este. Avalonia, 2008.
Farrar, Janet and Stewart. *Life and Times of a Modern Witch*. Phoenix Publishing, 1988.
Farrar, Janet and Stewart. *The Witches Way*. Robert Hale, London, 1984.
Fortune, Dion. *Moon Magic*. Wyndham Publications, Ltd., 1976.
Fortune, Dion. *The Sea Priestess*. Wyndham Publications, Ltd., 1976.
Fortune, Dion. *What is Occultism?* Weiser Books, 2001.
Fortune, Dion and Knight, Gareth. *The Circuit of Force*. Thoth Publishing, 1998.
Fortune, Dion and Knight, Gareth. *The Circuit of Force*. Thoth Publishing, 1998.
Fortune, Dion. *What is Occultism?* Weiser Books, 2001.
Harris, Mike and Burg, Wendy. *Polarity Magic: the Secret History of Western Religion*. Llewellyn, 2003.

Vs.

Exoteric Neopaganism

Toward a Minor Religion?

by Jon Hanna

"Je est un autre" ("I is an other") — Arthur Rimbaud

"There is nothing that is major or revolutionary except the minor." — Gilles Deleuze & Félix Guattari

An accusation that was, and still is, directed first at Gerald Gardner and then at Alex Sanders, is that they were too interested in popular attention. While the number of column-inches they provoked during their respective lifetimes stands as evidence for the prosecution, there are reams published in the last quarter-century or so that would bear evidence to the opinion that Gardner, Sanders, and their contemporaries within Wicca, had not been populist enough.

This publishing has expounded a form of modern pagan witchcraft that is directly or indirectly influenced by Wicca, but which is apart from its initiatory tradition. Many such practitioners identify their craft as also being *Wicca* (e.g. Scott Cunningham, D. J. Conway and Arin Murphy-Hiscock), some prefer not to use the term, but still see it as applicable to their practice (e.g. Silver Ravenwolf) and some distinguish themselves from it more vehemently while still having much in common with these practices (e.g. Ann Moura).

Of these practices, those which inform the bulk of such publication are much more exoteric than the original initiatory tradition of Wicca, with those who provide more complete instructional guides to would-be practitioners being exoteric by definition.

Such forms of witchcraft are a particularly prominent part of the wider Neopagan movement. As this wider movement has grown, there have been increasing numbers who identify with it, but not with any narrower grouping within it. While this Neopaganism is generally held to be a very diffuse movement, views expressed as belonging to such exoteric witchcraft are common among even those who do not identify with any grouping narrower than just Neopaganism, and there is definitely an exchange of ideas within it. As such, while it may be inaccurate to associate wider Neopaganism too closely with such forms of witchcraft, so too would it be inaccurate to hold them as completely distinct from each other.

The degree of distinction or overlap involved here is debated. *'Lumpers'* and *'splitters'* can be found among both those who are sympathetic to these movements and those who view one or more of them with some disdain. It will hopefully suffice here to note for the sake of precision that there are some that practice the earlier traditions of Wicca while also partaking of the more exoteric forms of modern paganism, before considering them as separate movements.

One item of commonality that is often claimed to be still shared by initiatory Wicca and exoteric Neopaganism is the form of dualism found expressed within them.

Hegel and Marx notwithstanding, the predominant public, exoteric expression of duality in Western metaphysics has long been the moral dualism of Christianity, reinforced by similar views being also found in the other Abrahamic faiths. Good opposes evil, heaven opposes hell, God opposes devil, and the individual is exhorted to strive toward the pole that is endorsed, and away from that condemned.

It is primarily in the esoteric that we find dualities and polarities where one is not valued over the other: The Hermetic Laws of Polarity and of Gender, for example, tells us that everything contains such dualities and the Law of Rhythm claims that motion between such poles is vital. The Qabalah meanwhile balances the two outer pillars as well as holding that each Sephiroth is both receptive to those above and transmits to those below. In the esoteric movements of the West, duality is not resolved through the eventual future annihilation of one side, but through unification, balance, or a perpetually cyclic dynamic.

Exoteric Neopaganism therefore, is unusual in being an exoteric Western religious movement that expresses a duality other than the Christian moral dualism.

At first glance, its sources seem obvious. Exoteric Neopaganism is after all, also unusual in the extent to which not only is it influenced by more esoteric perspectives (and those other influences it has, besides Wicca, are in many cases also esoteric), but also acknowledges or even boasts of that debt. This considered, we will not be surprised to find within it ideas that are more common among esoteric views.

However, this may be the myopia of hindsight, with its customary illusion of inevitability. While differences between earlier and later forms of modern paganism may strike one as requiring explanation as to their genesis, continuities seem less worthy of attention. However, unless the inertia of tradition suffices to explain such a continuity, it is just as remarkable as a difference. After all there *are* differences and changes that have arisen in attempts to develop exoteric and populist forms of Wicca. If people have chosen to abandon, amend or add practices, they have had a motive, but once embarked upon such a project of reform they will likewise require motivation for holding to what they retain. This is particularly so when the starting point is a relatively small group with a short public history in which people are not generally indoctrinated at a young age, all of which should reduce the effect of inertia in keeping practices constant by force of tradition, once it is no longer considered important to maintain such a tradition in its entirety.

Looking more closely at the polarities expressed, the continuity has not been as firm as one might think. Within Wicca, the most obvious duality found is that of male and female; the rites are led by a male–female partnership, initiations and elevations are conducted by women upon men and vice versa, and alternations between male and female occur throughout the entirety of the praxis.

The next most obvious is perhaps the alternation of winter and summer and death and life that finds expression through the sabbats and the use of the Persephone mythos, often termed 'the Descent of the Goddess'. A story much like that of Persephone (though comparable also to the earlier tale of Inanna), is referenced in relation to the Second Degree of Wicca. Among other interpretations, this story is a calendar myth, explaining the annual dying away and springing forth of life with reference to Persephone's wintering in Hades. Additions in some lines making use of the Gravesian concept of Oak King and Holly King bring another pairing to play on the cycle of seasonal festivals.

Finally, the symbolic opposition of Scourge and Kiss is another dualism that finds regular expression in the rites, being addressed throughout the liturgy. This latter, while it may be compared to oppositions found elsewhere (that of severity and mercy springs immediately to mind), is perhaps the most uniquely Wiccan in the mode of expression.

Arguably, another four polarities are the eight qualities that the *Charge of the Goddess* exhorts one to exhibit; beauty and strength, power and compassion, honour and humility, and mirth and reverence. Here each quality is paired with one that may be considered to be at odds with it, and hence one may consider them as four sets of polarities. I am inclined to disagree. One may, for example, neglect beauty in seeking strength, but one may just as well seek one through the other as is commonly done in any form of design. In those fields like engineering and software development, which owe a particular debt to mathematics, the idea of elegance as a combination of the two is highly prized in any design. Such a thought inclines me to see them as near-complements rather than diametrically opposed, and hence not to understand them as a set of polarities or dualities. However, I would not be vehement in arguing against anyone who did see them as such.

Vs.

Other polarities can perhaps be found. Certainly a more general view of polarity as a metaphysical principle may be vital to a practitioner's understanding of the meaning of Wiccan ritual or the mechanism by which it, both ritually and magically, operates along similar lines to the Hermetic Laws.[320] However, it is these three polarities — male/female, winter/summer that is also life/death and Scourge/Kiss — which find frequent and explicit expression throughout Wiccan praxis.

This is not the case with much exoteric Neopaganism, or even with many of the more esoteric-leaning forms of Wicca-influenced pagan witchcraft. The Scourge and Kiss are conspicuously absent: The scourge is often directly condemned if it is mentioned at all.[321] The kiss meanwhile does not just change in no longer being part of any duality, but is often less frequent, less pronounced, and may become little more than the alternative that one has to a handshake when introduced to a female guest at a dinner party.

The focus upon the male–female polarity of Wicca is also often changed and sometimes absent. It is true that it was referenced as part of what is probably the first attempt to codify a set of dogmas for Neopagan witchcraft, the American Council of Witches' *'13 Principles of Wiccan Belief'*,[322] though this in itself changes the point of continuity from one of tradition to one of doctrine. Other practices either remove the male–female polarity entirely, or else reduce the emphasis placed on it; sometimes to focus on sexuality apart from procreation and hence necessitating a removal of heterofocality lest a practice become implicitly heterosexist, and sometimes to remove considerations of sex from the practice in its entirety.[323] Those who view departures from Wiccan practices as progressive will quite confidently speak of the fertility-cult nature of Wicca in the past tense.[324]

Of the polarities that are central to Wicca, it would seem that only the combined polarities of summer and winter and of life and death expressed through *'The Descent of the Goddess'* remains wholly intact. Indeed, the Gravesian concept of Oak King and Holly King is perhaps even more prevalent in such exoteric expressions than they are within Wicca, where it is not ubiquitous. Everyone likes a good story, and the move away from the focus upon fertility in Wicca toward a concept of *'nature religion'* heavily influenced by late

---

[320] Farrar, Janet & Farrar, Stewart. *The Witches' Way*.
[321] See Drew, A. J., *Wicca for Couples, Making Magick Together* and Conway, D. J., *Wicca: The Complete Craft* for examples of this.
[322] Certainly, if not the first this was probably the first to have considerable impact. It remains referenced today, sometimes even outside of the United States, despite its expressly being concerned only with American interests.
[323] *op. cit.*
[324] Such as Grimassi, Raven., *Crafting Wiccan Traditions: Creating a Foundation for Your Spiritual Beliefs & Practices*.

twentieth-century ecological concerns, allowed these stories to flourish in an exoteric paganism. The place of the seasonal cycle in such a post-modern nature religion as Neopaganism is still not quite the same as within a fertility religion like Wicca, having spheres of concern that overlap but do not necessarily coincide.

The continuance of the importance of polarity into exoteric Neopaganism therefore does not continue the instances of this polarity. This strongly suggests that we cannot consider it a continuation at all. The polarity found in recent Neopaganism is itself recent and answers recent needs. What were those needs?

The answer can perhaps be found not by comparing exoteric and esoteric Paganisms, but by comparing exoteric Neopaganism with the more predominant exoteric religious movements. As stated above, most common polarity in such religious thinking is the moral duality found in Christianity. This comparison is very frequently made in explaining the form of dualisms found in both Wicca and exoteric Neopaganism alike.

Such a comparison may have originally been motivated by distinction; assuming an audience familiar with Abrahamic religion, it behooves any description of such a dualism to distinguish it from that which will first come to the audience's mind, so as to avoid false assumptions. However, this comparison has acquired the nature of a conflict; Neopagan polarity is not offered as opposed to monism (as its polytheism and duotheism is offered as opposed to monotheism) and then contrasted with moral dualism purely for the sake of clarity; but rather it is offered in direct opposition to moral duality.

Why might this alternative be desirable? Just as monism can be offered as an alternative to the dualism found in much esoterica, so too can it be offered as an alternative to moral dualism. For that matter, why reject moral dualism at all? Even those of us who have no place in our philosophies for absolute concepts of good and evil will find some acts sufficiently commendable or sufficiently abhorrent that we may as well use *'good'* and *'evil'* as a shorthand in our praise and condemnation (and ironically, it can be difficult to condemn moral dualism without falling into such language). That exoteric Neopaganism maintained such a rejection of moral dualism again calls for just as much explanation as when it excluded some other esoteric views.

Of course, some things just *feel* right. This doesn't obviate explanation, but rather moves it to the realm of psychology. Lacan suggested that identification of the Other was a necessary part of the identification of the Self, that one cannot learn to envision an *I* without also a *Not-I*. This psychological dualism would then mean that some element of dualism is likely to remain in one's view, including quite deeply in one's subconscious views, even if expressing a monist philosophy that rejected all dualism. To embrace a dualist philosophy while rejecting moral dualism cannot remove this sense of the Other, but it can have a better hope for success in holding a positive view of the Other.

In light of political and social views of Otherness, the attraction of this to those of the liberal or radical views that were predominant in Neopaganism in the late twentieth century are obvious. If this is our answer, then we should expect to see such an attempt to accept Otherness reflected in other aspects of Neopaganism. Indeed, we can. In particular, the very use of the word *pagan* speaks of Otherness; while modern pagans will generally view the word otherwise, for almost all of modern history, *pagan* and its equivalents in other European languages have demarcated an area of Otherness; there are Christians, Jews and Muslims, and then there are *pagans*. This may already have seemed inadequate by the nineteenth century when scholars of religion found that they could not usefully categorise Zen Buddhism and Roman State Religion under the same label, and was hence already undergoing a change in meaning.[325] To identify *oneself* as a pagan though, rejects the ethnocentrism involved in a different manner, by placing oneself directly in the midst of the entailed Otherness, and struggling against it from the other side of the divide.

The Neopagan community was unusual in the degree to which it did not so much find itself marginalised as a group, into the position of the Other (as with other religious minorities along with women, and racial and lingual minorities); nor was it formed from a confederacy of individuals who found themselves so marginalised (as with the gay and transgendered communities, and people with disabilities). Rather the modern Pagan communities arose from people expressly identifying themselves with those who had already been marginalised to the point of extinction; the pre-Christian pagans of Europe, the Middle East and North Africa. It can be understood therefore, as an act of what Deleuze & Guattari term *'becoming minor'*, of identifying with the *'minority'* (which may not numerically be a minority) in resistance to *'becoming fascist'*.[326]

This is all the more so, with those who identified themselves as Wiccan, or otherwise identified themselves as witches. Much recent consideration of the image of medieval witches that was common, both within and without modern paganism, toward the end of the twentieth century has focused on debunking the concept held at that time, specifically as it refers to the number and gender of those convicted of witchcraft, the severity of sentences, and the likelihood both of them representing any survival of pre-Christian practice and of modern pagan witchcraft (Wiccan or otherwise) representing any survival from them in turn. These more sceptical views have been largely accepted in much of the Neopagan community, and are used

---

[325] Tiele, Cornelis Petrus. 1902. "Religion." *Encyclopædia Britannica.* Ninth Edition.
[326] Deleuze, Gilles & Guattari, Félix, *Kafka: toward a minor literature.*

Vs.

to justify moves away from any tradition older than their own practice.[327] Still, the unfortunate witch of these twentieth century imaginings of the Burning Times remains a potent image, and of course was even more potent when believed to be historically accurate, as she was mere decades ago.

This image of the witch is almost a caricature of Otherness. She finds herself marginalised in her sex, sexuality, class, economic freedom, education and religion. Even lingual, ethnic and ablest discrimination may be directly reflected in the biography written for her. She is not just an Other, but stands for the Other in every case of marginalisation. Even more so the fairytale witch. While witches may be particularly quick to distance themselves from her, the fairytale witch lives strongly in the imagination. More than one fiction writer has reversed the normal distinction by calling her sort — rather than present day practitioners — the *'real witches'*, and psychologically at least, the argument may be with them.

With the position of the witch being considered by Feminists[328] and Feminist witches,[329] there was a significant move in how people who considered themselves witches reacted to the Otherness of the witch. While Gardner spoke as a witch to defend the witch from her marginalisation,[330] Feminist witches spoke as witches to defend *everyone* from *theirs*: in being not just *a* minority, but a minority that stood for all minorities, they claimed a position from which they could critique *all* oppression.

This also gave a sense of wider political relevance. While I have argued before that Neopagan politics where strongly influenced by Identity Politics[331] this comes at a cost of restricting their voice to matters of direct concern to themselves. A sense of *self-othering* could, even if it were only subliminally held, counter this by bringing with it a sense of moral authority to connect with, and resist, the othering of any group.

Otherness can also be embraced in the acquiring of an argot; a cant or secret language used only within the group. While lingual minorities may be marginalised, argots arise out of the very Otherness of its speakers. The place of codes and cyphers in witchcraft (magical alphabets) and magic takes on a new purpose in such a context in reinforcing the self-othering of the witch and the

---

[327] A justification which ironically both rejects longevity as a basis for judging the value of a tradition, yet also uses the same basis in holding that the older traditions do not have as sound a claim of longevity as once held.
[328] In, for instance, Dworkin, Andrea. *Woman Hating* and Daly, Mary. 1978. *Gyn/Ecology: The Metaethics of Radical Feminism.*
[329] Budapest, Zsuzsanna., *The Holy Book of Women's Mysteries* and Starhawk., *Spiral Dance: A Rebirth of the Ancient Religion of the Great Goddess.*
[330] In his works *Witchcraft Today* and *The Meaning of Witchcraft.*
[331] Hanna, Jon. 2010. *What Thou Wilt: Traditional and Innovative trends in Post-Gardnerian Witchcraft.*

pagan. A complete argot is not available for adoption, for while there are claims to such a Wiccan cant having once existed,[332] there isn't a sufficient lexicon to even allow for a few words, substituted for their English equivalents, to serve as shibboleths and signs of community solidarity as happens with cants like Polari, slangs, diaspora languages and languages that have been displaced by that of a coloniser.

A jargon can, however, serve such purposes as well as its immediate purpose of offering greater precision within a field. It is perhaps notable therefore that Neopagan jargon is often used more widely than might seem necessary. Further, terms have been acquired beyond those used by earlier modern pagans. We might expect this when new practices give them a context (such as *solitaire* being redefined to refer to a solitary witch, a term of little use to the coven-based practice of Wicca) or practices shift and the word carries over to a differing practice (such as the differences in what is meant by *Book of Shadows*). However, such specialised terminology has also been adopted in terms of items that were longstanding components of Wiccan practice. Not only have the Irish names of four festivals been adopted outside of Ireland, in countries where they may seem exotic rather than rooted and territorialised, but the lack of similarly exotic words for adoption for the equinoxes has led to coinages being used instead. Perhaps most remarkable of all sabbat names is that where *midsummer*, a word that existed in Anglo-Saxon and has the quality mark of any traditional English word — being used by Shakespeare — was considered less suitable than a modern coinage, *litha*, based more indirectly on Anglo-Saxon.

Further, these words are failures considered as jargon. Jargon offers precision at the cost of being obscure to outsiders, with any function as shibboleths being coincidental in design and secondary in value. The adoptions from Irish obscure the meaning in adding the question of whether and how the festivals were originally known by those names, as mentioned as far back as the tale of Cú Chullain's courtship with Emer, relate to the modern festivals.[333] The coinages *Ostara*, *Litha* and *Mabon* are even more obscure in the question of whether and how they differ from the previously used English terms.

The result is an altered form of English. To the linguistically conservative, coining jargon where none is needed is at odds with '*good*' English, a conservatism not confined to the politically conservative, if we consider the complaints of Orwell.[334] However, it can also be seen as being deliberately (if not necessarily consciously) at odds with English as a dominant and dominating language, comparable perhaps to the adoption of a coloniser's language in a

---

[332] Gardner, *The Meaning of Witchcraft*.
[333] Kinsella, Thomas., *The Tain*.
[334] Orwell, George, *"Politics and the English Language"*.

way that actively identifies with the colonised or otherwise marginalised that Deleuze and Guattari see in Kafka:

> "To hate all languages of masters. Kafka's fascination for servants and employees (the same thing in Proust in relation to servants, to their language). What interests him even more is the possibility of making of his own language—assuming that it is unique, that it is a major language or has been—a minor utilization. To be a sort of stranger within his own language; this is the situation of Kafka's Great Swimmer."[335]

We must note also, that this positioning of self-as-other in relation to English does not happen in relation to words of particular socio-religious history. The origins of *clergy* assumed a position of education and literacy in Christendom that no longer applies even to the Christian use of the word, and while it was used for non-Christian priests and religions as early as the fifteenth century, this was by analogy and such a sense is deemed obsolete by the *Oxford English Dictionary*. Yet here, where the colonising effect of combined religious and secular power — in Neopaganism's narrative of the conversion of Europe — has had a particularly strong effect upon the language, there is little attempt to distance paganism from such language, but rather a claim upon the status and prestige that the word brings. This is not an oversight or omission, for the social purpose of Neopagan jargon is not to replace English in the religious sphere, where it serves as a jargon in the pure sense, but rather to replace English in the everyday. It is not the mythic language of Neopaganism itself that is important here, but its jargon being absorbed into the vehicular and vernacular language of Neopagans. It makes the language of Neopaganism foreign in an act of 'becoming-minor.'[336]

Considered so, this offers a new perspective on one of the bones of contention within modern paganism: the use of the word *Wicca* by those outside of the initiatory lines which first identified themselves as such. A common explanation for the preference of this term to either *witchcraft* or *paganism*, is that *Wicca* offers a less shocking term, bringing less 'baggage' from other uses. Such a tactic would seem foolish though, when we consider that it requires that rather than deal with the negative nuances of *witch* and *pagan* one should first introduce a novel term, provoking distrust of the unknown, and then in explaining it *also* encounter the difficulties involved in the terms at first provided. It is a mysterious policy indeed, but when considered as another example of Neopagans becoming-minor by

---

[335] Deleuze, Gilles &Guattari, Félix., *op cit.*
[336] *ibid.*

making their own language foreign, the mystery disappears, and the tactic becomes reasonable.

With such an ideological position, a religious expression of a dualism that accepted difference but rejected the application of judgement values across the lines of that difference was a natural asset. The position of the pagan and the witch as Other allowed for the religion to find political expression, while such a dualism allowed the political ideology to find religious expression.

Such a duality may however find itself at odds with either the esoteric views of polarity or the political analysis of Othering that are its parents. Metaphysical dualisms often allow for polarity to be surpassed or for duality to be reconciled. A mystical experience of unity does not, however, translate well into exoteric doctrine. An individual may take an experience of unity with them, but still function in a world in which polarities exist. To accomplish the same act of uniting a duality in the rational manner required by exoteric doctrine must destroy the duality entirely; either the duality is deemed illusionary and the philosophy is really monism, or one side of the duality must conquer the other fully. Alternatively the dualism must be the only truth and the conflict with the other continue indefinitely.

The goal then becomes not unity, through an Hieros Gamos, but rather balance. Further, it is often a balance not just within certain polarities that are the focus of a practice, but within all polarities, particularly if the focus on male–female polarity inherited from Wicca is deemed to be heterosexist if not offset by other polarities being introduced. One might ask how a balance can be found in the polarity between balance and imbalance. This paradox is perhaps unfair (though perhaps also unavoidable much as paradoxes can prove to be in higher-order logic), but difficulties of a similar if more convoluted type may still arise. A mystical approach can cut the Gordian knot through irrational experience, but an exoteric approach can only abandon rationality if it does so permanently, and devalues reason entirely. One result could be a disinclination to make judgements, and indeed where esoteric practices often include the ability to make judgement among valued qualities (perhaps most explicitly in discrimination[337] being considered the virtue of Malkuth in the Qabalah), many Neopagans seem keen on adopting the warning in *Luke 6:37* against judging others.

Meanwhile, Neopaganism has been unable to maintain its own identification with the Other. The rejection of initiatory lineage and the disinclination toward judging has left it unable to define its own

---

[337] Colloquially, *discrimination* has become shorthand for *unfair discrimination*. While discriminating on irrelevant grounds, such as discriminating in employment on the grounds of sex or race, is obviously the very opposite of exercising discrimination on appropriate grounds, such as capability, the nuances the word has acquired would be another pressure toward a judgement-free position.

boundaries. In reaction we find Neopagan identity being policed through the concept of *'fluff bunnies'*. The precise meaning of this term will vary according to just which qualities or opinions a given Neopagan disapproves of in other Neopagans, and is not precisely defined, but the denomination is a very potent one. While it may have begun as an attempt to offer critiques of particular stances, it has quickly degenerated into little more than an insulting label to apply to some individuals whom Neopagans would like to Other within their own community. Neither the pagan nor the witch is the Other anymore but, perhaps surprisingly, the fluff bunny is.

Finally, the conditions that gave birth to late-twentieth century Neopaganism are no longer the conditions that influence it today. To those who remain politically radical, the claiming of a position of being particularly marginalised may seem self-indulgent, particularly as the historical understanding of medieval witchcraft and of its relationship to modern witchcraft have changed. Meanwhile, the growth of Neopaganism has given it a greater degree of independence from ideologies commonly associated with it in the seventies through to the nineties, just as it had previously broken free of the more conservative views common among the earlier modern paganism of Wicca and Ásatrú and among the early twentieth century magical orders.

We may then wonder if the dualism found in exoteric Neopaganism will undergo yet more change, or perhaps be abandoned. If what is suggested here has validity, then the motivation for such a form of dualism no longer exists as strongly as it did before. It seems likely, however, that it has now matured into a doctrine of sufficient import to be self-sustaining. I offered above that the inertia of tradition was not sufficient to keep practices alive in descendants of Wicca especially due to the small size of Wicca. This is not true of exoteric Neopaganism, which is considerably larger in the early twenty-first century than initiatory Wicca was in the late twentieth. Exoteric Neopaganism is also primarily transmitted by the written word, which remains preserved in print and on websites in a way that offers greater inertia than personal training.

In examining a form of duality found in exoteric Neopaganism, I have looked at both the religion and at the culture of the group in question. Often, people prefer to do one or the other, keeping a false separation between the spiritual or magical and the temporal. Considering the possible temporal advantages of spiritual and magical concepts is a promising approach, though to some that see them as inherently separate this may seem disrespectful. I think, however, that this offers a view in which exoteric Neopaganism stands more fully in its own right than in the shadow of Wicca (and likewise of Ásatrú, Druidry, and the magical orders of the twentieth

Vs.

century). Exoteric Neopaganism is often derided as a dilution,[338] without consideration of what it has been diluted *with*. This view of *dilution* is one-sided, and ignores the motivations and inspirations behind the changes within paganism of the last 20 or 30 years.

Bibliography
Budapest, Zsuzsanna. *The Holy Book of Women's Mysteries*. Newburyport: Weiser Books. First published as *The Feminist Book of Lights and Shadows*, 1976.
Conway, D. J. *Wicca: The Complete Craft*. Trumansburg: Crossing Press, 2001.
Cunningham, Scott. *Wicca: A Guide for the Solitary Practitioner*. St. Paul: Llewellyn Worldwide. 1998
Cunningham, Scott. *The Truth About Witchcraft Today*. St. Paul: Llewellyn Worldwide, 1988
Daly, Mary. *Gyn/Ecology: The Metaethics of Radical Feminism*. Boston: Beacon Press, 1978.
Deleuze, Gilles. Guattari, Félix. *Kafka: toward a minor literature*. Minnesota: University of Minnesota Press, 1986.
Drew, A. J. *Wicca for Couples, Making Magick Together*. Franklin Lakes: New Page Books, 2002.
Dworkin, Andrea. *Woman Hating*. New York: Plume, 1981. First published Dutton, New York, 1974.
Farrar, Janet & Farrar, Stewart. *The Witches' Way*. Blaine: Phoenix Publishing, 1984.
Gardner, Gerald. *Witchcraft Today*. New York: Citadel Press, 2004. First published by Rider, London, 1954.
Gardner, Gerald. *The Meaning of Witchcraft*. Newbury: Weiser Books, 2004. First published by Aquarian Press, 1959.
Grimassi, Raven. *Crafting Wiccan Traditions: Creating a Foundation for Your Spiritual Beliefs & Practices*. St. Paul: Llewellyn Worldwide, 2008.
Hanna, Jon. *What Thou Wilt: Traditional and Innovative trends in Post-Gardnerian Witchcraft*. Cathair na Mart: Evertype, 2010.
Kinsella, Thomas. *The Tain*. Oxford: Oxford University Press, 1970.
Orwell, George. *Politics and the English Language*. 1946.
Moura, Ann. *Green Witchcraft: Folk Magic, Fairy Lore & Herb Craft*. St. Paul: Llewellyn Worldwide, 2002
Murphy-Hiscock, Arin. *Solitary Wicca for Life: A Complete Guide to Mastering the Craft on Your Own*. Massachusetts: Provenance Press, 2005
Perseus, Enyo. *Diluting Wicca*
http://www.wargoddess.net/essay/dilutingwicca.php, 2001.
Ravenwolf, Silver. *To Ride a Silver Broomstick*. St. Paul: Llewellyn Worldwide, 1993.
Starhawk. *Spiral Dance: A Rebirth of the Ancient Religion of the Great Goddess*. San Francisco: Harper, 1989. First published, 1979.

---

[338] Quite literally so in Perseus, Enyo. 2001. *"Diluting Wicca"*.

Vs.

CONIUNCTIO

by Frater Jonathan Carfax

A thick, heavy incense hung in the air. Intoxicating olibanum, storax and forest cedar, sweet resin and aromatic wood coating everything in a fragrant fog. Flickering candlelight pierced its way through the smoke, illuminating two shapes writhing on the floor in regular rhythm to continuous loops of high wattage psytrance, erupting from strategically arranged speakers around the ritual space.

Invocations were cried out by one ritualist, ecstatic exclamations while laying back upon Persian-style cushions while the other worked between spread thighs. Hands passed over the body, arousing centres of energy that fanned a simple fire into a back-draft inferno primed to explode, like a coiling serpent poised to strike, fangs glistening with sacred poison of intoxication.

The energy erupted as the bodies arched. Shaking. A seizure of pure sacredness.

In response to the fire within, charged fluids rolled forth in the without, like those supporting the passage of a Venusian Botticelli. But rather than dispersal upon landfall they were caught by a mouth eager to receive the sacrament, a catalytic consumption, communion, buoyed by rapture and intent.

The music ended its tribalist momentum, and transitioned into stygian ambience. The energetic ebb induced sleep for both ritualists. Divine somnium. Hypnagogic dreaming.

"Wake up Jaq-e Channing."

"Hmmmph?"

"Wake up Jaq-e."

The second request was a female voice, whereas the first was definitely male. Jaq-e reached over and felt for her sleeping companion. Still there, not moving and heavily breathing. It was someone else. And the owners of these voices should not have been anywhere within Jaq-e's room, the door was locked.

Sitting up startled, she grabbed a blanket and covered herself as she surveyed the room. The candles were still burning, but with the incense having long since burnt out the room was clearer. In the candle light she could see a man in a three piece suit, seated on one of the bean bags in the corner of the room, grinning, looking something like a contented toad on a mushroom.

Vs.

He was old, bald. Fat. And familiar.

"Yes, it is who you think it is," said the woman's voice.

Jaq-e turned around to see the owner of the voice in the other corner of the room, seated on a swivel stool. This woman lit up another candle to bring further illumination to the room. She was an attractive older woman with bobbed hair, wearing something of a diaphanous gown tied tight at the waist. Jaq-e noticed from the cut of the dress that one of her breasts appeared to be missing, the curvature of the body missing part of the cleavage.

"I'm sorry, who are you both and how did you get in here?" stammered Jaq-e.

"Regrettably my dear, I am without one of my calling cards presently, but you can call me Your Highness, Prince Chioa Khan", said the smiling gentleman, lounging back deeper into the bean bag.

"Aleister. Call him Aleister. And I'm Florence. Florence Farr," said the woman, with only a touch of annoyance.

Clichéd hallucinations, thought Jaq-e, so much for imaginative creativity. Projections and thought forms. Pretty soon they will be unable to be sustained and dismissed.

"No Jaq-e, we are not mere thought forms. We are Florence Farr and Aleister Crowley," said Florence, gently but firmly, reading Jaq-e's mental assertions.

"Well, obviously we are not the Aleister Crowley and Florence Farr," interjected Aleister, *"but neither ghosts, nor gods, or imaginal figments. But by form and manner we carry something of their original essence and imprint because you invite us to, unconsciously, in order to converse with you."*

Florence interjected with a certain glee, *"In fact the real Crowley, Levi, whatever you want to call him, is spending some quality time back in incarnation currently."*

"As...?" queried Jaq-e, still coming to terms with the fact that two deceased persons of ardent esoteric admiration were seated before her.

"I believe he is spending the next decade as one of Sharon Osbourne's Chihuahuas," snorted Florence, delicately stifling the sound with a hand, *"I'm not sure whether his attraction to Ozzie's leg is some kind of karmic debt or whether..."*

"Back to present concerns Jaq-e," interrupted Aleister, shooting a filthy look at Florence, *"we are here to converse with you on matters of the utmost important. Much to discuss, my girl."*

"Yes, converse? As in...." trailed Jaq-e, then in realisation, *"my Holy Guardian Angel?"*

"Not just a pretty face then? Yes we both are, after a fashion, part of that entity. You have been a busy girl after all, and quite effective in your pursuit of the Great Work. We heard your call and were invoked by your inflamed soul yearning for devekut. But Jaq-e, before either of us are in a position to assist you to develop so as to traverse the

wastelands of Arabah, you will need to choose between us. Actually, it is not so much a choice: it is a test, and I think an easy test. Because one of us is in fact a manifestation of that which is but only a projection of your profane desires and expectations, and thus a chimera."

"And if I choose wrong?" asked Jaq-e.

"Well, you may not be any the wiser to be honest. Your own Ego will shape your experiences into that of a grand illusion. You may die contently mad," explained Aleister with a wry smile.

"And if I choose right?"

"You may die knowledgeably mad," he chuckled, *"Oh come now, you know very well that if you cross that great divide, this life as it presently stands is no longer...relevant – regardless of whether you choose return or cleaving."*

Yes, I know," replied Jaq-e, coming into a headspace of clarity and confidence, of realisation of the seriousness of the situation. She had reached the threshold she sought for many years, with many partners, through great effort and dedication. *"But why you...or her?"* she said, indicating Florence.

"Jaq-e, I like to think you are a child of the New Aeon, rejecting the old ways of working, embracing the heretic, a banner bearer for Ra-Hoor-Khuit. Florence is here for contrast, everything the New Aeon herald calls for us to reject," crooned Aleister leaning forward, arms open like an overly affectionate uncle.

"You over-inflated windbag," interjected Florence, stamping down her foot in protest. *"You and your phallocentricity dressed as mysticism! How many women, Priestesses, did you scar, degrade and neglect in your endeavours to manifest this Aeon of yours? Are the old rituals, the old Order really 'black'? They permitted an aspiring Priestess in an age of Victorian misogyny to occupy the throne of a Chief Adept? Worried the Osirian era might take a step backwards into a new matriarchal Asetian age?"*

Aleister laughed, *"Now Florence, even you don't believe that. I recall you writing: 'The old beauty is no longer beautiful; the new truth is no longer true,' is the eternal cry of a developing and really vitalised life. Our civilisation has passed through the First Empire of pagan sensualism; and the Second Empire of mistaken sacrifice, of giving up our own consciousness, our own power of judging, our own independence, our own courage. And the Third Empire is awaiting those of us who can see—that not only in Olympus, not only nailed to the Cross, but in ourselves is God."*

He paused and then grinned. *"Are you really as Old Aeon as you pretend? Are we really that different?"* teased Aleister.

"You like your Scarlet Women with initiative but still subservient, wildly creative but unstable, intellectually swift but in their place. Never in a position of Magisterial superiority. That is what I was, Aleister, and I saw right through you the day you applied for the

Second Order. It is I who paved the way for Priestesses such as Jaq-e to emerge, not you," retorted Florence.

"And what did holding sway over a dying Order of sentimental poets and coroners achieve? Where is your legacy? Like Osiris' lamentable form, the Golden Dawn is a corpse continually rewrapped in fresh bandages to minimise the stench, with a strap-on johnny to keep up appearances," snarled Aleister.

Jaq-e raised a hand trying to interject, to no avail as the words caught in her throat, the momentum of the debate intensifying before her.

"Really, Aleister, I fail to see how the Golden Dawn was anything but at the vanguard of liberating the intellectually astute Victorian woman into a Prophetess. Who else was going to offer such opportunities amongst the old crippled pseudo-masonic Orders?" questioned Florence.

"Florence, my dear, please don't mistake me. Your wit, intelligence and determination were, and still are, amongst the very few. But did it ever occur to you that the elevation of you and your fellow Priestesses into positions of power and authority may have been in spite of the Order, rather than because of it?" queried Crowley, "You fail to convince me that it was more than Societas Rosicruciana in a nice party frock," said Aleister, his voice a bored sneer.

"This is my problem with you," Florence sighed, "you hold a model Victorian gentleman's view of a woman's potential. That women such as I are the exception rather than the rule. And upon reflection of your philosophy, it runs the risk to reinforce this to the esoterically ambitious man of less than discerning faculties. It suggests a woman is more than a child but less than a man; a thing of fleeting beauty and eternal decay; the object of high art but rarely the artist; beholden to the need for procreation rather than the need to be an individual; not a facilitator of desire through truly mutual alchemy but the unworthy receiver of a man's psycho-sexual drives. And when our sexuality is acknowledged as a potent occult force on its own terms, it is essentially too dangerous for the unprepared man because it is that of a predator, vampiric and apocalyptic."

She continued, leaning forward, "The spiritually independent woman was born as reaction to the Victorian patriarchal sensibility, a catalyst for change there can be no doubt. Long before the announcement of your New Aeon, the years of the Fin de siècle were a cultural revolution of gender roles, art, politics, societal structures and spirituality. And it is this that gave birth to the Golden Dawn and it's participation by the New Woman."

"Maybe your New Woman movement was in fact part of the condensing energy leading to the announcement of the New Aeon," proposed Aleister before thundering in forceful prose, "But let her raise herself in pride! Let her follow me in my way! Let her work the work of wickedness! Let her kill her heart! Let her be loud and *adulterous! Let her be covered with jewels, and rich garments, and let her be shameless before all men!"*

"*It has always sounded to me that the arguments for woman of the New Aeon was one who is expected to be wantonly wicked and wild, non-conformist - but still in the service of men,*" replied Florence, "*I am not part of your New Aeon, Aleister. Have you ever considered your New Aeon pronouncement was not a commencement but a retrospective acknowledgment of a change that had already started amongst liberated women and men? The Golden Dawn was a product of that change. You, Aleister, were to a degree a product of that change...as much as I loathe to say it.*"

Standing, Florence towered over the seated Aleister to continue berating him, "*What characterises your New Aeon as anything more than just another apocalyptic movement riding on that spirit of change, one amongst many from the Fin de siècle? We were all talking about it, Yeats, Mathers, Blavatsky, and yes, even when I was writing the particular Flying Scrolls of the Order you mentioned. And some of us were working to prevent the manifestation of this change as a spiritual catastrophe, to make it an easier birth for humanity!*"

Aleister's eyes were cold and inscrutable. "*Yes, how did that insidious Sphere Group thing go in securing that world peace? You didn't exactly have the enthusiastic support of all your colleagues did you? Granted, Florence, we were all apocalyptic to some degree, but justifiably so I believe. At the end of the day my experiences bore the real fruit, no?*"

Before she had the chance to reply, he jumped out of the bean bag, making her take a defensive step back. "*You talk of culture, aesthetic, social structure. But I gave birth to a magical philosophy that cuts through into the decades that followed, Florence. Which philosophers and intellectuals are still perpetuating the Golden Dawn's legacy to humanity? Where are the avant-garde artists and musicians singing your praises and using you as a cultural reference point? You didn't change society, you merely hitched a wagon to the train of change, mere passengers.*"

Waving his hand in dismissal Aleister continued, "*More accept the Law year upon year. I don't need people to be affirmed Thelemites by conscious decision or act. Like Christian values, my dear, Thelemic freedom will slowly infuse into the popular consciousness. Individual freedom and expression triumphing over the hive behaviour and social norms.*"

Florence stepped closer and held up her hand to silence him. "*Aleister, I do believe you are confusing your cult of personality with your philosophical ideals. The lines between the Crowleyites and the Thelemites are blurred at the best of times. But that is nothing new is it? Like Stansfeld Jones, Kenneth Grant, your offspring have been regarded as darlings or devils, by you and your followers, depending on how much they interpreted the Law consistently with your views or how far out on the limb they ventured,"* mused Florence. *"Furthermore, it would seem to me that part of your New Aeon reinforces structures of the old, of class division and fights against the reforms from that which arose from socialist worker organization. You hearken for the slave class that supported the upper echelons of society. Not really a model of true Hermetic Brotherly Love, is it now?"*

Aleister clapped in amusement, *"I do recall that fellow Oscar Wilde wrote something to the effect that socialism would promote individuality by freeing men from manual labour to pursue the development of their soul. I believe he also observed that the trouble with socialism is that it takes up too many evenings! Ha! I fear I can only agree with him on the latter. And I still need my chimney swept. My dear, Thelema is for all people, the doctor, the politician, the whore, the housewife, the ditch digger. I fear your Old Aeon version of Hermetic Brotherly Love, dressed as esoteric socialism, would fulfil Mr Wilde's worst fears of exaggerated altruism. Misguided charity reinforcing a bad situation, rather than allowing an individual the opportunity to liberate themselves. Didn't a certain shepherd say something about passing on the fine arts of trout angling rather than being a fishmonger to society?"*

"So, Aleister, in this pursuit of liberation, of women's individuality in a man's world, does this mean that all women need to be strapping on a metaphorical phallus? Would you not agree that the 'thrust' of the sexual energy driving the manifestation of this Aeon, according to you, tends to be described from the perspective of the enthroned good king Nebuchadnezzar, rather than the one attending court? That the woman, while desirable, appears to not be critical and little more than a consecrated vessel?" asked Florence.

"Alchemy requires its flasks, its Pelicans, my dear," retorted Aleister.

"The self-sacrifice of the alchemical Pelican, a nourishing sacrament of blood," observed Florence, *"assuming of course that the magic of this Aeon really requires a penis at all to manifest the energies of change. I do believe some among your successors have had a more open mind about the role of the vagina in generating the sacraments for alchemical transformation."*

"In fact," continued Florence with a building enthusiasm, *"I do believe you fear the vagina, dear Aleister, Vagina Dentata. Scared it is going to bite your cock off with its teeth perchance?"*

"But this is the very unfounded fear of many 'unconventional' men of your time. The inevitable consequence of natural conjunction," shrilled Florence in a crescendo, *"just as the female praying mantis decapitates her partner in the process. An unfounded fear that natural coition is destructive, and woman is the protagonist of this act. It is no surprise then, from your point of view, that one should instead often institute a different sacrament of a most obvious substitution, a fellow gentlemen's pleasure!"*

Vs.

"*Florence, biology has provided us with unalterable and inviolate characteristics that are sacred instruments in their own right. The union of opposites is a biological and metaphysical reality, following a natural formula,*" said Aleister. "*But, providing the two ritualists differ spiritually and in gender – whether this be in actuality or by voluntarily adopting the energetic manifestation of the opposite, other substitution is indeed available and equally valid.*"

"*Er... I don't like men,*" offered Jaq-e in a half-hearted interjection.

Aleister turned to look at Jaq-e for the first time since the debate began. He smiled. "*Oh, she speaks. At last. That will serve you well. Sorry Soror, what did you say? You don't like men?*"

"*Aleister, our dear charge here is a sapphist,*" stated Florence, "*and while she has something of the tom about her, I don't think you should presume that certain instrumentality of your preference has any immediate significance to her methods.*"

"*Eh?*" said Aleister.

"*Oh come now, did you miss that the rite inducing our manifestation was through a touch of furious velvet tipping,*" giggled Florence. "*Her ritual partner sleeping over there is another woman, you silly man.*"

"*It's not that I don't like men. I just don't, you know, do them. Mundanely or ritually,*" ventured Jaq-e "*and it hasn't seemed to be a problem. Well obviously not, you are both here after all...*"

"*This was always one of your problems, Aleister,*" added Florence. "*Women have been producing the nectar of illumination for sacramental purposes for centuries in many traditions, you however chose to focus only on the sacrament you could provide to your Scarlet Woman. Fortunately some of your Thelemic successors have had good sense to recognise that this is not a 'black rite'.*"

Aleister bombastically refuted the charge. "*I do believe I am on the published record as stating that: every man, and every woman, and every intermediately-sexed individual, shall be absolutely free to interpret and communicate Self by means of any sexual practices soever, whether direct or indirect, rational or symbolic, physiologically, legally, ethically, or religiously approved or no, provided only that all parties to any act are fully aware of all implications and responsibilities thereof, and heartily agree thereto.*"

"*Provided the adoption of female energetic manifestation is more than mere animality, rampant carnality or inevitable morbidity. And in the same breath, that the energetic manifestation of man is not restricted to brutal force, a beast acting blindly and driven by mere instincts alone,*" responded Florence. "*Aleister, maybe I do converge with you on this point. That it is the act, and the harnessing of the energies itself that matter, and less so under what circumstances, with who and through what orientation we may choose to express that.*"

Vs.

With an indifferent gallic nod of agreement, Aleister turned to Jaq-e. *"Something you need to overcome is this dualistic interplay. The addictive rapture of the dance of Nut and Geb is at best unstable, impermanent and in fact an abomination if sought as a place of permanence, rather than a state to be ultimately destroyed. It is but a step to a more profound and everlasting transformation. There is ultimately only the None and the Many."*

With these words a certain awareness dawned on Jaq-e, something remembered. She turned and scrambled through a bookcase and pulled out a well thumbed book. A copy of translations from the *Nag Hammadi* library, her eyes found and fixed on the *Gospel of Thomas*, and read out loud:

"Jesus said to them, When you make the two one, and when you make the inside like the outside, and the outside like the inside, and the above like the below, and when you make the female one and the same, so that the male be not male, nor the female female... then you will enter the kingdom."

"I think I have made my decision," stated Jaq-e, looking at them both. It was then that all the candles in the room suddenly burst into an illumination greatly out of proportion to their diminutive size. A photonic majesty of colours bathed Jaq-e, her eyes partially rolling back into her head.

Aleister raised an eyebrow in surprise and turned to face Florence. They both rose and approached one another, open hands raised before them as they touched palms.

"Who would have thought she might choose that which was not presented a choice?" chortled Aleister with a certain satisfaction. Florence nodded in agreement.

A visual metamorphosis ensued, a melding of shapes transforming into a sexless manifestation of purest *coniunctio*, the outline of bioluminescent wings falling to the floor, spreading horizontally and a third pair reaching upwards as metaphysical muscles and tendons stretched the wingspan filling the room like a peacocks tail, on each feather the eye of the Divine.

A final exchange emitted from the seraphic entity as the personalities of Aleister and Florence collapsed into non-being to give way to the Holy Guardian Angel's true form.

"Don't gloat, Aleister. You would not have had a chance getting this close to me 150 years ago."

"Dear Florence, did you ever consider that our respective universal essences were purposely divided for love's sake, for the chance of union?"

Vs.

OF THE NATURE OF THE SOUL

Phaedrus 246a - 254e (The Soul as Charioteer)

by Plato

> *Note: the image of the Soul as Charioteer, trying to maintain control over two wild and opposing forces symbolised by the horses in this text, is one that may be familiar to a number of practitioners in the Western Mystery Tradition. Plato's Chariot has found its way into the traditional image of the Major Arcana of the Tarot numbered VII – The Chariot, in which a charioteer holds the reins of one white horse and one black horse (or sometimes sphinxes). This model of the soul as dual in nature can also be related to modern Pagan religions such as Wicca, in which the each individual soul, and the soul of the Universe, is split into masculine and feminine, God and Goddess. In the practice of alchemy the prima materia is also split through various processes into its opposing elements – the White Queen and the Red King – which are then reunited in a Sacred Marriage that eventually creates the Philosopher's Stone. It is easy to focus on the two opposing horses that are drawing the chariot in this analogy and in the VII Chariot Arcana from the Tarot pack; however it should always be remembered that the single, individual Charioteer is the ultimate controller and unifier of the opposing forces. Thus, Plato's Chariot analogy indicates a dual universe that in turn is only One.*

Of the nature of the soul, though her true form be ever a theme of large and more than mortal discourse, let me speak briefly, and in a figure. And let the figure be composite - a pair of winged horses and a charioteer.

Now the winged horses and the charioteers of the gods are all of them noble and of noble descent, but those of other races are mixed; the human charioteer drives his in a pair; and one of them is noble and of noble breed, and the other is ignoble and of ignoble breed; and the driving of them of necessity gives a great deal of trouble to him.

I will endeavour to explain to you in what way the mortal differs from the immortal creature. The soul in her totality has the care of inanimate being everywhere, and traverses the whole heaven in divers forms appearing - when perfect and fully winged she soars upward, and orders the whole world; whereas the imperfect soul, losing her wings and drooping in her flight at last settles on the solid ground - there, finding a home, she receives an earthly frame which appears to be self-moved, but is really moved by her power; and this composition of soul and body is called a living and mortal creature. For immortal no such union can be reasonably believed to be; although fancy, not having seen nor surely known the nature of God, may imagine an immortal creature having both a body and also a soul which are united throughout all time. Let that, however, be as God wills, and be spoken of acceptably to him.

And now let us ask the reason why the soul loses her wings! The wing is the corporeal element which is most akin to the divine, and which by nature tends to soar aloft and carry that which gravitates downwards into the upper region, which is the habitation of the gods.

The divine is beauty, wisdom, goodness, and the like; and by these the wing of the soul is nourished, and grows apace; but when fed upon evil and foulness and the opposite of good, wastes and falls away.

[...]

As I said at the beginning of this tale, I divided each soul into three - - two horses and a charioteer; and one of the horses was good and the other bad: the division may remain, but I have not yet explained in what the goodness or badness of either consists, and to that I will proceed. The right-hand horse is upright and cleanly made; he has a lofty neck and an aquiline nose; his colour is white, and his eyes dark; he is a lover of honour and modesty and temperance, and the follower of true glory; he needs no touch of the whip, but is guided by word and admonition only.

The other is a crooked lumbering animal, put together anyhow; he has a short thick neck; he is flat-faced and of a dark colour, with grey eyes and blood-red complexion; the mate of insolence and pride, shag-eared and deaf, hardly yielding to whip and spur. Now when the charioteer beholds the vision of love, and has his whole soul warmed through sense, and is full of the prickings and ticklings of desire, the obedient steed, then as always under the government of shame, refrains from leaping on the beloved; but the other, heedless of the pricks and of the blows of the whip, plunges and runs away, giving all manner of trouble to his companion and the charioteer, whom he forces to approach the beloved and to remember the joys of love. They at first indignantly oppose him and will not be urged on to do terrible and unlawful deeds; but at last, when he persists in plaguing them, they yield and agree to do as he bids them. And now they are at the spot and behold the flashing beauty of the beloved; which when the charioteer sees, his memory is carried to the true beauty, whom he beholds in company with Modesty like an image placed upon a holy pedestal. He sees her, but he is afraid and falls backwards in adoration, and by his fall is compelled to pull back the reins with such violence as to bring both the steeds on their haunches, the one willing and unresisting, the unruly one very unwilling; and when they have gone back a little, the one is overcome with shame and wonder, and his whole soul is bathed in perspiration; the other, when the pain is over which the bridle and the fall had given him, having with difficulty taken breath, is full of wrath and reproaches, which he heaps upon the charioteer and his fellow-steed, for want of courage and manhood, declaring that they have been false to their agreement and guilty of desertion. Again they refuse, and again he urges them on, and will scarce yield to their prayer that he would wait until another time. When the appointed hour comes, they make as if they had forgotten, and he reminds them, fighting and neighing and dragging them on, until at length he, on the same thoughts intent, forces them to draw near again. And when they are near he stoops his head and puts up his tail, and takes the bit in his teeth. Then the charioteer is worse off than ever; he falls back like a racer at the barrier, and with a still more violent wrench drags the bit out of the teeth of the wild steed and covers his abusive tongue and -- jaws with blood, and forces his legs and haunches to the ground and punishes him sorely. And when this has happened several times and the villain has ceased from his wanton way, he is tamed and humbled, and follows the will of the charioteer, and when he sees the beautiful one he is ready to die of fear. And from that time forward the soul of the lover follows the beloved in modesty and holy fear.

And so the beloved who, like a god, has received every true and loyal service from his lover, not in pretence but in reality, being also himself of a nature friendly to his admirer, if in former days he has blushed to own his passion and turned away his lover, because his youthful companions or others slanderously told him that he would be disgraced, now as years advance, at the appointed age and time, is led to receive him into communion. For fate which has ordained that there shall be no friendship among the evil has also ordained that there shall ever be friendship among the good. And the beloved when he has received him into communion and intimacy, is quite amazed at the good-will of the lover; he recognises that the inspired friend is worth all other friends or kinsmen; they have nothing of friendship in them worthy to be compared with his. And when this feeling continues and he is nearer to him and embraces him, in gymnastic exercises and at other times of meeting, then the fountain of that stream, which Zeus when he was in love with Ganymede named Desire, overflows upon the lover, and some enters into his soul, and some when he is filled flows out again; and as a breeze or an echo rebounds from the smooth rocks and returns whence it came, so does the stream of beauty, passing through the eyes which are the windows of the soul, come back to the beautiful one; there arriving and quickening the passages of the wings, watering them and inclining them to grow, and filling the soul of the beloved also with love.

And thus he loves, but he knows not what; he does not understand and cannot explain his own state; he appears to have caught the infection of blindness from another; the lover is his mirror in whom he is beholding himself, but he is not aware of this. When he is with the lover, both cease from their pain, but when he is away then he longs as he is longed for, and has love's image, love for love (Anteros) lodging in his breast, which he calls and believes to be not love but friendship only, and his desire is as the desire of the other, but weaker; he wants to see him, touch him, kiss, embrace him, and probably not long afterwards his desire is accomplished. When they meet, the wanton steed of the lover has a word to say to the charioteer; he would like to have a little pleasure in return for many pains, but the wanton steed of the beloved says not a word, for he is bursting with passion which he understands not; -- he throws his arms round the lover and embraces him as his dearest friend; and, when they are side by side, he is not in a state in which he can refuse the lover anything, if he ask him; although his fellow-steed and the charioteer oppose him with the arguments of shame and reason.

After this their happiness depends upon their self-control; if the better elements of the mind which lead to order and philosophy prevail, then they pass their life here in happiness and harmony -- masters of themselves and orderly -- enslaving the vicious and emancipating the virtuous elements of the soul; and when the end comes, they are light and winged for flight, having conquered in one of the three heavenly or truly Olympian victories; nor can human discipline or divine inspiration confer any greater blessing on man than this. If, on the other hand, they leave philosophy and lead the lower life of ambition, then probably, after wine or in some other careless hour, the two wanton animals take the two souls when off their guard and bring them together, and they accomplish that desire of their hearts which to the many is bliss; and this having once enjoyed they continue to enjoy, yet rarely because they have not the approval of the whole soul.

They too are dear, but not so dear to one another as the others, either at the time of their love or afterwards. They consider that they have given and taken from each other the most sacred pledges, and they may not break them and fall into enmity. At last they pass out of the body, unwinged, but eager to soar, and thus obtain no mean reward of love and madness. For those who have once begun the heavenward pilgrimage may not go down again to darkness and the journey beneath the earth, but they live in light always; happy companions in their pilgrimage, and when the time comes at which they receive their wings they have the same plumage because of their love.

Vs.

Extract from Thunder, Perfect Mind

A Gnostic text from the Nag Hammadi Library.

> *Note: this text, discovered in 1945 in the Nag Hammadi Library in Upper Egypt, has been viewed by many as spoken by the feminine principle of the Divine. Some have said it is Sophia, or Wisdom. It is included here because it uses a style of writing that was common at the time of its conception (2nd-3rd century CE) in Greece called identity riddles, in which a series of paradoxical statements are given about an individual or subject. Within these opposing statements lie truths about the subject matter; however, the real trick – and possibly one of the intended purposes – of this text is to reach the still, silent centre-point in the mind that transpires after reading so many paradoxical statements. In a similar way to the age-old riddle* 'What is the sound of one hand clapping?' *the purpose of the text is not to find the answer, but to find no answer and thus achieve Unity.*
>
> *Full text online Gnostic Society Library at http://www.gnosis.org/naghamm/thunder.html*

For I am the first and the last.
I am the honoured one and the scorned one.
I am the whore and the holy one.
I am the wife and the virgin.
I am [the mother] and the daughter.
I am the members of my mother.
I am the barren one
and many are her sons.
I am she whose wedding is great,
and I have not taken a husband.
I am the midwife and she who does not bear.
I am the solace of my labour pains.
I am the bride and the bridegroom,
and it is my husband who begot me.

Vs.

I am the mother of my father
and the sister of my husband
and he is my offspring.
I am the slave of him who prepared me.
I am the ruler of my offspring.
But he is the one who begot me before the time on a birthday.
And he is my offspring in (due) time,
and my power is from him.
I am the staff of his power in his youth,
and he is the rod of my old age.
And whatever he wills happens to me.
I am the silence that is incomprehensible
and the idea whose remembrance is frequent.
I am the voice whose sound is manifold
and the word whose appearance is multiple.
I am the utterance of my name.

[...]

[I am ...] within.
[I am ...] of the natures.
I am [...] of the creation of the spirits.
[...] request of the souls.
I am control and the uncontrollable.
I am the union and the dissolution.
I am the abiding and I am the dissolution.
I am the one below,
and they come up to me.
I am the judgment and the acquittal.
I, I am sinless,
and the root of sin derives from me.
I am lust in (outward) appearance,
and interior self-control exists within me.
I am the hearing which is attainable to everyone
and the speech which cannot be grasped.
I am a mute who does not speak,
and great is my multitude of words.

INDEX

A

Abel 16, 25, 26, 27, 28, 38, 39, 41
Adam 29, 36, 40, 42, 43, 44
Aeschylus 134, 137, 140, 143
Aesir 192, 193
Ahriman 35
Ahura-Mazda 35
Al-Khidir 41
Allah 35, 36
Andromeda 18, 52, 53, 54, 57, 58, 59, 60
Annwfn 29, 109, 111
Aphrodite 130, 131, 133, 135, 138, 139, 140, 141, 142, 143, 145, 146, 147, 204
Apollo 15, 25, 30, 33, 132, 143
Aradia 29, 42, 198
Aratus 53
Arawn 29, 31, 109
Ares . 17, 31, 130, 131, 132, 133, 134, 135, 136, 137, 138, 139, 140, 141, 142, 143, 144, 145, 146, 147
Aristophanes..................... 26, 33, 137
Artemis 15, 25, 155, 159, 160, 198
Arthur, King........... 100, 111, 112, 216
Asclepius 163
Asmodeus 43
Astarte 43
Asvins .. 150, 151, 161, 163, 164, 165, 166
Athena . 130, 131, 132, 133, 134, 135, 136, 139, 140, 141, 142, 143, 144, 145, 148
Atho 43
Attis 38
Axis Mundi 32
Azael 42

B

Baal 43
Baba Yaga..................................... 47
Babalon 204
Baldur 40, 195, 196, 197

Baphomet 24, 28, 33
Beli.. 25
Beltane................18, 29, 52, 54, 112
Bhagavad Gita 72, 76
Binah................................22, 25, 214
Black Book of Carmarthen ...109, 111, 113
Blodeuwedd 109, 113
Bondye................................117, 121
Book of Thoth.............................. 27
Bran 25
Brigid.. 25

C

Cailleach 25
Cain 16, 25, 26, 27, 29, 31, 33, 38, 39, 40, 41, 42, 45
Calan Mai......................17, 108, 112
Cassiopeia 53, 59, 60
Castor 17, 150, 151, 152, 153, 154, 156, 157, 158, 159, 161, 162, 164, 166, 167
Cepheus 53, 58, 59
Cetus 53, 59
Charge of the Goddess .205, 206, 218
Chesed 21
Chokmah 21, 25, 214
Chronos 116
Circe 204
Codex Regis 191
Corpus Hermeticum 67
Creiddylad.............109, 111, 112, 113
Crowley, Aleister................19, 27, 229
Culhwch ac Olwen 109, 111
Cycnus................................132, 133

D

Danbala 63, 64
Dead Sea Scrolls 38
Dee, John 68
Demeter 146, 152, 193, 194
Diana 25, 29, 41, 42, 43, 198
Diomedes.................................132, 134

Dioscuri 150, 151, 152, 153, 154, 155, 156, 157, 158, 159, 160, 161, 162, 163, 164, 165, 166, 167
Dumuzi .. 17, 169, 172, 173, 174, 175, 176, 177, 178, 188, 189, 190

E

Eden 35, 40, 42, 206
Elohim 28, 201
Emerald Tablet 67
Enki 177, 182, 184, 188
Enlil 183, 188
Enoch 40, 42
Epona 110
Ereshkigal 16, 17, 25, 43, 176, 178, 180, 181, 183, 184, 185, 187, 188, 189, 190
Erichthonius 138
Eve 16, 25, 26, 27, 29, 35, 38, 40, 43, 44, 101
Exodus 39
Ezili 62, 63

F

Farr, Florence 19, 229
Fortune, Dion 208, 213
Freyja 17, 191, 192, 193, 194, 196, 197, 198, 199, 204
Freyr 192, 193, 194
Frigga 17, 191, 192, 193, 194, 195, 196, 197, 198, 199

G

Gallu 176
Gawain 17, 100, 101, 102, 103
Geburah 22
Gemini 27, 32, 33, 164, 165, 167
Genesis 26, 27, 28, 30, 36, 38, 39, 40, 44, 201
Gilgamesh 169, 184, 186
Gog 25
Green Man 41, 101, 105
Gronw 109, 113
Gugulanna 184
Gwawl 109, 110
Gwynn ap Nudd 109, 111, 112
Gwyrthyr 109, 113

H

Hades 28, 30, 31, 155, 218
Hafgan 29, 109
Hekate 204, 214
Helen ... 133, 152, 153, 154, 155, 158, 159, 160, 165, 166
Helios 15
Hephaestus 17, 130, 131, 132, 133, 136, 137, 138, 139, 140, 141, 142, 143, 144, 145, 146, 147, 148
Hera 130, 131, 132, 139, 140, 141, 142, 143, 144, 146, 147
Hercules 132, 133, 144, 165
Hermaphrodite 21
Hermes ... 30, 31, 33, 58, 67, 137, 163
Hesiod 132, 136, 137, 166
Hestia 138, 146
Hieros Gamos .. 16, 63, 173, 174, 178, 225
Hippolyta 132, 134
Hod 22
Holda 41
Holly King 15, 108, 110, 112, 113, 218, 219
Homer .. 130, 133, 136, 137, 138, 139, 142, 143, 144, 145, 152, 153, 156
Homeric Hymns 152, 153, 167
Hopkins, Gerard Manley 58

I

Iblis 36
Idas 154, 156, 157
Iliad 133, 135, 137, 139, 142, 143, 144, 145, 152
Imbolc 28, 168
Inanna .. 16, 17, 25, 43, 169, 170, 172, 173, 174, 175, 176, 177, 178, 180, 181, 182, 183, 184, 188, 189, 190, 218
Innini 17, 169, 170, 171, 172, 173, 174, 175, 176, 177, 178
Ishtar 17, 43, 169, 170, 172, 173, 174, 176, 180, 184, 185, 186, 187, 190
Isis 16, 214

J

Jesus 25, 28, 38, 112, 235
Job 36, 38
John Barleycorn 41
John the Baptist 25, 112

Jubal 25, 40
Juno 141, 196

K

Kali 74
Kether 22, 25
Kundalini 33, 78

L

Lamech 40, 41
Leda 150, 152, 153, 154
Leucippides 154, 157, 159, 166
Levi, Eliphas 24, 70
Leviticus 39, 42
Lilith 16, 25, 26, 27, 29, 42, 43, 44, 45, 204
Lleu 109, 113
Lludd 111, 112
Lokasenna 193, 195, 197, 198
Loki 15, 40, 193, 195
Lucet 30, 32
Lucifer .. 25, 29, 32, 35, 36, 37, 38, 41, 42, 43, 44, 45
Lugus 30
Luke 28, 225
Lumiel 35, 36, 43
Lwa 61, 62, 63, 64
Lynceus 154, 156, 157

M

Magdalene 25, 39
Magog 25
Malkuth 22, 225
Mani 38
Marassa. 17, 115, 116, 117, 118, 119, 120, 121, 122, 123, 124, 125, 127, 128
Mars 133, 134, 141, 142
Maryaj 18, 61, 62, 63, 64
Matthew 28
Maya 75, 79, 123
Medusa 53, 55, 57, 59
Mercury 32
Merlin 25
Metamorphoses 56, 59, 60, 164
Metis 145, 146
Michael 36, 37, 38
Mithras 38
Montalban, Madeline 39, 43, 44

Moon 15, 18, 21, 22, 26, 27, 29, 31, 91, 92, 93, 94, 98, 125, 164, 167, 203, 204, 205, 213, 214, 215

N

Naamah 25, 29, 40, 41, 42, 43, 45
Nanna 183, 188
Nemesis 153
Neopaganism. 18, 216, 217, 219, 220, 221, 224, 225, 226
Nereids 53, 55
Netzach 21
Nimue 204
Njord 192, 193, 196
Noctifera 28
Nodens 32, 112
Nuit 53, 57

O

Oak King 15, 108, 110, 112, 113, 218, 219
Odin 15, 192, 193, 194, 195, 196, 197, 198
Odyssey 130, 137, 138, 152, 156
Ogou 63
Old Testament 38, 40, 42, 116
Olympus 136, 137, 143, 144, 145, 147, 148, 230
Orpheus 132
Osiris 16, 32, 231
Ovid 56, 59, 60, 141, 142, 162, 164

P

Pausanias 133, 135, 143, 154, 155, 157, 158, 159, 160, 166
Pegasus 53, 59
Persephone 113, 155, 194, 218
Perseus 18, 52, 53, 54, 55, 56, 57, 58, 59
Phaedrus 19, 236
Phaenomena 53
Philo 39
Philosopher's Stone 15, 236
Plato 19, 26, 30, 65, 67, 145, 236
Poetic Edda 191, 193, 194, 195
Pollux 17, 150
Polydeuces .. 150, 151, 152, 153, 154, 156, 157, 159, 161, 162, 164, 166, 167
Poseidon 53

Prakrti 71, 72, 73, 74
Prometheus 137, 143
Prose Edda 191
Psychopomp 30
Purusa 71, 72, 73, 74, 75, 76
Pwyll 29, 32, 109, 110
Pwyll, Prince of Dyfed 109

Q

Qabalah 21, 217, 225
Quetzalcoatl 38
Qur'an 36, 38, 39

R

Ra 116, 230
Red Book of Hergest 109
Revelations 36
Rhea 116, 145
Rhiannon 109, 110
Rig Veda 150, 165, 166
Rigatona 110

S

Sagittarius 32, 33
Samadhi 64, 76, 77, 78
Samael 29, 38, 42
Samkhya Karika 71, 72, 73
Saturn 32, 190
Selene 15, 166, 214
Seraphim 29
Set 16, 33, 54
Shakespeare, William ... 108, 113, 223
Shakti .. 18, 71, 72, 73, 74, 75, 76, 77, 78, 79
Shamash 42
Shekinah 43, 44
Shemyaza 42
Shield of Heracles 131, 132
Shiva ... 18, 71, 72, 73, 74, 75, 76, 77, 78, 79
Sir Gawain and the Green Knight .. 17, 100
Sol Invictus 32
Sol Niger 96
Spare, Austin Osman ... 18, 80, 81, 83
St George 41
Sturluson, Snorri ... 191, 193, 196, 199
Sun 15, 18, 21, 22, 26, 29, 32, 91, 92, 94, 95, 98, 125, 164, 165, 167, 203
Symposium 26, 30

T

Tammuz 17, 169, 172, 176
Tantra 73, 77
Tarot 15, 18, 27, 30, 32, 33, 91, 92, 93, 95, 99, 116, 117, 118, 236
Tettens 30, 31
Theocritus 152, 154
Theseus 154, 155, 159, 166
Thor 27, 193, 196
Thunder, Perfect Mind 19, 209
Tiphereth 22
Tiw 31
Torah 39
Traditional Witchcraft 16, 26, 30, 35
Tree of Life 21, 22, 25, 214
Tubal 25, 29, 42, 45
Tubal-Cain 26, 40, 142
Tyndareus 151, 152, 153, 156, 166

U

Upanishads 72, 76

V

Vanir 192
Venus 30, 43, 164, 180, 196
Virgin Mary 199, 207
Vodou 15, 17, 18, 61, 63, 64, 115, 116, 117, 118, 119, 120, 122, 123, 124, 125, 126, 127, 128, 129
Vortigern 25

W

Weland 142
White Book of Rhydderch 109
Wicca . 15, 18, 28, 201, 205, 206, 207, 208, 210, 216, 217, 218, 219, 220, 223, 224, 225, 226, 236
Woden 28, 30, 31, 32
World Tree 32

Y

Yahweh 35, 36, 38, 39, 42, 43, 44
Yesod 22

Z

Zenda-Vesta 35

Vs.

Zeus 26, 53, 130, 131, 132, 133, 137, 140, 141, 142, 143, 144, 145, 146, 147, 148, 150, 152, 153, 156, 157, 164, 165, 166, 238

Zohar 42, 44

ALSO AVAILABLE FROM AVALONIA...
WWW.AVALONIABOOKS.CO.UK

From a Drop of Water
A Collection of Magickal Reflections on the Nature, Creatures, Uses and Symbolism of Water

Edited by Kim Huggens
(Various Contributors)

From A Drop Of Water is a unique collection of 17 essays by some of the foremost modern esoteric writers, pagan scholars and magickal practitioners. Each contribution reflects the writer's own understanding and passion for Water, and in doing so they share their unique insights, experiences and their diverse research on the subject with the reader

Both Sides of Heaven
A collection of essays exploring the origins, history, magic and nature of divine winged messengers, angels, demons and fallen angels.

Edited by Sorita d'Este
(Various Contributors)

BOTH SIDES OF HEAVEN is a collection of 18 essays by some of the foremost modern esoteric writers, occult scholars and magicians. In their personal contributions they share their experiences, research and unique insights into the spiritual realms of the mysterious beings who have played such an important and inspirational role in human spiritual history.